The Nature of the Transnational Firm

The theory of the transnational corporation is now a topic of central importance to economics. Transnational corporations play an increasingly
important role in the world economy, and their enormous size and power
make them a subject of great interest and concern to consumers, producers,
nation states and international organizations, as well as to researchers.

Christos Pitelis and Roger Sugden have brought together leading theorists
in this area to present a wide variety of perspectives on the nature of the
transnational firm. The volume is unique in that it incorporates both orthodox
and radical theories, providing new insights and suggesting areas of potential development.

With its emphasis on a wide-ranging approach to the theory of the transnational firm, the book will be immensely helpful to everybody interested
in the topic, students and professional economists alike.

Christos N. Pitelis is Lecturer in Managerial Economics at the University
of St Andrews, and Roger Sugden is Senior Lecturer in Industrial Economics
and Director of the Regulatory Research Unit at the University of
Birmingham.

The Nature of the Transnational Firm

Edited by Christos N. Pitelis
and Roger Sugden

London and New York

First published 1991
by Routledge
11 New Fetter Lane, London EC4P 4EE

Simultaneously published in the USA and Canada
by Routledge
a division of Routledge, Chapman and Hall, Inc.
29 West 35th Street, New York, NY 10001

Phototypeset in 10pt Times by
Mews Photosetting, Beckenham, Kent
Printed and bound in Great Britain by
Biddles Ltd, Guildford and King's Lynn

British Library Cataloguing in Publication Data

The Nature of the Transnational Firm.
　1. Multinational companies
　I. Pitelis, Christos II. Sugden, Roger
　338. 88

ISBN 0-415-05271-8
ISBN 0-415-05748-5 (Pbk)

Library of Congress Cataloging in Publication Data

The Nature of the Transnational Firm / Edited by Christos N. Pitelis
　and Roger Sugden.
　　　p.　cm.
　　Includes bibliographical references and index.
　　ISBN 0-415-05271-8 (hbk). – ISBN 0-415-05748-5 (pbk)
　　1. International business enterprises. I. Pitelis, Christos.
　II. Sugden, Roger.
　HD2755.5.N42　　1990
　338.8′8–dc20　　　　　　　　　　　　　　　　　　　90-37020
　　　　　　　　　　　　　　　　　　　　　　　　　　　　CIP

To our wives
Ιωάννα and Nicky

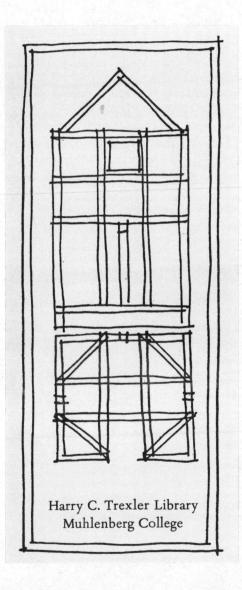

Contents

Contents

Figures and tables

Contributors

John Cantwell
Lecturer in Economics
University of Reading

John H. Dunning
ICI Research Professor of International Business
University of Reading and State of New Jersey Professor of
International Business, Rutgers University

Edward M. Graham
Research Fellow
Institute for International Economics

Jean-François Hennart
Associate Professor of International Business
University of Illinois at Urbana-Champaign

Neil M. Kay
Professor of Business Economics
University of Strathclyde

Christos N. Pitelis
Lecturer in Managerial Economics
University of St Andrews

Roger Sugden
Senior Lecturer in Industrial Economics, Director of the
Regulatory Research Unit
University of Birmingham

Mohammad Yamin
Senior Lecturer in Economics
Nottingham Polytechnic

Abbreviations

E(E)C	European (Economic) Community
FDI	foreign direct investment
HKC	Hymer-Kindleberger-Caves
HOS	Heckscher-Ohlin-Samuelson
LDC	less developed country
MNC	multinational corporation
MNE	multinational enterprise
OL	ownership and location
OLI	ownership/location/internalization
PCM	product cycle model
R&D	research and development
TNC	transnational corporation

Chapter abstracts

Christos N. Pitelis and Roger Sugden

CHAPTER 1
ON THE THEORY OF THE TRANSNATIONAL FIRM
CHRISTOS N. PITELIS AND ROGER SUGDEN

The opening chapter provides a relatively brief introduction to the volume. It identifies and discusses three main aims: to give the intellectual contribution of transnational corporation theorists its rightful place in the vibrant transaction costs research programme; to reassert the importance of concerns which more traditionally occupied the theory of the transnational firm but which have recently been inappropriately overrun by internalization analysis; to acknowledge and stimulate the catholicism of transnational theory by presenting, in one volume, discussions which span the various wide-ranging approaches that characterize the literature. The chapter also outlines the volume's structure, which is largely although not exclusively influenced by the chronological emergence of theories. Finally, it explains two less important issues: the deliberate overlap between chapters; the fact that when referring to essentially the same entities some chapters use the term 'transnational' and others the term 'multinational'.

CHAPTER 2
A SURVEY OF THEORIES OF INTERNATIONAL PRODUCTION
JOHN CANTWELL

A vast amount of work has focused on the transnational firm. The aim of chapter 2 is to survey a crucial segment of this, namely the different theories of international production that have been developed over the last thirty years or so. Cantwell presents a wide-ranging, detailed and critical assessment. Besides its value *per se*, the chapter provides a largely implicit perspective on the position of the other contributions to the volume within the wider literature.

In the first main section studies are grouped under five headings. Four of these refer to alternative frameworks, which are each argued to contain different approaches with common theoretical foundations. Of the four, two are based on alternative theories of the firm; what Cantwell calls the market power or Hymer theory of the firm, and what he calls the internalization or Coasian theory of the firm. The third is based on the analysis of competitive international industries – associated with Raymond Vernon and more recently Rhys Jenkins, for instance – and the fourth is denoted macroeconomic developmental approaches, seen to date from Raymond Vernon's earliest product cycle model. The fifth heading that Cantwell identifies is the eclectic paradigm. This is argued to be distinct because it incorporates elements from all the other frameworks, can be applied at microeconomic, mesoeconomic or macroeconomic levels, and performs an essentially different role. There is recognition and discussion of overlaps across these frameworks, which are also compared and contrasted.

This is pursued in the second section, where it is argued that differences between approaches can be explained by the fact that they address different questions. The point is explored by examining the role of ownership advantages and locational influences in the context of explaining firm growth and international competitiveness. This leads into a concluding section where Cantwell contemplates some possible future developments for theories of international production. His concern is dynamic issues and his speculations focus in particular on the role of technology.

CHAPTER 3
A REASSESSMENT OF HYMER'S CONTRIBUTION TO THE THEORY OF THE TRANSNATIONAL CORPORATION
MOHAMMAD YAMIN

One of the most influential and important contributors to the literature on transnational corporations has been Stephen Hymer. His work has been influential *per se* and has inspired many authors. But it has also been misunderstood and unappreciated. This is the message of chapter 3.

Yamin outlines and comments upon Hymer's famous analysis of firms' advantages leading to international operations. However, he then looks at a second, related yet underplayed analysis based upon the 'removal of conflict'. This sees international operations arising because rivals co-operate to increase profits. Interestingly, it is observed that the only detailed case histories of international operations in Hymer's Ph.D. thesis involve the removal of conflict rather than the possession of advantage, yet it is still the former which has been disregarded.

In the light of this, Yamin argues that the alleged difference in approach between Hymer's earlier and later work is more superficial than real. Whilst his later writings focused on broader, systemic issues, this so-called radical phase implicitly incorporated a generalization of his removal of conflict approach. Yamin also offers an explanation for the partial appreciation and use of Hymer's work – for instance, pointing to parallel developments in the literature on trade theory – and in so doing suggests that removal of conflict may be more relevant for today than for thirty years ago, when Hymer was first writing.

The chapter's final section comments on the relationship between Hymer's analysis and the internalization approach. Yamin argues that the two views are less divergent than is sometimes believed. More positively, it is suggested that their respective concern with market power and transaction costs may be fused into a more fruitful, integrated approach.

CHAPTER 4
THE TRANSACTION COST THEORY OF THE MULTINATIONAL ENTERPRISE
JEAN-FRANÇOIS HENNART

More recent and nowadays more influential than the ideas conventionally associated with Stephen Hymer is so-called internalization or, in modern parlance, transaction cost analysis. Whilst it has been criticized – and indeed some of the criticisms are reflected in this book – most see such analysis as at least extremely important. In line with this, the theme of chapter 4 is that transaction cost analysis provides a general theory of economic organization and accordingly is significant to our understanding of transnationals.

Hennart begins with a detailed, readable discussion designed to show that transaction cost theory can account for all the major types of transnational corporation. The bulk of his argument focuses on natural market imperfections and thus non-pecuniary externalities – as against the structural market imperfections and pecuniary externalities focused upon by Stephen Hymer. He examines first horizontal and then vertical investments, looking at the role of knowledge, goodwill, small-number conditions, information asymmetry and quality control. In so doing Hennart highlights some empirical tests, a feature of the entire chapter.

He then examines, relatively briefly, the explanatory powers of transaction cost theory more generally. This discussion of joint ventures and contracts – including licensing and franchising – recognizes that transnationals are simply one of various ways to organize economic activity. It throws light on the nature of transnationals by attempting to explain why particular options are chosen.

The chapter's third and final main focus is on some directions for future research. It is suggested that much theoretical and empirical work remains to be done. Particular concern is expressed about the lack of attention to organization costs within firms and the point that the presence of transaction costs in markets is not a sufficient condition for the existence of transnationals. Drawing on some of his earlier work, Hennart discusses the view that firms can be more efficient than markets when the latter fail because their method of organization is radically different from that used in markets, i.e. because they rely primarily on behaviour constraints rather than price constraints.

CHAPTER 5
THE ECLECTIC PARADIGM OF INTERNATIONAL PRODUCTION: A PERSONAL PERSPECTIVE
JOHN H. DUNNING

In a series of papers and books over the last thirty years John Dunning has been developing an eclectic approach to the understanding of transnationals. Initially identified as the eclectic theory, this has been renamed the eclectic paradigm. It is the most recent analysis to command widespread influence. In chapter 5 Dunning presents his personal perspective on the approach.

The chapter highlights issues that the eclectic approach does and does not address, explores the evolution of Dunning's thinking and explicitly confronts criticisms that the approach has attracted.

In the first section Dunning distinguishes the eclectic paradigm from, for instance, internalization theory by examining the phenomena different approaches address. He sees his main concern as relatively general, namely an explanation of the level and pattern of foreign value-added activities by all firms from a particular country or group of countries. This contrasts with an interest in explaining why a particular firm extends its territorial boundaries, where he finds internalization analysis very persuasive. The section considers how these issues have occupied different scholars and suggests that the former has deeper roots, for instance having similarities in spirit to Raymond Vernon's product cycle analysis and Stephen Hymer's Ph.D. thesis, whereas the existence and growth of particular firms have been in issue only since the mid-1970s.

The evolution of Dunning's thinking receives its most explicit attention in the second section. For example, his concern with ownership and location advantages is traced to his 1958 productivity study. The section also acknowledges a change in the way the eclectic approach has used internalization analysis. It is argued that his earlier writings saw internalization advantages arising from the way ownership advantages are exploited rather than in their own right. This is now seen to be too extreme, and Dunning argues that the benefits of internalization *per se* must be related to assets the firm possesses prior to the act of internalization.

Some criticisms of the paradigm are addressed in the following section. For example, he discusses the variables highlighted by the analysis, and in justifying the separation of ownership, location and internalization factors presents a policy argument. The chapter explores at length the importance of firms' strategic response and of dynamic effects. This introduces the most recent advances in Dunning's thinking, for instance that there is a continuous, two-way interaction between the configuration of ownership, location and internalization variables and the strategy of firms. It also introduces an examination of the investment development cycle, which he first presented in 1979. Finally the section concludes with a look at conglomerate investment.

CHAPTER 6
MULTINATIONAL ENTERPRISE AS STRATEGIC CHOICE: SOME TRANSACTION COST PERSPECTIVES
NEIL M. KAY

Observing that some form of transaction costs approach is the dominant theme in many accounts of transnationals' behaviour – a point reflected in the preceding two chapters of this book – chapter 6 assesses the transaction cost issue.

The context for the assessment is a stylized discussion of four corporate strategies: specialization, diversification, transnationalism and joint venture. Kay suggests that supply-side pulls imply a lexical ordering of these strategies and then argues that the very existence of the ordering depends upon the presence of transaction costs. This illustrates how he unambiguously believes that transaction costs are significant. However, talk of there being only one transaction cost approach is dismissed and indeed Kay distances himself from some seminal work in the area. In particular, having recognized that it seems obvious that Williamson's work should be used in deepening understanding of transaction costs, Kay argues that doing so poses major and insurmountable problems. This argument occupies a large part of the chapter.

Given that the Williamson approach sees the emergence of a transnational as involving a strategic decision to adopt a hierarchical structure rather than a market solution, the chapter studies his analysis of corporate strategy and structure in general. For example, it considers his views on how strategies and structures evolve and on the nature of transactions. It argues, among other things, that Williamson's focus on assets specialized to a particular use or user is very limiting and that his definition of a transaction has consistency problems. Kay then turns to the comments Williamson makes about the existence of transnationals in particular. In doing so he builds upon the earlier discussion of asset specificity and transactions.

Following this, attention moves from Williamson to a more detailed examination of the joint venture strategy. This focuses on differences between ventures involving Japanese and Western firms and thus leads to a discussion of joint venture versus transnationalism in the context of an opening European market after 1992.

CHAPTER 7
STRATEGIC MANAGEMENT AND TRANSNATIONAL FIRM BEHAVIOUR: A FORMAL APPROACH
EDWARD M. GRAHAM

Graham's starting point is the observation that literature on industrial organization recognizes that large firms in concentrated industries make their decisions 'strategically', i.e. bearing in mind the likely reaction of rivals. His chapter is essentially an introduction to the use of such strategic interaction analysis as a means of understanding firms' decisions to produce in various countries.

The chapter initially presents a simple and relatively formal analysis, using a two-firm, two-market, constant cost, perfect information model. This focuses on Cournot equilibria and on collusion to maximize joint profits. A typical conclusion, for example, is that a firm's decision to become a transnational is influenced by whether or not its rival becomes a transnational, and in turn by its costs relative to the rival's (a result which Graham recognizes is consistent with the analysis in Hymer's Ph.D. thesis). It is also suggested that if there is cross-investment, such that both firms produce in both countries, there may be collusion over price/output decisions to maximize joint profits yet simultaneously efforts by each firm to lower costs. The chapter then looks at a slightly more complicated model. This allows for costs to decrease over time as a result of 'learning by doing' and for imperfect information. The analysis here is less formal and picks up the earlier concern with costs.

Throughout, Graham is concerned with the applicability of his analysis to the real world. Indeed, in one sense the foundation of his chapter is the assertion that in the real world strategic interaction is a key characteristic of firms' behaviour. However, this concern with realism is explicitly seen in the particular attention given to Japan and Japanese-based firms. For example, he notes that Japanese-based firms seem to have adopted aggressive pricing tactics when producing and selling in new markets and wonders if this might be explained by a preference for Cournot equilibria rather than joint profit maximization, following the implications of his formal model. Similarly an explanation based on economies of learning is also contemplated.

CHAPTER 8
THE IMPORTANCE OF DISTRIBUTIONAL CONSIDERATIONS
ROGER SUGDEN

On the basis that transnationals are merely a specific type of firm, this chapter begins to explain why there are transnational corporations by examining two answers to the 'Why firms?' question. Internalization analysis, seen to concentrate on efficiency implications, is unfavourably compared to Stephen Marglin's analysis of the rise of factories. Accordingly it is suggested that a Marglinian approach, emphasizing the characteristics of a firm's activities and consequently distributional considerations, has interesting implications for analysing transnationals. The bulk of the chapter is therefore devoted to providing such an approach.

Drawing on a wide pool of literature, Sugden presents a general theoretical framework. He places rivalry and collusion at the centre of analysis and discusses two sets of reasons explaining transnationals' existence. First, that they arise because a firm defends itself against rivals, fearing the latter will undermine its market position. Second, because a firm attacks rivals, seeking to undermine their market positions. The distributional implications of this approach are discussed, for instance in terms of unemployment and monopoly pricing.

Attention then turns to more specific issues: a theoretical and empirical investigation of labour market domination. In the context of the general theoretical framework, a 'divide and rule' hypothesis is advanced: by dividing workers into country-specific groups, employers improve their bargaining position, thereby gaining at the expense of workers. This is explored using evidence on wage levels in different types of firm, the views of participants in firms and actual cases of firms dividing workers. The conclusion is that 'divide and rule' provides at least a contributory reason for the existence of some transnationals. Again it is clearly argued that distribution is the crucial welfare concern, not efficiency.

CHAPTER 9
THE TRANSNATIONAL CORPORATION: DEMAND-SIDE ISSUES AND A SYNTHESIS
CHRISTOS N. PITELIS

The final chapter discusses and builds upon two themes: first, the need for an alternative synthesis of supply-side explanations of transnationals' existence; second, the view that the theory of the transnational corporation, both generally and in the rest of this book, has concentrated on supply-side explanations to the detriment of the demand side.

Pitelis argues that other studies synthesizing supply-side explanations have taken an eclectic yet in one sense partial view of the literature. In contrast he uses an internalization concept to encapsulate monopolistic advantage, transaction costs and 'divide and rule' analyses. Moreover he does so in a way that overturns the efficiency-only property typically associated with internalization.

He then argues that supply-side approaches have concentrated on the choice between institutional forms, given that internationalization is to occur, not an explanation of why there should be internationalization in the first place. Explicitly building on a long tradition of mainstream and other literature, the chapter contends that rectifying this bias is where demand-side factors are useful; in short, demand-side deficiencies are claimed to be a general incentive for firms to internationalize production.

However, this demand-side analysis needs synthesizing with the supply-side synthesis. This is also addressed by Pitelis. In doing so he distinguishes *ex ante* and *ex post* reasons for transnationals. *Ex ante* (the presence of transnationals) the transnational form of internationalization is chosen instead of alternatives, for various supply-side reasons – for example, because it economizes on transaction costs. However, once one firm has crossed national borders it is suggested that others will do the same because of inter-firm and inter-nation rivalry. The latter supply-side factors are seen as primarily *ex post* explanations for transnationals.

Pitelis also considers how investment between developed economies is consistent with his analysis, and presents evidence on the matter. He concludes with a brief discussion of some policy implications. This chapter is less optimistic than much other literature about the effects of transnationals' presence.

1 On the theory of the transnational firm

Christos N. Pitelis and Roger Sugden

The past quarter of a century has witnessed a dramatic surge of interest in the theory of the transnational corporation. This is demonstrated, for example, by the exponential growth of publications in the area.

One obvious explanation is the increased and increasing importance of such firms in the world economy, a point reflected in analysis of the growth and spread of transnationals contained in the likes of Stopford and Dunning (1983), Dunning and Pearce (1985), Dicken (1986) and United Nations (1983, 1988). This prominence, alongside the power which transnationals can potentially accumulate by virtue of their often enormous size and the nature of their activities, makes the firms a natural cause of concern for consumers, other producers, nation states and international organizations alike. Hence they are also a source of research interest.

In the view of the present authors, however, another perhaps equally important reason for this interest is the emergence of a new research programme in the theory of the transnational firm: the internalization of markets approach. According to this, transnationals arise owing to the existence of especially 'natural' market failures, more specifically to the relatively high costs 'naturally' attached to market transactions. It is argued that such costs are internalized by the transnational, which thus can be seen as an institutional device for economizing on market transaction costs.

To the extent that this insight is accurate, even partly, its implications are significant. In particular, it suggests that the policy stance of some states towards transnationals needs to be radically reconsidered. For instance, if policy is based on the conventional structure–performance approach of industrial organization analysis – the sort of thing reflected in some earlier work on transnationals – any departures from perfectly competitive market structures should be viewed with suspicion. Accordingly, for example, the large transnational should be seen as a potential target for state intervention. But if transnationals represent a solution to market failures, rather than a cause of such failures, states with policies inimical to transnationals should alter their stance. Perhaps this crucial implication is one explanation for the large literature that the internalization of markets approach has spawned.

Whatever the reason, the emergence of internalization analysis certainly explains the existence of this volume, at least in part. Looking beyond the transnational corporation literature, internalization analysis has acquired a prominent position in economics, particularly in industrial organization theory. This has been mirrored by a rapidly expanding literature and a number of collections and/or texts, for example Putterman (1987), Clarke and McGuiness (1987), Jacquemin (1987), Thompson and Wright (1988). Despite the fact that transnational corporation theorists, most notably McManus(1972) and Buckley and Casson (1976), have developed independently and simultaneously the internalization-transaction costs framework, their contributions have remained largely unrecognized by industrial organization theory. One reason seems to be that the theory of the transnational is often seen as a special case of the theory of the firm, so that contributions in the general area have received most attention. Another may be the prolific and influential writings of Oliver Williamson, who has relatively little to say on transnationals directly. In any case, we consider it appropriate that the intellectual contribution of transnational corporation theorists to the vibrant transaction costs research programme be given a fair hearing. One of the main aims of this volume is to serve this belief.

This is not merely a case of putting the record straight. More importantly, for example, it may enable industrial organization theorists to learn from their transnational corporation counterparts. Having said this, however, learning in the other direction is also required. In fact the failure to appreciate this requirement may be another reason explaining the lack of recognition for transnational corporation theorists concerned with internalisation.

Initially industrial organization theory emphasized 'structural' market failures, such as monopoly, and then considered 'natural' market failures. The anti-trust implications of this development were therefore seen as a challenge to an orthodoxy which viewed monopoly with suspicion. They still are. Moreover, in making its challenge, transaction costs theory attempted to position itself *alongside* the mainstream industrial organization perspective. This has been achieved.

In stark contrast, in the theory of the transnational, transaction cost analysis has arguably attained a *dominance*, and has done so fairly quickly. Despite Hymer's (1960) original focus on 'market power' aspects of transnationals' behaviour, most recent contributions to the theory of the transnational totally reject such considerations. Transactional failures are seen to dominate and little attention is paid to the attainment of monopoly power through, for example, strategic behaviour.

Such dominance is unsatisfactory, partly because transaction costs theory has now received substantial criticisms from various quarters in the industrial organization literature; see, for example, Francis *et al.* (1983), Malcolmson (1984), Hodgson (1988), Fourie (1989) and Kay (1990), to mention just a few. These criticisms may no longer justify total reliance on a transaction costs explanation of the transnational corporation. They certainly need incorporation into the transnationals literature, and a failure to recognize this may account for the by-passing of transnational theorists.

For instance, Malcolmson's (1984) argument that market power may be achieved via economizing on transaction costs is particularly important; it suggests that internalization theorists cannot ignore the sort of concerns that more traditionally occupied transnational corporation theory. In other words, it forcefully reintroduces into the theory of the transnational the sort of concerns which were prominent when the Hymer-Kindleberger tradition was taken more seriously and which are also seen in 'global reach' analyses – see, for example, Barnet and Muller (1974). Accordingly the importance of such concerns to an understanding of transnationals needs to be stressed and emphasized once more. Achieving this reassertion is the second major aim of the volume.

Furthermore, in pursuing this and our first aim we also hope to encourage a full and genuine integration of industrial organization and transnational corporation theory. As reflected in our discussion thus far, these two areas tend to be seen as distinct. We have suggested, for instance, that they can learn from each other. But ultimately more than this is needed: industrial organization should move towards the analysis of global industries. That is, it should appreciate that what happens in many industries in many countries can only be really understood if the industry is seen in a global context. The evidence for this is provided by the literature on the significance of transnationals, more specifically on their growth, spread and influence. Correspondingly, it should be appreciated that in an analysis of global industries transnational firms are the leading protagonists. Thus at least elements of industrial organization theory and transnational corporation theory need to be fused into one and the same thing. Perhaps this volume can encourage this integration, albeit in a very small way, by at least bringing together the two strands in pursuit of its other objectives.

However, this is essentially a secondary concern; more important, in a sense, is our third main aim. Criticisms of the transaction costs approach are not the only reason for exploring alternative ideas. The theory of the transnational firm has been possibly unique in the way it has attracted and recognized a multitude of explanations for the emergence and implications of such firms. Our impression is that over the years transnational corporation theory has shown a tolerance and encouragement of a wide range of approaches that is unusual compared to economics more generally. Given the recent dominance of transaction cost analysis, this may appear paradoxical. Yet even in this period the presence of alternative explanations has been willingly accepted. Among the different approaches there have been theories emphasizing oligopolistic interdependence, capital's attempts to subjugate labour through divide-and-rule strategies, and macroeconomic demand-side considerations. There have also been attempts to provide syntheses, most notably Dunning's 'eclectic' analysis. Such catholicism should be acknowledged and stimulated, not least because it is crucial for real understanding and progress in any area of study. Consequently it makes sense to present, in one book and alongside the dominant transaction cost analysis, discussions which span the various wide-ranging theories on transnationals. To the best of our knowledge no such book exists. Filling this gap is the third major aim of this volume.

In order to achieve the above objectives we have requested some of the principal contributors to the theory of the transnational to provide a discussion of what they perceive as the 'state of the art' in the theory, either in general or in the particular area they are associated with and themselves favour. We hope that in so doing we have produced a unique volume, one which incorporates major existing contributions to the theory of the transnational but which also provides new insights and areas of potential development. Hence this volume should be particularly helpful to everybody interested in the theory of the (transnational) firm, students and professional economists alike.

The structure of the volume is as follows. Following this introduction, John Cantwell sets the scene with a comprehensive, critical survey of the different theories of international production. Besides its value *per se*, chapter 2 provides a largely implicit perspective on the position of the other chapters within the wider literature. The order in which Cantwell deals with the theories is in the spirit of the more general layout of the volume. (See the abstracts at the beginning for more depth on the contents of each chapter.)

Turning to the chapters that take a more detailed look at various issues, their ordering is largely although not exclusively influenced by the chronological emergence of theories. Thus chapter 3 provides Mo Yamin's reassessment of Hymer, the most prominent figure in the modern history (i.e. last quarter-century) of transnational corporation theory. Although Hymer has been extremely influential and inspiring, Yamin argues, he has also been misunderstood and unappreciated. This is followed in chapter 4 by an authoritative, sympathetic and wide-ranging appreciation of internalization analysis, which we have already noted is more recent and nowadays more influential than the ideas conventionally associated with Hymer. Jean-François Hennart's theme is that transaction cost analysis provides a general theory of economic organization and accordingly is significant to our understanding of transnationals. Chapter 5 turns to the most recent analysis to command widespread influence: John Dunning's 'eclectic' approach. This brings together some of Hymer's work and transaction cost analysis. In the chapter, Dunning presents his personal perspective on the approach; highlighting issues it does and does not address, exploring the evolution of his own thinking and explicitly confronting criticisms the approach has attracted.

To a greater or lesser extent both Hennart and Dunning (and indeed Yamin) are concerned with transaction costs. This interest is maintained in chapter 6, where Neil Kay provides an affinitive critique of the concept. In some ways Kay's discussion could have been comfortably slotted between chapters 4 and 5. However, Kay gives explicit, detailed attention to Williamson's 'markets and hierarchies' approach and therefore to an important aspect of industrial organization theory. This occupies a large part of the chapter. Moreover the context of his assessment is a stylized discussion of different corporate strategies – specialization, diversification, transnationalism and joint venture. Both these concerns mean that his paper fits nicely alongside Monty Graham's chapter 7. This starts with the observation that industrial organization literature recognizes that large firms in concentrated industries make their decisions strategically, i.e. bearing in mind the likely reaction of rivals. Writing in a tradition which dates back to the Hymer-Kindleberger approach, Graham provides an up-to-date introduction to the use of such strategic interaction analysis as a means of understanding firms decisions to produce in various countries.

Oligopolistic interaction is also at the heart of chapter 8, which focuses on the more radical monopoly capital literature and Stephen Marglin's work on factories; see especially Marglin (1974). Emphasizing distributional considerations, Roger Sugden provides an alternative general theoretical framework and in this context suggests that transnationals arise to subjugate labour. The chapter represents one of the most recent contributions to transnational theory. The same is true of chapter 9. This is an appropriate, yet personal, conclusion in so far as it attempts to synthesize earlier analyses, i.e. work represented in chapters 2 to 8. Furthermore Christos Pitelis suggests that the theory of the transnational, both generally and in the rest of this volume, has concentrated on supply-side explanations to the detriment of the demand side. Thus he also transfers the focus of attention to yet another aspect of transnational firm theory and synthesizes this with more widely recognized arguments.

Finally, two relatively less important explanatory comments are in order. First, the contents of ensuing chapters to some extent overlap. We have not attempted to edit away this overlapping. Partly this is because different views on the nature of the transnational firm inevitably have similar points of departure, similar issues to comment upon, and so on. Partly it is because we feel each chapter should be readable separately. Whilst the book as a whole is designed to be a coherent and useful piece of work, at least some readers on at least some occasions may wish to study particular chapters in isolation. The work is presented with this in mind. Second, when referring to essentially the same entities some chapters use the term 'transnational' and others the term 'multinational'. This has been left to author preference. In a collection of papers explicitly intended to reflect wide-ranging opinion across a particular subject, anything else would be inappropriate. The choice between labels is founded on their different connotations; at its simplest, this stems from the term 'multinational' suggesting a firm associated with many nations, transnational a firm which crosses national borders. However, the reasons for authors choosing between the terms is irrelevant to this volume. What does matter is that both are widely used in the literature and that there is no reason for this to be denied. In not trying to impose one term rather than the other we are simply reflecting, albeit in a very minor way, the tolerance which typifies the transnationals literature more generally.

REFERENCES

Barnet, Richard J., and Muller, Ronald E. (1974) *Global Reach*, New York: Simon & Schuster.

Buckley, Peter J. and Casson, Mark C. (1976) *The Future of the Multinational Enterprise*, London: Macmillan.

Clarke, Roger, and McGuiness, Tony (1987) *The Economics of the Firm*, Oxford: Blackwell.

Dicken, Peter (1986) *Global Shift*, London: Harper & Row.

Dunning, John H. and Pearce, Robert (1985) *The World's Largest Industrial Enterprises*, Aldershot: Gower.

Fourie, F.C.V.N. (1989) 'The nature of firms and markets: do transaction approaches help?', *South African Journal of Economics*.

Francis, Arthur, Turk, Jeremy, and Willman, Paul (1983) *Power, Efficiency and Institutions*, London: Heinemann.

Hodgson, G. (1988) *Economics and Institutions*, Oxford: Polity Press.

Hymer, Stephen H. (1960) *The International Operations of National Firms: a Study of Direct Foreign Investment*, Cambridge, Mass.: MIT Press.

Jacquemin, Alexis (1987) *The New Industrial Organization*, Oxford: Oxford University Press.

Kay, Neil M. (1990) 'Markets, false hierarchies and the evolution of the modern corporation', *Journal of Economic Behavior and Organization*.

McManus, J.C. (1972) 'The theory of the multinational firm', in G. Paquet (ed.) *The Multinational Firm and the Nation State*, Don Mills, Ont.: Collier-Macmillan.

Malcolmson, J. (1984) 'Efficient labour organisation: incentives, power and the transaction costs approach', in Frank Stephen (ed.) *Firms, Organizations and Labour: Approaches to the Economics of Work Organization*, London: Macmillan.

Marglin, Stephen A. (1974) 'What do bosses do? The origin and functions of hierarchy in capitalist production', *Review of Radical Political Economics*.

Putterman, Louis (1987) *The Economic Nature of the Firm: a Reader*, Cambridge: Cambridge University Press.

Stopford, John M. and Dunning, John H. (1983) *Multinationals: Company Performance and Global Trends*, London: Macmillan.

Thompson, Steve, and Wright, Mike (1988) *Internal Organisation, Efficiency, and Profit*, Oxford: Philip Allen.

United Nations (1983) *Transnational Corporations and World Development: Third Survey*, New York: United Nations.

—— (1988) *Transnational Corporations and World Development: Fourth Survey*, New York: United Nations.

2 A survey of theories of international production

John Cantwell

In the 1970s and early 1980s it became fashionable to search for general theories of international production which encompassed all the contributions of earlier writers thought to be significant. These were sometimes advanced as general theories of the multinational corporation (MNC), the main institutional agent of international production, or general theories of foreign direct investment (FDI), the major means by which international production is financed.[1] When confronted with evidence on certain types of international production that their 'general' theories did not seem to explain, the proponents of such theories all too frequently seemed to respond either by dismissing the relevance of the evidence or by adapting their terminology to accommodate it. To the extent they succeeded their theories became increasingly cumbersome and less operational (as discussed by Buckley, 1983).

By the late 1980s the limitations of particular theoretical approaches as catch-all explanations of international production seem to have become clearer even to their keenest advocates. This has led work in the field in two directions. First, within each approach there has been an effort to extend or develop theories to broaden their coverage, while allowing for the influence of other factors perhaps better explained by other complementary theoretical approaches. One issue that most schools of thought have identified as particularly requiring attention is the dynamic aspects of international production. This chapter therefore concentrates on theories of the growth of international production, and of changes in its composition, from various different perspectives.

Second, an attempt has been made to avoid fruitless confrontation between alternative theories setting out spuriously to encompass one another, by constructing a general framework of analysis of international production which represents the common ground between different theoretical approaches but is not inextricably wedded to any of them. It also provides a framework for helping to articulate the real areas of disagreement and to decide between alternative theories where they offer genuinely competing explanations of the same phenomenon. This general framework has been developed by John Dunning, and since it deliberately draws on a variety of theoretical approaches it is known as the eclectic paradigm (Dunning, 1977, 1981, 1988a). The eclectic paradigm combines elements of quite different approaches to international production, and so it should not be misunderstood as itself another general theory: 'precisely because of its generality, the eclectic paradigm has only limited power to explain or predict particular kinds of international production; and even less, the behaviour of individual enterprises,' (Dunning, 1988a; 1).

Theoretical diversity is to be expected in the field of the economics of international production as much as in any other area of economics. However, it is one of the virtues of the eclectic paradigm that it makes clear that such diversity is attributable not only to a variety of ideological standpoints. There are three additional reasons to expect theoretical diversity in this case. First, international production may be of a resource-based, import-substituting, export-platform or globally integrated kind, each of which raises distinctive considerations and each of which affects home and host counties in different ways.

Second, and related to this, the use of particular theories often reflects the issues addressed and the questions asked. Theories of international production have drawn on six separate branches of economic theory (Cantwell *et al.*, 1986): the theories of international capital movements, trade, location, industrial organization, innovation and the firm. To give examples of possible approaches, those whose concern is with the MNC *per se* tend to rely on a particular theory of the firm, while those interested in FDI for its own sake may place special emphasis on a theory of international financial flows.

Third, international production can be analysed at three levels: macroeconomic (examining broad national and international trends), mesoeconomic (considering the interaction between firms at an industry level) and microeconomic (looking at the international growth of individual firms). It is quite natural that macroeconomic theories of international production should have often relied heavily on theories of trade, location and (in the case of FDI) the balance of payments and exchange rate effects; mesoeconomic approaches tend to be derived from industrial economics, game theory and the theory of innovation; while microeconomic thinking is grounded upon the theory of the firm.

Using this distinction between different levels of analysis, the main theories of international production can be grouped under four headings. These constitute four alternative theoretical frameworks, since approaches within each share certain common theoretical foundations. However, each of them can be further subdivided between particular theories or approaches, and they are not always mutually exclusive. The first two are based on alternative theories of the firm; the market power or Hymer theory of the firm, and the internalization or Coasian theory of the firm. The third group are macroeconomic developmental approaches, while the fourth are based on the analysis of competitive international industries.

It should be noted that, as already suggested above, the eclectic paradigm, is not an alternative analytical framework in the same sense, since it incorporates elements from all four types of approach and can be applied equally well at micro or macro levels. It is, rather, an overall organizing paradigm for identifying the elements from each approach which are most relevant in explaining a wide range of various kinds of international production, and the wide range of different environments in which international production has been established.

The next section reviews the four major types of approach to international production, together with the eclectic paradigm. The following one examines the relationship between different approaches in the perspectives they offer on the growth of the firm and international competitiveness. This leads into a concluding section on how the various approaches have attempted or are attempting to treat the dynamic aspects of international production, with some speculation on future developments in the analysis of international production. Since much of the literature has been concerned to emphasize the role played by technology in the growth of the MNCs, this features heavily in the discussion.

A SURVEY OF THE MAJOR THEORIES OF INTERNATIONAL PRODUCTION

The theory of international production dates from 1960, when Hymer, in a doctoral dissertation eventually published in 1976, showed that the orthodox theory of international trade and capital movements did not explain the foreign operations of MNCs (see Cantwell *et al.*, 1986). In particular, it did not explain two-way flows of FDI between countries, and still less between countries with similar factor proportions. His explanation of why firms move abroad and establish international production was based on a theory of the firm and industrial organization. Since that time, four major theoretical frameworks for the analysis of MNCs have emerged, and a fifth overall framework attempts to bring strands from each together. The first two are based on particular theories of the firm, and although their advocates sometimes claim that they are general theories, they are unlike the eclectic paradigm, which is a general all-encompassing framework which need not be tied to any particular theory of the firm or MNC development. The other two frameworks suggested here also collect together somewhat different approaches, derived from adaptations of the theory of international trade or economic development and the theory of oligopolistic competition or technological innovation respectively.

The first theoretical framework used to analyse international production is that passed down by Hymer, based on the view of the firm as an agent of market power and collusion. It comes in both non-Marxist and Marxist versions, the latter dating back to Baran and Sweezy (1966). Two of the clearest recent statements of this framework can be found in Newfarmer (1985) and Cowling and Sugden (1987). (See also chapters 3 and 8.)

The second is the internalization approach, based on a Coasian or institutionalist view of the firm as a device for raising efficiency by replacing markets; it has been advanced as a general paradigm by Rugman (1980), though less extravagent claims are made for a similar approach by Buckley and Casson (1976, 1985), Williamson (1975), Teece (1977), Caves (1982), and Casson (1987), amongst others. (See also chapter 4.)

Approaches based on the analysis of competitive interaction in international industries include later (Mark II) versions of the product cycle tradition (Vernon, 1974; Graham, 1975; Flowers, 1976; Knickerbocker, 1973), the technological accumulation approach (Pavitt, 1987; Cantwell, 1989b), the internationalization of capital approach (Jenkins, 1987), and in a development context the work of those whom Jenkins terms neo-fundamentalist Marxists (Warren, 1980).

Macroeconomic developmental approaches come in various forms, covering the earliest versions of the product cycle model (PCM Mark I), which trace back to Vernon (1966) and Hirsch (1967); the approach of the Japanese economists Kojima (1978) and Ozawa (1982); the investment–development cycle (Dunning, 1982) and stages of development approach (Cantwell and Tolentino, 1987), and – though these are rather different – approaches that deal with the role of financial factors in FDI (Aliber, 1970; Rugman, 1979; Casson, 1982).

The final framework is the eclectic paradigm developed by Dunning (1977, 1988a), which as its name suggests combines elements of all the other four in such a way that it is compatible with various different theoretical approaches. It can be applied at a macroeconomic or mesoeconomic level, but since it is discussed in the literature in a microeconomic context with reference to theories of the firm it is reviewed immediately after the first two approaches in the survey which follows. (See also chapter 5.)

The market power approach

The earliest articulation of a rounded-out theory of international production separate from the theory of international trade and capital movements can be traced back to Hymer (1976). In the traditional neoclassical approach economically advanced countries, owing to their relative abundance of capital but scarcity of labour, have low rates of profit or interest but high wage rates prior to international transactions. They therefore tend to export goods requiring capital-intensive production methods to less advanced labour-abundant countries; or, as a partial substitute for this, to export capital direct through FDI in developing countries. Capital thereby flows from countries in which the interest rate is low (owing to the abundance of capital) to those in which it is high (owing to capital scarcity).

The traditional classical and Marxist approaches reached similar conclusions, though by following a different line of reasoning. It was argued that there is a tendency for the rate of profit to fall (or in some versions a tendency towards underconsumption) in an advanced capitalist country. This provides an incentive to foreign investment in countries at an earlier stage of development, where capital can be employed more profitably. If the rate of profit at home has been driven down, owing to the intensity of competition, as in Adam Smith's story, then foreign investment in underdeveloped countries serves as an outlet for surplus capital. In Marxist accounts the rate of profit falls either because of a rise in the capital–output ratio (the organic composition of capital) or because of a fall in the share of profits in income (the rate of exploitation). It then follows that there are likely to be investment opportunities in economically backward countries with low capital–output ratios or which permit a super-exploitation of a weakly organized labour force. Alternatively foreign investment and trade involve the search for new markets in underdeveloped countries and regions, owing to the inadequacy of local consumption or demand.

Although theorists sometimes react only slowly to changes in the reality they endeavour to explain, such traditional explanations could not survive for long without severe adaptation in the period after 1945. It was true that before 1939 the bulk of international trade and investment ran between industrialized and developing countries, often in accord with colonial or other historical connections. However, this changed rapidly in the post-war period. In 1950 around three-fifths of manufacturing exports from Europe, North America or Japan were directed to the rest of the world, but by 1971 only just over a third (Armstrong *et al.*, 1984: 215). Even more dramatically, two-thirds of the world's stock of FDI was located in developing countries in 1938, but this had fallen to just over a quarter by the 1970s, where it has remained since (Dunning, 1983b: 88). In other words, international production is now organized principally between the industrialized countries.

Clearly, the conventional explanations of international production which were essentially constructed at a macroeconomic level were in need of substantial revision if they were to remain useful. They did not explain cross-investments between countries at an advanced stage of development, let alone the cross-investments within the same industry which became increasingly important from the 1970s onwards. Hymer's response was to apply a theory of the firm within its industry to establish the determinants of internationalization.

Hymer's particular theory of the firm sees it as a means by which producers increase the extent of their market power. A definition of market power can be taken from Sanjaya Lall, whose work at the time was identified with this approach:

> Market power . . . may . . . be simply understood as the ability of particular firms, acting singly or in collusion, to dominate their respective markets (and so earn higher profits), to be more secure, or even to be less efficient than in a situation with more effective competition. . . . The concept may, of course, be applied to buyers (monopsonists) as well as sellers.
>
> (Lall, 1976: 1343)

Originally applied to international production by Hymer (1976), this theoretical approach has been used recently by those such as Savary (1984), Newfarmer (1985) and Cowling and Sugden (1987).[2]

The main idea is that in the early stages of growth firms steadily increase their share of domestic markets by means of merger as well as capacity extension, and that as industrial concentration (and market power) rises so do profits. However, there comes a point at which it is no longer easy to further increase concentration in the domestic market, as few major firms remain, and at this stage profits earned from the high degree of monopoly power at home are invested in foreign operations, leading to a similar process of increased concentration in foreign markets.

The notion that firms everywhere seek out collusive arrangements as the major means by which they keep profits high is reminiscent of Adam Smith, but the market power school have gone further. According to Smith, competition between firms remained a spur to increased investment and technological change, whereas for those who have emphasized the role of market power in MNC activity investment is not so much an independent response to competition as a means of further extending collusive networks. MNCs are believed to invest in foreign operations to reduce competition and increase barriers to entry in their industry, and by increasing the degree of monopoly power they may even (in the longer term) have an adverse effect on the efficiency of foreign plants.

The market power theory of the firm is therefore clearly at odds with the alternative theory that the central objective of the firm is to raise its internal efficiency as the means of increasing profits. To the extent that MNCs raise research and productivity in their foreign operations, and improve efficiency through co-ordinating different types of plant and different types of technology, the effects on profitability in international industries may be ambiguous. Higher internal efficiency within MNCs may increase competition amongst them, making it more difficult for them to divide markets by agreement, and reducing profitability (or at least offsetting the gains due to greater efficiency). If this continues it may act as a disincentive to a further extension of international production, but in this view greater short-run efficiency is to be understood simply as a source of increased market power, which is likely to reduce the extent of investment in greater efficiency in the future.

The market power approach is often associated with the industrial organization literature, in which it is commonplace to argue that a more concentrated market structure is allied to greater collusion and a higher share of profit. It should be noted, though, that in Hymer's original version it was a theory of the firm and of the behaviour of the firm rather than a theory of industrial organization in the modern sense. In Hymer (1976) the firm appears as an active rather than a passive agent. Hymer followed Bain (1956) in viewing the firm as actively raising entry barriers and colluding with other firms in its industry. In the market power theory the primary causal link runs from the conduct of firms to market structure rather than vice versa. MNCs are seen as building up a position of market power at home, and then in their respective international industries. Their movement abroad is hastened by depression in the home market, which may result in part from their own diminishing incentive to invest, owing to their ever more extensive market power and collusive agreements.

Kindleberger's (1969) interpretation of the Hymer story placed it more firmly in the industrial organization tradition, which revolves around a structure–conduct–performance model. In Kindleberger's restatement the MNC was seen as a function of market structure characterized by monopolistic competition between differentiated products, rather than as an agent involved in oligopolistic interaction with other firms. The more recent writings of Newfarmer (1985) and Cowling and Sugden (1987) have moved back towards the Hymer stance, in that while their argument is set in an industrial organization context, they emphasize the (anti-competitive) impact of MNCs on host country market structure.

The use of an industrial organization context by more recent authors partly reflects a change in the issues and the institutions under study themselves. Hymer's objective had been to investigate why national firms went abroad, rather than to evaluate the operations of existing MNCs. Today the concern is with the way in which international industries are organized. Cowling and

Sugden (1987) contend that internationalization is undertaken not only as a means of increasing the market power of firms in final product markets, but also to raise the share of profits in two ways. First, the greater ability to shift production between alternative locations strengthens the bargaining power of firms in negotiations over wages and conditions of work. Second, by 'putting out' work previously done within the firm to a network of dependent subcontractors, both locally and internationally, the position of collectively organized trade unions in large plants is weakened. This is then integrated with the 'monopoly capitalism' argument of Baran and Sweezy (1966) or the stagnationist argument of Steindl (1952): a combination of a rising share of profits and an increasing market power (which reduces the incentive to invest) leads to a slower growth of demand, and secular stagnation eventually at an international level.

Within the market power approach, as is the case within all the frameworks considered, differences of emphasis can be detected. Hymer was concerned with the relationship between the efficiency with which production is organized within the firm and the extent of market power and collusion. By contrast, Cowling and Sugden (1987) make almost no mention of the technological efficiency of production other than with reference to the organization of work. They are much more concerned with the distribution of income between wages and profits. Indeed, Sugden (1983) suggests that the pursuit of a higher profit share necessarily entails inefficiency as MNCs geographically spread production as a means of increasing their bargaining power through a 'divide and rule' strategy. Certain of the differences between authors and approaches to international production can therefore be attributed to differences in the issues addressed.

Internalization

The alternative theory of the firm which has been applied to international production derives from the work of Coase and lays emphasis on the efficiency with which transactions between units of productive activity are organized. This modern theory of the 'internalization' of markets as it is applied in the case of international production (see Buckley and Casson, 1976) is based on Coase's (1937) criticism of neoclassical economics. The framework of analysis, like the neoclassical theory of trade and investment, is based on exchange between individuals or groups of individuals, but it introduces the transaction costs of such exchange, which vary in an arm's-length or market relationship as compared with a co-operative relationship. Where the transaction costs of an administered exchange are lower than those of a market exchange, then the market is internalized and the collective efficiency of the group is thereby increased. Apart from the existence of ecomomies of scope across activities, the direct co-ordination of transactions may reduce the costs associated with information impactedness, opportunism, bounded rationality and uncertainty (for a summary see Caves, 1982).

It is argued that intangible assets such as technology are especially costly to exchange in arm's-length transactions. By thinking of the exchange of technology as a transaction that is internalized when the firm has a horizontally integrated network of production, horizontal integration is treated by analogy with vertical integration. Firms that invest abroad in R&D facilities are therefore treated in exactly the same way as firms that invest in a venture to extract natural resources and secure supplies of raw materials; both are internalizing markets, and it is simply that they internalize markets for different commodities.

Where markets are internalized through the common ownership and control of the groups that are involved in exchange with one another, the transaction cost approach suggests the appropriate institutional arrangement on which co-operation between the parties is likely to be founded. At one extreme are joint ventures over which the MNC exerts little direct control, or a largely decentralized MNC in which internal markets regulated by transfer prices have replaced external markets, as emphasized by Rugman (1981). Indeed, where the MNC internalizes an externality (an external economy or diseconomy) it may create an internal market where no external market existed previously (Casson, 1986a). At the other extreme is the organizational structure stressed by Williamson (1975), that of globally integrated multinationals in which control is centralized and hierarchical. This distinction is discussed in Kay (1983).

Of course, there is an overlap of the spectrums spanned by market and administrative co-ordination, in that where market exchange is characterized by monopolistic or monopsonistic elements, the MNC may exercise control over its contractual partner without resort to 'internalization'. Strictly speaking, in the transaction cost approach the firm is defined as the direct organizer of non-market transactions. However, the firm or MNC might equally well be defined as the controller and co-ordinator of an (international) network of production or income-generating assets (Cowling and Sugden, 1987). If so, the firm may exercise control over production which it has subcontracted out but for which it is the monopsonistic buyer. Transactions are of an external market kind, but production may be controlled and co-ordinated from a single administrative centre. In this respect the internalization framework offers a theory of the choice between different modes of transacting rather than a theory of the (boundaries of) the firm.

To be of use in empirical work this approach needs to be operationalized in a workable model of transaction costs (Casson, 1981; Buckley, 1983), but the variables thought to be especially significant are the regularity of transactions between the parties, and the complexity of the technology exchanged. Transaction cost analysis may also require adjustment to take account of the distribution of the gains from exchange under different institutional arrangements (as suggested by Sugden, 1983). Thus the MNC may not favour the most efficient or lowest-cost arrangement if its profit share is higher under another. By the internationalization of production MNCs may weaken the effectiveness of trade union organization, and increase the share of profits.

Advocates of the internalization approach have also recognized the possibility that MNCs may increase profits through the restriction of competition in final product markets, and that this may offset the generally superior allocation of resources associated with MNC activity:

> Welfare losses arise where multinationals maximise monopoly profits by restricting the output of (high technology) goods and services . . . where vertical integration is used as a barrier to entry . . . [or] because they provide a more suitable mechanism for exploiting an international monopoly than does a cartel.
>
> (Buckley, 1985: 119)

However, they believe that, even in the presence of monopolistic elements, the creation of new internal markets generates sufficient improvements in efficiency that overall cost minimization remains the overriding motivation of the growth of the firm:

> The internal market . . . in the long run will stimulate both the under-taking of R&D and its effective implementation in production and marketing. Consequently, dynamic welfare improvement is likely to result.
>
> (Buckley, 1985: 119)

Although in the past internalization theorists and the market power school have claimed theirs as a general theory of the firm (and hence of the MNC), they have each addressed rather specific aspects of the firm's operations. Unlike in the market power argument, in the transaction cost approach the structure of the final product market is of only secondary interest. The emphasis is on achieving profit maximization through the efficient exchange of intermediate products, rather than through the exclusion of (potential) rivals in the final product market.

For this reason the counterfactuals with which international production is compared are different. Internalization theorists have treated the alternative to international production as being the licensing of a local firm (or inter-firm trade in intermediate products), or exports from the home country (and no local production). The market power school have instead treated the alternative as being independent local production, which is driven out or diminished by the direct local presence of the MNC (or, to a lesser extent, by its licensing a local competitor). In this respect, it is quite possible for work in the internalization tradition to take into account influences deriving from competition or collusion in final product markets or the distribution of income, just as certain of the market power group going back to Hymer himself made allowance for efficiency considerations. However, disagreement between these approaches remains in the sense that the choice of theoretical issues on which to concentrate is not arbitrary but reflects what each camp believes to be the most important historical driving forces underlying the growth of the modern firm.

The eclectic paradigm

The eclectic paradigm grew out of a desire to synthesize elements from the two competing theories of the firm and certain other approaches to international production considered below. However, it was not intended to be a complete synthesis, as it is not possible to encompass fully a set of theories which address rather different questions and rely on different views of the world. It was therefore soon acknowledged that it was not itself another theory. It was instead intended to provide an overall analytical framework for empirical investigations which would draw the attention of the analyst to the most important theories for the problem at hand. It also provided a framework for a comparison between theories, by establishing the common ground or the points of contact between them, and clarifying the relationship between different levels of analysis and the different questions which theorists have been concerned to address. Thus, for example, internalization theory may be the most relevant under certain circumstances or when answering certain kinds of questions (such as those related to backward vertical integration into resource extraction), while the determinants of the competitive strategy of firms in their final product market may be more pertinent in other cases (such as technological competition or co-operation).

In the eclectic paradigm it is contended that MNCs have competitive or 'ownership' advantages *vis-à-vis* their major rivals, which they utilize in establishing production in sites that are attractive owing to their 'location' advantages. According to Dunning, two types of competitive advantage can be distinguished; the first is attributable to the ownership of particular unique intangible assets (such as firm-specific technology), and the second is due to the joint ownership of complementary assets (such as the ability to create new technologies).[3] MNCs retain control over their networks of assets (productive, commercial, financial, and so forth) because of the 'internalization' advantages of doing so. Internalization advantages arise from the greater ease with which an integrated firm is able to appropriate a full return on its ownership of distinctive assets such as its own technology, as well as directly from the co-ordination of the use of complementary assets, subject to the costs of managing a more complex network.[4]

Dunning (1988a) describes the internalization advantages that result from the co-ordination of the use of complementary assets as 'the transactional benefits . . . arising from a common governance of a network of these assets, located in different countries' (p. 2). That such benefits can be enjoyed only through co-ordination within the firm rather than by market co-ordination is said to be the result of transactional market failure. Three reasons are given for transactional market failure (Dunning, 1988a, b). First, risk and uncertaintly may be significant in transactions carried out across national boundaries. Second, where there are externalities, benefits external to the transactions concerned may not be captured by parties transacting at arm's length. Third, there may be economies of scope through the direct co-ordination of interrelated activities.

More will be said about ownership advantages in due course, since they have been the subject of considerable debate in the literature. However, there are two points that must be clarified at the outset. First, there may appear to be an overlap between those ownership advantages which are due to the joint ownership of complementary assets and those internalization advantages which derive from the co-ordinated use of such assets. In fact the distinction here is rather like the distinction between the advantages of owning particular assets such as patented technology and the internalization advantages of retaining control over their use in order to ensure that the full return on them is appropriated by the firm that holds proprietory rights.

None the less, while ownership advantages that derive from particular assets can normally (in principle, at least) be sold – such as in the licensing of the use of a technology to another firm – there is in general no market for ownership advantages of a more collective kind. Examples of the collective type of ownership advantage are the overall organizational abilities of the firm, the experience and entrepreneurial capabilities of its managers taken together, the reputation and creditworthiness of the firm in international capital markets, its political contacts and its long-term business agreements with other firms. This kind of ownership advantage goes beyond any particular asset or any one individual, and in general cannot be sold outside the firm but is usable only within it.

One such collective ownership advantage is the ability of the firm to generate new technology, which will eventually result in a stream of new ownership advantages of a particular kind. This example will serve to illustrate the distinction between collective ownership advantages at the level of the firm as a whole and the internalization advantages of the co-ordinated use of assets which are associated with them. Consider a firm which holds a strong position in a certain branch of the chemical industry and which uses its innovative potential to expand into the development of a technologically related chemical process. Suppose for the sake of argument that, to date, scientific and technical effort in the related sector has been concentrated outside the home country of the firm, so that its development work in this area is undertaken primarily in a subsidiary located in some foreign centre of excellence for the process concerned. A specialized R&D unit is established in the foreign country which is linked up with the parent firm's R&D facilities.

Now the ability of the firm to set up production in the foreign country and to initiate a new research programme there is due to its initial ownership advantage, which consists of established technology and an innovative strength in chemicals. The firm then gains internalization advantages through the co-ordination of R&D in home and host countries, which extends its original ownership advantage by increasing its capacity to innovate in both related sectors. In other words there is a progressive interaction between ownership advantages (the possession of technology and the ability to innovate) and internalization advantages (the international co-ordination of R&D facilities). Ownership and internalization advantages increase alongside one another in the case of successful international growth.

The second point that requires clarification at this stage is that the concept of ownership advantages is open to two possible theoretical interpretations. It is apparent from the discussion above that the market power theory of the firm perceives ownership advantages principally as anti-competitive devices which act as barriers to entry against other firms. Meanwhile, the competitive international industry approach considered below sees ownership advantages as competitive weapons which sustain a process of competition between rivals. For this reason ownership advantages are 'sometimes called competitive or [sometimes called] monopolistic advantages' (Dunning, 1988a: 2).

In conventional neoclassical or industrial organization analyses of market structure in which competition and monopoly are treated as opposites, to describe advantages as competitive or monopolistic would suggest a contradiction in terms. This is how matters also appear on the whole to the market power school, whose work is one variant of the industrial organization analysis. In their view if the larger firms in an industry have stronger ownership advantages this reduces the number of firms in the sector and increases the extent of collusion amongst those that remain, thereby restricting competition and implying a higher degree of monopoly power.

However, this contrasts with the classical approach to competition, which saw it as a process rather than a market structure. In the dynamic view of competition what matters is not the number of firms in an industry but the mobility of resources (within firms, as well as in terms of the entry and exit of new firms) and the balance of forces between firms in an industry. In this context in an oligopolistic industry Jenkins (1987) argues that competition and monopoly coexist. Firms compete through the continual creation of quasi-monopolistic positions, such as the creation of a new technology ahead of the field. It will be necessary to return to this issue in later sections.

As the eclectic paradigm is an overall organizing framework rather than a theory, it has no definite view of competition built into it. Nor does it depend *a priori* on a particular theory of the firm. It is capable of providing expression either to the internalization approach, in which the firm grows by displacing markets which operate in a costly and imperfect way, or the market power theory, in which it is the growth of the firm that is the essential cause of market imperfections and failure. The eclectic paradigm incorporates elements of both these alternative theories of the firm, since it allows that ownership advantages may act as barriers to entry and sources of market power. However, Dunning himself accords priority to internalization and supposes that competition is more important than collusion amongst MNCs: 'It is not the orthodox type of monopoly advantages which give the enterprise an edge over its rivals – actual or potential – but the advantages which accrue through internalisation . . .' (Dunning, 1988b: 32). Indeed, the latest terminology in which the eclectic paradigm has been couched (Dunning, 1988a, b), suggesting that the growth of the firm is a function of market failure, owes much to the internalization approach. While particular ownership advantages and the internalization advantages of appropriating rents are attributed to structural market failure, collective ownership advantages and the internalization advantages of co-ordinating the use of complementary assets are said to be due to transactional market failure.

Despite the priority which Dunning gives to the internalization over the market power theory of the firm, it would still be wrong to make the eclectic paradigm synonymous with the internalization approach, as is sometimes done in literature reviews. The more general nature of the eclectic paradigm has already been stressed, and this allows it to give equal weight to theories of macroeconomic locational advantages, and the interaction between the firm and its macroeconomic environment. Thus 'The theory of foreign-owned production stands at the crossroads between a macroeconomic theory of international trade and a microeconomic theory of the firm' (Dunning, 1988b: 19). In the same way the eclectic paradigm can be used to set out arguments that derive from competitive international industry approaches.

In this case interest also switches away from the analysis of the firm or MNC as such, towards the impact of the activity of one firm on that of another, and the interrelated development of the firm and its industry.

Competitive international industry approaches

Of the theoretical frameworks considered here there are two combinations which have conflicting perspectives, even though ideas from one might be used to qualify the other. The different perspectives of the market power and internalization theories of the firm have already been discussed; the market power and competitive international industry approaches are similarly opposed, though for slightly different reasons. Both relate to final product markets and are set out in the context of an oligopolistic industry. However, while the market power school suppose that, in general, internationalization lowers the extent of competition and increases collusion amongst firms, competitive international industry approaches share the view that in general the growth of international production tends to be associated with rivalry and to sustain the process of technological competition amongst MNCs. Also, the latter are genuinely mesoeconomic (industry-level) approaches and do not constitute another theory of the firm; they begin from the interaction between firms and the progress of industrial development, rather than examining the implications of behaviour inherent in the nature of the firm itself.

The earliest oligopolistic theories of international production (in the rivalrous as opposed to the market power sense) were later versions of the product cycle model, and similar extensions of the product cycle approach. In 1971 Vernon recognized that the original PCM was losing its explanatory capacity, and in 1974 he suggested a modified (Mark II) version which introduced oligopolistic considerations (Vernon, 1971, 1974). After the initial innovatory phase of the product life cycle, established firms were seen as preserving their position through the existence of scale economies in place of technological leadership.

In this case the reason for relocating production abroad (import-substituting investment) as a product matured was no longer a matter of simple profit maximization in the face of a changing pattern of demand as income levels in other countries caught up. The emphasis shifted towards risk-minimizing strategies, with the aim of avoiding price warfare in a mature oligopoly. On the assumption of a high ratio of fixed to total costs in an industry characterized by economies of scale, security became a more important consideration for the firm relative to profitability. Vernon argued that this led to cross-investment (that is, intra-industry production) to reduce the threat of subsidiary price-cutting in the domestic market of each large firm, despite the potential cost-minimizing benefits of concentrating production in just one or a few locations.

This idea of intra-industry production as an 'exchange of threats' became crucial to the work of Graham (1975, 1978, 1985). According to Graham, oligopolistic interaction between firms in an industry increases as firms grow, since (following product cycle reasoning) the capital-intensity of production rises and economies of scale become more important as the product line matures. As the ratio of fixed to total costs rises the consequence of rivals adopting aggressive price-cutting stratregies becomes potentially more damaging, and so each firm increasingly takes account of risks as well as returns. In doing so it may have to accept some trade-off between security and profitability (Rothschild, 1947).

The notion of the search for security is also at the heart of the market power theory of the firm, though in this case it is achieved through monopolization and collusion and is generally supposed to be in line with profitability (Cowling and Sugden, 1987). Indeed, Hymer and Rowthorn (1970) had argued on this basis that the leading firms in each industry would have to aim to have a similar geographical distribution of sales or production as one another, at which point collusive agreements to ensure security would reach a peak. However, in Graham's (1975) historical account, while industrial stability and an avoidance of price warfare had typically been maintained before 1914 by collusive agreements and cartels, the exchange of threats was seen as a non-collusive alternative, which since 1960 had become the more usual means of reducing risk. With an exchange of threats competition is preserved, but in a stable rather than a cut-throat form.

To emphasise the difference with the analysis of the market power school, Graham (1985) goes beyond the product cycle framework and suggests that intra-industry production involving the cross-investments of MNCs in the same sector will generally act to accelerate new product development and introduction. He therefore reaches the very opposite view to that of Hymer and Rowthorn (1970) or Cowling and Sugden (1987): 'interpenetration of national markets by MNCs based in different countries – assuming that no merger of major rivals results – acts to reduce the likelihood that collusion can be successfully undertaken globally' (Graham, 1985: 82).

The notion of oligopolistic interaction can also be combined with various other non-product cycle ideas on the firm. Sanna Randaccio (1980) combined oligopolistic interaction with Penrose's (1959) theory of the growth of the firm. She hypothesized that the ability of a firm to gain an increasing share of an individual market through local production was a function of the share of that market already held. Firms with a smaller existing share would be able to grow rapidly, with a lower risk of setting in motion a damaging competitive warfare. To allow a stable competitive process to continue to run smoothly, it was therefore in the interests of US firms to switch resources away from domestic growth and towards the expansion of their European production (starting from a smaller base), just as it was in the interests of European firms to expand their US operations.

Meanwhile, returning to the exchange of threat view of oligopolistic interaction, Casson (1987) has attempted to integrate it with the internalization theory of the firm. In this case, in order to examine the implications for rivalry of different relative market shares, Casson's model makes the determinants of long-run market share exogenous. Depending upon the relative strength of firms, an exchange of threats (establishing a foothold in the major markets of rivals) may be used to preserve price stability.

In recent years work has also begun on technological competition between the MNCs in an international industry, rather than on the effect of oligopolistic rivalry on price competition. The quotation from Graham above suggests a connection between technological competition and the rise of intra-industry production. Cantwell (1989b) shares Graham's view that the increasing internationalization of manufacturing production has helped to sustain technological competition between MNCs. Following the idea that MNC expansion can be linked to a process of technological accumulation within the firm (Pavitt, 1987), innovation and the growth of international production are seen as mutually supportive.

The term 'technological accumulation' encapsulates the view that the development of technology within a firm is a cumulative process. That is, the creation of new technology is to be understood as a gradual and painstaking process of continual adjustment and refinement, as new productive methods are tested and adapted in the light of experience. In any firm there is a continual interaction between the creation of technology and its use in production. For this reason, although a group of firms in a given industry are likely to have similar lines of technological development (similarities which may be increased through collaborative R&D projects, through drawing on the results of publicly funded research, and through imitation), the actual technological path of each is to some degree unique and differentiated. The acquisition of new skills, and the generation of new technological capacity, partially embodied in new plant and equipment, must be a goal of every firm in an oligopolistic industry if it is to maintain and increase its profits. Even where new technology is acquired from outside the firm, it must be gradually adapted and integrated with its existing production methods.

The notion of technological accumulation is consistent with the ideas of Rosenberg (1976, 1982), Usher (1929) and the earlier work of Marx on technological change through systematic adaptation. More recently,

Atkinson and Stiglitz (1969), Nelson and Winter (1977) and Stiglitz (1987) have spoken of 'localized' technological change in the context of the previous technological evolution and learning experience of the firm.

While the product cycle theory supposed that an individual act of technology creation was then diffused abroad, in the technological accumulation approach the use of technology in new environments feeds back into fresh adaptation and (depending upon the state of local scientific and technical capability) new innovation. When production is located in an area that is itself a centre of innovation in the industry concerned, the firm may gain access to research facilities which allow it to extend technology creation in what are for it previously untried directions. In recent years technological accumulation has frequently been organized in international networks, or in other words integrated MNCs. At one time MNCs may have been simply the providers of technology and finance for scattered international production; today they have become global organizers of economic systems, including systems for allied technological development in different parts of the world.

The technological accumulation approach therefore addresses the question of why it is that technology is developed in international networks rather than in a series of separately owned plants. Part of the answer is provided by internalization theory, which focuses on why MNCs as opposed to purely national firms have come into existence. That is, if the initiating firm is to appropriate a full return on its technological advantage, and if it is to co-ordinate the successful introduction of its new technology elsewhere, then it must exercise direct control over the network as a whole. However, this may be not so much a feature of the market for technology, which is the focus of internalization theory, as a feature of the very nature of technological development itself.

Suppose for a moment that the act of exchanging technology between firms does not present a problem, in that a reasonable price for such an exchange can always be readily agreed. Now consider an international industry in which constituent firms produce more or less identical products for the same international markets. However, each firm has its own quite specific process technology, derived from a distinct technological tradition (say, different chemical processes with a similar end result). In this situation, if technological accumulation is continuous in each firm, raising its productivity or lowering its costs along a given line of technological development, then no firm would abandon its existing pattern of innovation and buy in all its technology from a competitor. It would be far more costly, and perhaps even impossible, for a firm to switch into a completely new line of technological development, by comparison with the costs of the potential seller of technology simply extending its own network. Some exchanges of technology between existing firms will take place, since alternative lines of technological accumulation in the same industry are often complementary to one another. However, where technology is bought in it must be adapted to and incorporated into an existing stream of innovation, and this adaptation becomes part and parcel of the on-going process within an established firm of generating its own technology.

In the case outlined, the retention of technology within each firm has little to do with any failure or malfunctioning of the market for technology, but everything to do with the close association between the generation and the utilization of a distinctive type of technology within each firm. By extending its own network, each firm extends the use of its own unique line of technological development, and by extending it into new environments it increases the complexity of this development. The expansion of international production thereby brings gains to the firm as a whole, as the experience gained from adapting its technology under new conditions feeds back new ideas for development to the rest of its system. For this reason, once they have achieved a sufficient level of technological strength in their own right, firms are particularly keen to produce in the areas from which their major international rivals have emanated, which offer them access to alternative sources of complementary innovation. This offers one explanation of the increase in intra-industry production in the industrialized countries (Cantwell, 1987b).

This is founded on the belief that innovation is location-specific as well as firm-specific (Cantwell, 1989b). The scientific and technological traditions of each country, the shared experience of its researchers and production engineers and the communication between them across companies, the nature of its educational system, and its common business practices – all contribute to the distinctiveness of the path of technology development undertaken in each location. By drawing on innovations of various kinds depending upon the conditions prevailing in the relevant local research centre MNCs develop a more complex technological system. The attractiveness of locations for other research-related investments may well be strengthened in the process. The involvement of foreign MNCs in research in centres of innovation has a direct effect on broadening the scope of local technological capability, and an indirect effect through its competitive stimulus encouraging other firms to extend their local research programmes. The process helps to establish locational poles of attraction for research-related activity.

The technological accumulation approach suggests two major reasons why the growth of international production has been associated with sustained technological competition between MNCs in manufacturing industries. First, internationalization has supported technological diversification, since the form of technological development varies between locations as well as between firms. By locating production in an alternative centre of innovation in its industry the MNC gains access to a new but complementary avenue of technological development, which it integrates with its existing lines. By increasing the overlap between the technological profile of firms competition between MNCs is raised in each international industry, but so also are co-operative agreements as the number of technological spill-overs between firms increases as well. Spill-overs occur where technologies are created by a firm which lie outside its own major lines of development but which may be of greater use within the main traditions of another firm.

Second, and partly because of the first factor, today there are a growing number of connections between technologies which were formerly quite separate. This greater technological interrelatedness has brought more firms, and especially MNCs, into competition with one another. These two elements have been associated with the growth of what are sometimes called 'technological systems' in MNCs. Where MNCs in a competitive international industry are all attracted to certain centres of innovation to maintain their overall strength, then research and research-related production may tend to agglomerate in these locations (Cantwell, 1987c).

Some similar themes appear in the internationalization of capital approach of Jenkins (1984, 1987). In his view the growth of international production is just one aspect of a trend towards a more integrated world economy. As a result of this trend in each industry products and processes have become increasingly standardized across countries, while firms safeguard their competitive position through the continuing differentiation of products and technology. Once again, the growth of MNCs is seen as part of a competitive process, in which each firm attempts to gain competitive advantages through innovation, and only in certain circumstances do they enter (for a time) into collusive arrangements.

According to Jenkins, if nationalistic governments in LDCs prevent the entry of MNCs this only reduces the speed of adaptation to the requirements of international competition, but does not allow them to avoid such adaptation altogether. Marxists such as Warren (1980) go further and argue that FDI helps to promote local capitalist development and economic advance. They emphasize oligopolistic competition between MNCs of different national origins. They reject the idea that MNCs provide host LDCs with inappropriate technology, and contend that this is simply a defence of economic backwardness (Emmanuel, 1982).

In the opinion of Jenkins (1987), the emphasis that Baran and Sweezy (1966) and the Marxists that followed them placed upon monopoly, and their downplaying of oligopolistic competition between MNCs, can be traced back to a time when the USA and its firms held a hegemonic position in the world economy. Since then newer MNCs from Europe, Japan and now the Third World have been growing rapidly. The increasing internationalization of R&D also suggests that MNC growth has helped to sustain technological competition. The use of the market power approach as a *general* theory of international production therefore has a somewhat dated feel about it.

However, competitive international industry approaches allow for co-operation and collusion between firms, and for the weakening of local firms as a consequence of MNC expansion under certain circumstances. Inward investment may have competitive or anti-competitive effects on host country industries (Cantwell, 1989b). It has been argued that in modern international industries a competitive impact from MNC growth in one location and an anti-competitive effect in another are two sides of the same coin (Cantwell, 1987c). Where indigenous firms enjoy a strong technological tradition in the sector in question the growth of international production provides a competitive stimulus which encourages an increase in local research-related activity, while where such a tradition is weaker the research of local firms may be displaced by simpler, assembly types of production organized by foreign MNCs. The faster growth and upgrading of activity in one location are then achieved at the direct expense of the downgrading of another, as different stages of production become geographically separated.

Macroeconomic developmental approaches

It was argued above that the earliest neoclassical and Marxist macroeconomic theories of foreign capital movements could not deal satisfactorily with the growth of international production between industrialized countries at a similar stage of development. The more modern macroeconomic theories of international production which address this question are currently at a rather more rudimentary stage of development than are microeconomic or mesoeconomic theories (for a survey see Gray, 1982). They have tended to attract less attention than theories of the firm since the demise of the product cycle model or PCM (Giddy, 1978; Vernon, 1979). However, their origins go back to the same period, the early 1960s. They emerged as a result of criticisms of the traditional theory of international trade, just as Hymer's work represented a criticism of the traditional theory of international capital movements.

The product cycle itself was in the first instance a purely microeconomic idea which had been familiar for some time in business schools, but which was applied by Vernon (1966) to topical discussions on patterns of international trade and the balance of payments. Vernon's criticism of conventional trade theory also called attention to the rapid rise of international production amongst US firms in Europe at that time. In the Heckscher – Ohlin – Samuelson (HOS) theory trade (or FDI, where capital movements substituted for trade) should be greatest between countries whose proportional factor endowments are most dissimilar. This could not explain the tremendous post-war expansion of trade and investment in manufacturing industry between the US and Europe. Nor could a theory which assumed that trade automatically balances in accordance with comparative advantage offer any assistance in explaining regular US trade surpluses in the 1950s.

The role of technological factors in addressing these issues had already been clear to some authors in the 1950s. As is well known, Leontief (1954) referred to the significance of skilled labour in US export industries. Meanwhile, in linking trade imbalances with the monetary side of the balance of payments, Johnson (1958) suggested that the persistence of a dollar shortage in Europe after the Second World War may be explained by the lag with which innovation in Europe followed that in the USA. Then in the early 1960s two important papers on trade theory appeared. Posner (1961) pioneered a 'technology gap' theory of that part of trade based on innovating and learning faster than others; the link with the problems confronted by Leontief and Johnson are evident. At around the same time Linder (1961) argued that the main motor of trade was a similarity of income levels and patterns of demand, suggesting that trade flows are greatest between countries with similar factor endowments.

The PCM attempted to combine elements from both the Posner and the Linder theories of international trade, and to do so in such a way that the growth of US FDI in European manufacturing became part of the story. The essential argument is that high incomes and demand in the USA fostered innovation, especially in consumer durables produced by labour-saving techniques. This gave US firms a competitive lead which they exploited initially through exports and then through import-substituting investment in the region (Europe) catching up. Eventually, as products matured, trade in the sectors concerned would return to a cost-determined comparative advantage pattern, with MNCs losing technological advantages and having to rely on barriers to entry in marketing and distribution instead.

Apart from the original work of Vernon (1966) and Hirsch (1967), the PCM is explained clearly by Wells (1972) and in the studies of Hufbauer (1965, 1970). Detailed critical summaries can be found in Cantwell (1987a), Vernon (1979), Giddy (1978) and Buckley and Casson (1976). One reason for the demise of the PCM is that the technological leadership enjoyed by the USA in the 1950s and early 1960s gave way to a more balanced technological competition between the USA, Europe and Japan. Indeed, it is now Japan which has a regular trade surplus and whose firms are investing heavily in US manufacturing. Another reason is that the PCM deals only with import-substituting investment, but since the 1970s the global integration of affiliates within MNCs has become steadily more important.

In his criticism of the PCM Kojima (1978) relied heavily on the distinction between import-substituting (trade-displacing) and offshore or export-platform (trade-creating) types of investment. An unfortunate pro-Japanese anti-American slant was given to his argument by a presumption that through its effects on trade import-substituting investment damaged welfare while export-platform investment improved it, and by his labelling the former 'American-type' and the latter 'Japanese-type'. Apart from the fact that there are many US firms with export-platform investments in South East Asia, and many Japanese firms with import-substituting investments in Europe and the USA, there is no reason why import-substituting investments must reduce the overall extent of trade at a macroeconomic level (as opposed to the level of the individual firm) unless certain restrictive assumptions are made. Moreover, there is evidence to suggest that export-platform investments are more likely to be of an enclave kind, with little technology diffusion to host-country firms (Dunning and Cantwell, 1990), and therefore they may play a lesser role in host-country industrial adjustment and welfare.

Kojima's position owes much to his interpretation of FDI (unlike Vernon) within an HOS model. Import-substituting investment was therefore seen as a replacement of trade in accordance with comparative advantage (investment emanating from an advantaged home country), while export-platform investment involved firms in an industry comparatively disadvantaged in the home country. As an extension of this argument, Kojima and Ozawa (1985) claim that global welfare is increased where international production helps to restructure the industries of each country in line with dynamic comparative advantage.

The underlying developmental process described by Vernon and Hirsch and by Kojima and Ozawa have many similarities despite the broader nature of the Kojima–Ozawa argument, and despite the differences in the theories of trade they employ. The Kojima–Ozawa approach applies particularly to a country which is growing rapidly, such as in recent years Japan, Germany or the newly industrializing countries. As local firms innovate and steadily upgrade their domestic activity, they have an interest in relocating their less sophisticated types of production in countries at an earlier stage of development. Although they still possess the technological and organizational know-how to sustain this simpler production, it may be more profitable to do so abroad, and to concentrate on higher value-added activities in the now more developed home environment. In other words, as in the PCM, firms relocate 'mature' or 'maturing' lines of production in countries which are still a step behind the home country.

Apart from export-platform investments, Ozawa (1979, 1982) pays particular attention to resource-based investments. Again, in a country experiencing rapid industrial growth, and especially in a 'Ricardian' one such as Japan, lacking in natural resources, the rate of domestic expansion is likely to be constrained by resource availability. Home-country MNCs then have a direct interest in investing in resource-related development abroad as a means of supplying their own domestic markets. As they develop their manufacturing operations at home and in other industrialized countries, they may wish to move basic resource processing and simple manufacturing activities close to the site of resource extraction. In this case, the objectives of MNCs are in line with the development strategies of host countries.

This is an interesting idea, particularly when it is not assumed to be peculiarly true of Japanese MNCs alone, and once it is stripped from the intellectual straitjacket of the HOS model in which Kojima had confined it. Today, Japanese MNCs are at least as concerned with oligopolistic investments in the USA and Europe as with resource-based and export-platform investments in less developed countries (LDCs). It is now the newer Third World multinationals that are especially oriented to LDCs.

The major problem with Kojima's use of the HOS model is that it cannot be assumed that the industries in which a country has its greatest innovative potential are those in which it currently enjoys a comparative advantage (Pasinetti, 1981; Cantwell, 1989b). This indeed is the lesson of Japan's own post-war history, in which she successfully encouraged local technological development in sectors in which she began with a comparative disadvantage. With the assistance of foreign MNCs through licensing agreements (Ozawa, 1974) some comparatively disadvantaged industries were transformed into comparatively advantaged ones.

Moreover, it was precisely Vernon's point that import-substituting investment need not emanate from a sector in which the home country has a comparative advantage (unlike in the HOS model). A country which holds technological leadership may be a net exporter in some comparatively disadvantaged as well as in comparatively advantaged industries, owing to the technological edge of its firms. This is what gives it a regular trade surplus. If the innovative lead is lost (in the PCM as products mature) then production is relocated in accordance with underlying cost-determined comparative advantage. Kojima should also welcome this type of industrial adjustment if his argument were to be applied consistently.

A more general macroeconomic approach is the investment-development cycle, advanced by Dunning (1982). This is based upon the proposition that the level of inward and outward direct investment of different countries, and the balance between the two, depend upon their national stage of development. The poorest countries have very little inward or outward FDI, and consequently a level of net outward investment that is close to zero.

Countries at somewhat higher levels of development attract significant amounts of inward direct investment, but as the outward investment of their own firms is still limited they register negative net outward investment. Past some point outward direct investment takes off, and for countries at yet higher levels of development net outward investment begins to increase, until for the most developed countries it returns to zero and beyond this becomes positive.

Empirical evidence for the period since the mid-1970s presented by Tolentino (1987) suggests that this formulation may now require some qualification. Countries now seem to be embarking on outward direct investment more rapidly and at a much earlier stage of development than they once were. Apart from the fast growth of MNCs from Japan and Germany, a wide range of smaller industrialized and Third World countries have become significant sources of outward direct investment. The increasing internationalization of production has become a general phenomenon.

Dunning (1986) has elaborated upon the investment–development cycle by arguing that the character and composition of the outward direct investment of a country's firms (as well as its level) vary with the national stage of development. Early foreign ventures are frequently resource-based, but as firms mature they move beyond investment in a single activity or product and adopt a more international perspective on the location of the different types of production in which they are involved. Such MNCs are increasingly responsible for directly organizing an international division of labour in place of markets, and so the character of their activity and their ownership advantages become further removed from the conditions of their home countries.

Cantwell and Tolentino (1987) have extended this idea to argue that the outward direct investment of countries itself tends to follow a developmental course over time. Beginning from resource-based activity with fairly limited technological requirements, MNC involvement shifts towards gradually more sophisticated types of manufacturing. For the mature multinationals of Europe and the USA such an evolution has been going on for over a hundred years. The changing industrial composition of investment is associated with a changing geographical composition as well; resource-related investment in LDCs has been overtaken by research-related investment in industrialized countries.

The evolution of Japanese multinationals since the 1960s has been compressed into a much shorter time span. Investments in resource-related activity in South East Asia led the way in the 1960s and early 1970s, but today interest has shifted to the manufacturing investments of Japanese firms in Europe and the USA. Kojima (1978) had claimed that Japanese MNCs were to be distinguished from US MNCs by their comparative lack of technological advantages, and by their orientation towards developing-country resource development and industrialization rather than oligopolistic competition with other developed-country multinationals. This now appears to have simply been a reflection of the early stages of development of Japanese multinationals.

Although Third World MNCs are nowhere near as advanced as the modern Japanese multinationals, the sectoral and geographical composition of their activity is also evolving much more rapidly than did the investments of the traditional source countries (Cantwell and Tolentino, 1987). There has been a general trend towards the internationalization of business which is common to the firms of all countries. As a result, Third World MNCs have tended to embark on multinational expansion at an earlier stage of their development than did industrialized-country firms.

The arguments of Cantwell and Tolentino (1987) and more recently Ozawa (1990) have established a link between competitive international industry and macroeconomic approaches to the growth of international production. It is suggested that the types of industries involved in international expansion vary with the characteristics of a country and the stage of development which it has reached. In turn, the industrial composition of international production influences its macroeconomic consequences.

Considering a stylized example, industrialization in a resource-scarce country may lead local manufacturing firms into backward vertical integration abroad. These investments may be thought of as supply-side driven, though their effect is to promote faster growth in the home country. Import-substituting investments in manufacturing in other industrialized countries may follow, attracted by foreign demand (as in the PCM), but quite possibly helping in due course to stimulate (further) outward investments from the host countries concerned. The eventual result may be a system of interlocking investments in each major industry, in which supply-side factors come to regulate the composition of activity in each location and the international division of labour. The geographical concentration of research activity may become cumulative over time (Cantwell, 1989b), while Ozawa (1990) suggests that restructuring in Japan has reached a Schumpeterian phase in which research-led industries are to the fore, and in which Japanese firms establish research-related foreign operations to tap into cultural diversities and creative human resources in Europe and the USA.

Macroeconomic developmental approaches relate the investment position of national groups of firms to the industrial progression of their home country. They may be demand-side or supply-side driven; in the PCM the growth of demand leads the relocation of production, while in the arguments of Kojima and Ozawa or Cantwell and Tolentino the emphasis is on supply-side opportunities and constraints in the course of industrial restructuring. However, in each case the underlying development process has both demand-side and supply-side aspects to it.

As mentioned above, it is also possible to trace the macroeconomic effects of international production that are likely to result within the market power approach. If international collusion between MNCs rises over time it would create a stagnationist tendency at a macroeconomic level (Cowling and Sugden, 1987). In addition to this, Pitelis (1987) argues that an increasing concentration of market power in the largest MNCs, and the growing importance of pension funds and other such financial institutions, have led to a steady rise in the economy-wide propensity to save, creating a further demand-side pressure towards stagnation. While this is a description of the macroeconomic effect of MNCs in the market power framework, it does not provide an alternative macroeconomic explanation of the growth of international production. It is true that Marxist writers, particularly around the turn of the century, had argued that a lack of demand in the industrialized countries would lead to imperialist investments in the search for new markets, to alleviate the effects of the concentration of capital at home. However, as noted above, this early kind of macroeconomic explanation cannot account for a rapid growth of cross-investments between countries which are all alleged to suffer from the same slackening of investment opportunities.

Macroeconomic theories of international production can also be extended to take account of financial influences on FDI. Part of the original product cycle idea was that a country whose firms became innovative leaders would establish a strong export position, accompanied by outward direct investment to support the international growth of the country's firms. This was true of Britain in the nineteenth century, of the USA in the early post-war period, and of Japan and Germany more recently (Cantwell, 1989a). A country in this position may be expected to sustain an overall balance of payments surplus (before short-term capital movements) and hence a strong currency. The strength of the domestic currency then provides an additional motive for outward direct investment by local firms. It can thus be argued that longer-term movements in exchange rates reflect underlying trends in industrial competitiveness, reinforcing the effect of real influences on the growth of international production.

As Europe and Japan caught up with the USA in the 1960s her export position weakened, and the US dollar ceased being a strong currency in short supply. However, under the terms of the Bretton Woods pegged exchange rate system the dollar was not allowed to depreciate in response to balance of payments difficulties. As a result the dollar was widely viewed as being overvalued. This overvaluation contributed to yet higher outward investment, since US interests were able to buy up European firms and assets more cheaply in dollar terms, which offered a secondary, financial explanation for the high level of US FDI (emphasized by Aliber, 1970).

Matters are not so clear-cut in the period of general internationalization across the firms of many countries in the 1980s. European and Japanese MNCs have expanded their US operations throughout the last decade. Inward direct investment in the USA remained buoyant when the US dollar was strong between 1982 and 1985, just as when it was weaker in the early 1980s and late 1980s. However, there is some evidence to suggest that inward direct investment was particularly high (rising above an upward trend) in 1979–82 and since 1986. For this reason, Dunning (1988b) argues that events in international currency markets can affect the timing of FDI but not its long-term trend. Aliber's theory of FDI emanating from strong currency areas offers 'some interesting ideas about the *timing* of FDI and particularly that of foreign takeovers; and of fluctuations around a long term trend' (Dunning, 1988b: 15). Yet he also rightly notes that 'In many respects, it is a better extension of the traditional portfolio capital theory to incorporate market failure than a theory of FDI *per se*' (Dunning, 1988: 15).

In other words, Aliber's approach represents a return to the traditional theory of international capital movements, from which Hymer's (1976) work had led a departure. In the traditional theory, currency valuation and relative interest rates determine foreign investment flows, but factors related to the growth of firms and industries do not. The general trend towards internationalization, the substantial interpenetration of MNC activity in one another's domestic markets, and changes in the sectoral composition of international production can be explained only by the newer theories which have been emphasised here.

The various approaches to modelling the growth of international production differ over their choice of focus for a driving force underlying this expansion, related to the level of their analysis. In the technological accumulation approach it is the conditions for technology creation and its effective and efficient use in production. In the market power approach it is the widening of collusive networks and the restriction of competition in each national market. For internalization theorists whether international production expands or contracts depends upon changes in the transaction costs of operating in a wider set of markets (including the market for technology), relative to the costs of the direct co-ordination of trans-actions. In most macroeconomic approaches it is the developmental position of countries and their firms. For theorists who focus on the foreign direct investment flows associated with international production rather than international production itself (such as Aliber, 1970) it is the functioning of currency and financial markets. For business economists whose method is to provide a series of case studies of MNCs (such as Stopford and Turner, 1986), the driving force is individual managerial or entrepreneurial strategies. These approaches are not always mutually exclusive, and the following section examines some points at issue between them.

POINTS AT ISSUE BETWEEN THE DIFFERENT THEORIES OF INTERNATIONAL PRODUCTION

To a large extent the differences between the approaches outlined above can be accounted for by the fact that they have addressed different questions, and in doing so different levels of analysis have been appropriate. The recognition of this variety of interest has led to a retreat from the search for a general theory of international production, as remarked upon at the start. Perhaps the most important distinction is that theories of the firm have naturally been interested in the existence of the firm or the MNC in itself, and issues related to it, while competitive inter-national industry and macroeconomic approaches have been concerned with a broader set of issues, focusing on the interaction between the growth of the firm and the location of production. This distinction, and the possibility of combining insights gained from these alternative perspectives, are considered below. The implications for the ways in which different authors have interpreted the existence and growth of the firm are examined in the earlier part of this section. The role attributed to the interplay between the growth of MNCs and the changing location of production is considered towards the end of this section, while some suggestions for cross-fertilization between approaches are set out in the final section.

Firstly, in comparing different views on the existence and growth of the firm, it is necessary to refer to an area of residual or unresolved debate between the alternative schools of thought on international production. On the face of it the debate concerns the place of ownership advantages in the growth of the firm or MNC. However, this disguises disagreements (or differences of emphasis) over the role of efficiency considerations in the organization of the firm, and over the significance of competition between firms in their final product markets. In a nutshell, competitive international industry approaches suppose that ownership advantages which raise the efficiency of the firm are a necessary condition for its survival *vis-à-vis* its rivals in an oligopolistic market. A strengthening of its ownership advantages relative to these rivals will enable it to increase its market share, or in other words to grow faster than its competitors. Internalization theorists have instead examined the efficiency of firms in terms of how the exchange of intermediate products is organized, in which process ownership advantages and inter-firm competition in final product markets are secondary questions. The market power school also take the view that ownership advantages associated with greater efficiency need not be regarded as a necessary condition for the existence of the firm or MNC, but for different reasons. They emphasize the conditions prevailing in final product rather than intermediate product markets, but deny that firms necessarily raise efficiency, and think of oligopolies in terms of a gradual extension of collusion, with the establishment of ownership advantages as barriers to entry.

To illustrate the difference, in the technological accumulation approach each firm in an industry internally generates a succession of innovations or ownership advantages, which constitute the basis of both their domestic and their international production. The ability to innovate in a growing sector is itself an ownership advantage which is a function of the past technological experience of the firm. These ownership advantages are oligopolistic advantages, essential to survival in an international oligopoly. The most innovative firms in an industry create a faster stream of more effective ownership advantages, and in so doing they increase their international production more rapidly and raise their world market share. The weakest firms lose market share, and if a firm lost all ownership advantages it would be quickly driven out of both domestic and international markets. However, firms with the fewest or weakest ownership advantages in general hold their position more easily in domestic markets than in international markets, owing to government support, consumer loyalty, the closeness of local business contacts, and so forth.

Ownership advantages are defined with reference to the (oligopolistic) final product market. They are advantages which lower the unit costs and raise the profit margins of given firms relative to others in the same industry. A firm with weak ownership advantages, and certainly one with none at all, has high unit costs relative to others in its industry, and consequently suffers consistent losses. A firm with strong ownership advantages (measured, for example, by a high share of patenting activity) will have a larger market share, and if its ownership advantages become stronger (its share of patenting rises) then its market share increases. Empirical investigation of competition between the world's largest firms has confirmed that companies whose share of international patenting is greater than their international market share in their industry, at a given point in time, experience a faster rate of growth and hence a rising market share in the ensuing period (Cantwell and Sanna Randaccio, 1989).

Firms which lose ownership advantages face higher unit costs and lower profits, and a reduction in their market share. In the limit, a firm with no ownership advantages at all, though it is difficult to imagine such an extreme case in any existing industry, would lose market share until it was taken over or driven out altogether. Firms of MNCs therefore require ownership advantages as a necessary condition of their continued existence, and the stronger are their advantages the faster the rate of international growth they are able to sustain.

Against this, it is sometimes claimed by writers in the internalization tradition that ownership advantages are not necessary for the existence of MNCs and international production, apart from the advantages created by internalization itself (Buckley and Casson, 1976; Casson, 1987). By this they mean that firms may grow relative to intermediate pro- duct markets where producers trading with one another merge their operations, irrespective of the ownership advantages of the production units concerned. Hence they are referring strictly to the transition from national firms combining to form multinational firms, by means of the internalization of the intermediate product markets which previously linked them.

However, to conclude from this that ownership advantages are not a necessary condition of international production is a very misleading way of putting matters. At least one of the individual production units that combine to form an MNC must have ownership advantages, so that the MNC has too. For firms to grow relative to their competitors in final product markets, or indeed simply to retain their share of final product markets, ownership advantages are necessary. The generation of ownership advan- tages, achieved mainly through innovation, is necessary for competitive success and indeed survival. Firms that fail to accumulate technology and related ownership advantages are either driven out of business, or taken over by firms that have the capacity to do so.

The ownership advantages of each firm represent its particular differen- tiated area of strength as against its major rivals, which determines the level and rate of change of its market share. Ownership advantages relate to production costs while internalization relates to transaction costs, though there is an interaction between the two. The internalization of intermediate product markets may complement ownership advantages but it is not a substitute for them. A group of firms each of which has no ownership advantages and therefore makes losses will not suddenly become profitable merely by organizing transactions among themselves more efficiently. They will only reduce their losses. In any event, the benefits of internalization tend to be greater where each participating affiliate begins with strong ownership advantages, owing to the potential for economies of scope, technological complementarities, and so forth. Just as compatible ownership advantages may encourage internalization, so internalization may serve to increase (or in some cases to decrease) the firm's subsequent capacity to innovate or its ownership advantages. The existence of such interaction, though, does not make the concepts logically inseparable from one another.

The need for ownership advantages applies to both national firms and MNCs, although it is especially true of MNCs, since inefficient firms may be able to survive longer in their own domestic markets. Moreover, the most innovative firms whose ownership advantages are strongest are more likely to take over firms whose ownership advantages are weak than vice versa. The international networks of MNCs expand directly through the independent establishment and extension of their own ventures, together with take-overs or mergers with firms whose technological activity (ownership advantages) is complementary. Once MNCs are created they may gain additional advantages from the international co-ordination of activity, in part through the enhancement of their technological strengths by way of a more geographically and industrially diversified research programme. The international co-ordination of research and production is therefore supportive of technological advantages, not a substitute for them, nor a sufficient condition for their generation.

The debate over the necessity or otherwise of ownership advantages is largely a discussion that has proceeded at cross-purposes, since as discussed above different approaches have been set up to answer different questions. Internalization theory endeavours to explain why firms in general displace intermediate product markets in general, or why MNCs in general displace international trade in intermediate products, and in addressing this issue, it is not necessary to refer to ownership advantages. The existence of ownership advantages on the part of firms plays no role in the Coasian theory in deriving the existence of firms themselves, the joint ownership of assets being explained by the replacement of markets.

However, while this is a sufficient theory of the existence of firms considered as a whole without reference to any final product market (in place of atomistic competition), it is not a sufficient theory of the growth of a particular firm or a particular group of firms *vis-à-vis* other firms. To explain why one firm displaces another, or why, for example,

Japanese MNCs have grown at the expense of US firms, then relatively stronger ownership advantages are necessary. The relative strength of technological ownership advantages is in general the principal determinant of variations in unit costs or productivity across firms (particularly in industrialized countries). Variations in unit costs are in turn necessary to explain why certain firms grow faster than their competitors in a given final product market.

In this respect, internalization theory has addressed a different issue from competitive international industry approaches; it is concerned with the extent of firms as a whole, as opposed to markets in general (or what might be thought of as the degree of concentration of ownership), rather than the process of competition between already existing firms. For a particular firm or a particular group of firms ownership advantages are a necessary condition for establishing and preserving international production.

To appreciate how the role attributed to ownership advantages varies between theories, it is useful to draw a distinction between what is normally understood as a theory of the firm and the separate development of theories of the growth of the firm. In the theory of the growth of the firm as developed by Penrose (1959) internally generated growth associated with firm-specific ownership advantages is central. The growth process is inherent to the firm which directs its internal resources towards expansion:

> While external inducements and difficulties have been widely discussed, little attention has been paid, in a systematic way at least, to the equally important internal influences on the direction of expansion. . . both an automatic increase in knowledge and an incentive to search for new knowledge are, as it were, 'built into' the very nature of firms possessing entrepreneurial resources of even average initiative. . . . I have placed the emphasis on the significance of the resources with which a firm works and on the development of the experience and knowledge of a firm's personnel because these are the factors that will determine the response of the firm to changes in the external world and also determine what it 'sees' in the external world. . . . Unused productive services are, for the enterprising firm, at the same time a challenge to innovate, an incentive to expand, and a source of competitive advantage.
>
> (Penrose, 1959: 66, 78, 79–80, 85)

The purpose of this rather lengthy quotation is to clarify the difference between the theory of the growth of the firm, in which internal ownership advantages are critical, and the Coasian theory of the firm, in which they are not. The Coasian theory of the firm emphasizes the conditions of exchange of intermediate products initially in markets external to the firm, which lead firms to internalize the markets in question. Internalization thus offers a theory of the firm or the extent of the firm rather than its growth; except in as much as any static theory can be made dynamic by referring to changes in levels. Thus, despite the claim that the 'original objective of the approach adopted by Buckley and Casson (1976) was to use the concept of the internalisation of markets to develop a model of the growth of the firm' (Buckley, 1988: 182), it is not inherently a theory of growth in the way that the Penrosian theory and the allied competitive international industry approaches based on internal ownership advantages are.

Given this distinction between theories of the internally generated growth of the firm in competition with others, and the internalization theory in which the motive force for growth lies outside the firm, it is not surprising that internalization writers have tended to treat ownership advantages as given. At least until now, internalization theory has concentrated on the issue of technology transfer and the institutional form it assumes, rather than variations between firms in their ability to generate technology. Even when considering oligopolistic interdependence in the form of an exchange of threats, Casson (1987) assumes constant long-run market shares, or in other words fixed and exogenous ownership advantages in the way they have been defined here.

A similar downplaying of the role of ownership advantages can be found in Kojima's work on Japanese MNCs and the recent literature on Third World MNCs, in which it is sometimes claimed that investments in LDCs require no ownership advantages on the part of the firms that make them. It is certainly true that it may be the smaller, relatively weaker firms in an international industry which make export-platform investments in labour-intensive production, while the more advanced firms invest in research-related production in the industrialized countries. However, this need not be the case in the Kojima–Ozawa story, since it may be the same firms which upgrade their production at home while redeploying less sophisticated types of activity in countries at an earlier stage of development. Even if it is the case all that this entails is that the ownership advantages of such smaller newer MNCs lie in a simpler type of manufacturing and in their access to commercial outlets, not that they have no ownership advantages at all. It is simply that the more sophisticated types of international production require stronger ownership advantages (a stronger technological base) than other types, which is scarcely surprising.

Note also that ownership advantages are not always necessarily in the specific sector in which investment takes place. Consider, for example, a diversified take-over by an international conglomerate. Ownership advantages are therefore to be understood as providing a firm with a general ability to expand, and the stronger are these advantages the faster the speed of international expansion that it is able to sustain. It is true that where a conglomerate chooses to move into an unrelated sector its motive is essentially of a financial kind, and may be better explained by a theory of FDI (such as that of Aliber, 1970, or Rugman, 1979) than a theory of international production. The ownership advantages of such firms may well be of a financial rather than a technological kind.

Where firms rely on technological ownership advantages they invest in production in areas related to their existing strengths. Of course, where they produce in foreign centres of innovation they may also gain access to a new stream of complementary technological developments. Investment may be motivated mainly by the objective of strengthening their ownership advantages. In such cases the original ownership advantages of firms are built upon, consolidated in their existing fields and extended into new areas. There is a progressive interaction between the growth of international networks and the strength of ownership advantages.

The other confusion about ownership advantages that is often found in the literature is that, as noted above, they are frequently described as monopolistic advantages. Perhaps a further reason why internalization theorists have insistently criticized the concept of ownership advantages is because of this interpretation, associated with the market power approach. The origins of this terminology go back to Kindleberger (1969), who recast Hymer's work to associate MNCs with the existence of a particular market structure, that of monopolistic competition (within which each participating firm has some monopolistic advantage). Hymer himself believed that firms actively sought to raise barriers to entry and to collude with other firms in their industry, and that market structure was a product of their behaviour and the extent to which they succeeded in making lasting collusive agreements, rather than the other way around. In Kindleberger's restatement the MNC was seen as a function of a market structure characterized by monopolistic competition between differentiated products, rather than as an active agent engaged in oligopolistic interaction with other firms.

In Hymer's approach the strength of ownership advantages amongst the leading firms reflects the degree of monopoly power in a sector. However, strictly speaking, even in his framework ownership advantages should be thought of as oligopolistic and not monopolistic advantages.[5] This is even more true in competitive international industry approaches such as that based on technological accumulation. Firms accumulate differentiated but overlapping technologies, irrespective of whether they produce identical or different final products. MNCs are therefore involved in technological competition with other members of an international oligopoly. Where it suits them they may arrive at certain co-operative arrangements, such as in cross-licensing agreements. Each participant in the international oligopoly has certain specific advantages based on its own previous technological experience. The relative strength of the ownership advantages of each firm determines both their rate of growth *vis-à-vis* their competitors, and their attitude towards co-operative arrangements with other firms in the same sector. In this view the extent of collusion is a less important determinant of profits and growth than the strength of advantages, and is instead essentially also a product of the latter. Collusion comes and goes as the balance of advantages between firms change.

The different perspective of the various approaches as to the operation of locational influences can now be considered. The dividing line here is essentially between the two theories of the firm, which tend to treat location as exogenous (to be determined by some other theory), and the macroeconomic and mesoeconomic approaches, in which locational factors are themselves influenced by the growth of firms. To give an illustration of a process of continual interaction between ownership and location advantages, consider the case of a modern global manufacturing industry in which MNCs benefit from direct access to any of the main locationally advantaged centres of technological development. By investing in research and production in these sites they increase their own competitiveness (ownership advantages), as well as the competitiveness of production in the countries concerned and their attractiveness to other firms (location advantages). In this case ownership and location advantages are not independent.

Looking back historically, the location advantages of countries also helped to determine the pattern of technological specialization of each country's firms, or in other words the sectors in which they had the greatest capacity for generating ownership advantages. For example, Rosenberg (1976) has shown that US firms emerged from the industrial revolution with advantages in woodworking technologies due to the plentiful availability of local timber supplies, while British firms developed advantages in metalworking and coal-related technologies due to local coal deposits.

Internalization theorists have tended to take location advantages and technological ownership advantages as given and exogenous, in order to focus attention on the form of linkages between plants. Neoclassical trade and location theorists have gone even further, and in many cases simply assumed away technological ownership advantages (all firms have access to the same technology) in order to focus on purely locational factors. The market power school treat technological advantages as barriers to entry, while typically taking location as exogenous.

This is not to say that the market power and internalization approaches have ignored locational factors. Hymer (1975), for example, suggests that firms locate activities in accordance with a hierarchy, with high-grade activities in industrialized countries and low-grade activities in LDCs. Newfarmer (1985) and Bornschier and Chase-Dunn (1985), who take a market power view, similarly distinguish between central and peripheral locations in an international industry. While retaining the internalization perspective, Casson (1986b) has also suggested a model of the international division of labour. Indeed, internalization theorists have recognized that the growth of the firm may influence location; for example 'internalisation allows international transfer price manipulation that will bias location towards inclusion of low tax locations (Buckley, 1988: 182). It is simply that those who have analysed the growth of international production from the viewpoint of the theory of the firm have not on the whole attached very much significance to the interaction between the growth of the firm and the changing location of production. For this reason they have often disregarded those elements of macroeconomic explanations which have attempted to do just this: 'Elsewhere I have attempted to show that even this macro explanation must rely on micro aspects to achieve its explanatory cutting edge' (Buckley, 1988: 186).

This contrasts with the product cycle approach, the Kojima–Ozawa analysis and the various competitive international oligopoly theories, which have all stressed the interaction between the growth of the firm and the location of production and the consequences for the structure of industrial production and trade. Macroeconomic theories of international production make location advantages depend on macroeconomic factors related to countries and their level of development, while mesoeconomic approaches emphasize the locational factors specific to an international industry (see Gray, 1982, for a discussion of whether location advantages can be treated as purely macroeconomic). Naturally, the focus of interest and the level at which analysis is conducted affect the treatment of location in theories of international production.

THE DEVELOPMENT OF A DYNAMIC ANALYSIS OF INTERNATIONAL PRODUCTION

As a rule, macroeconomic and competitive international industry approaches to international production are by their very nature dynamic, as they have usually been concerned to describe a process over time. Theories of the firm, although they have attracted a greater literature, have addressed only certain types of question on the dynamics of international production. The internalization approach has asked why firms in general (the visible hand) have expanded relative to markets in general (the invisible hand). The particular issue which has attracted most attention is the idea of an evolution in the business of firms, from exports (through a sales agent), to licensing a foreign company, to the establishment of international production (Buckley and Casson, 1981; Teece, 1983; Nicholas, 1986).

This section considers how theories of the firm may be extended or adapted to take account of the wider evolution of international production linked to the cumulative development of technology through the international networks of MNCs. The technological accumulation approach emphasizes the connection between the generation of technology and the growth of production, both within firms and in terms of the distinctive geographical pattern of innovation and research-related production that develops in each industry. This evolutionary view of the growth of international production may usefully be combined with insights from the theory of the firm, and the theory of the growth of the firm.

Two possible extensions of internalization theory might be considered which would broaden the approach. First, attention can be paid to the interrelationship between the growth of the firm and the changing location of production, which has already been raised in the context of other approaches as suggested in the previous section. Second, the transaction cost framework might be usefully combined with a theory of entrepreneurship, innovation or the changing technology and organization of production within the firm.

Whereas the theory of cumulative technological change, like the work of the classical economists, is a theory of production (and the changing technology of production), as it stands the Coasian theory of the firm, like the neoclassical economic thinking of which it is a criticism, is a pure theory of exchange. Exchange takes place under a variety of institutional arrangements, in markets or within the firm. It is worth noting that Nelson and Winter (1982) make use of certain aspects of the work of Williamson and others in developing their evolutionary theory of economic change. However, in order to make the Coasian theory of the firm itself evolutionary it would be necessary to specify how transaction costs are themselves influenced by the growth and technological innovation of firms.

As Casson (1986a) has pointed out, while transaction cost theory specifies conditions under which non-market institutional arrangements will obtain (for example, within the firm), it does so at present to the exclusion of any active role for managerial strategy. In other words, while a theory of the MNC, couched in terms of an exchange framework, can explain the existence of the MNC or the firm, it has still left the firm itself as a passive reactor to transactional circumstances. As remarked above, it relates to the external influences on growth, and not to the internal sources of growth which make the firm inherently dynamic when under competition in its final product market. Changes in the organization or control of production are merely a response to changes in the costs of various exchange relationships in markets or otherwise. This procedure may be justified if one is concerned only with the internalization of intermediate product markets actively replacing trade between independent parties.

However, difficulties are encountered when this approach is applied to the historical evolution of say, import-substituting international production; take, for example, the growth of investment by US firms in Europe in the 1950s and 1960s. Part of the reason is that locational factors were responsible (faster growth in Europe). While this helps to explain the initial direction of the investment, it does not explain how manufacturing MNCs steadily grew in the post-war period. Nor does a change in political risk provide a complete explanation. It might be suggested that, where markets in intangible assets such as technology become in some sense more imperfect, the transaction costs of market exchange rise, and horizontally integrated MNCs tend to grow. But it seems most implausible to argue that any international markets were operating more imperfectly in the late 1950s and the 1960s by comparison with the 1930s.

Within this framework, the explanation is presumably in part that the transaction costs of co-operative relationships fell even faster than the costs of using the market mechanism. Yet one of the main reasons for this was the growing experience of firms in international production in the industrialized countries, initially of US firms in Europe. To avoid falling into a static tautology (that is, that international transaction costs fell because of the growth of the MNC, and the MNC grew because of lower internal transaction costs) this must be set in a dynamic framework, whereby the interaction between transaction costs and the growth of firms is set out. Transaction costs depend upon the technological and productive activity of the firm. The international growth of firms is part of an evolutionary process. This also helps to call attention to other aspects of the explanation: in this case, the generation of strong technological ownership advantages by US firms, and the greater locational advantage of producing in Europe in the 1960s.

Internalization theory when taken independently is at its strongest when discussing vertical integration, such as the backward integration of manufacturing companies to secure raw material supplies, including natural resources (Casson *et al*, 1986), or their forward integration into distribution or sales agencies (Nicholas, 1983, 1985). When it comes to the international expansion of manufacturing production itself a pure theory of exchange is on weaker ground. It has been claimed that the horizontal integration of manufacturing plants can be explained by the transaction costs of exchanging technology at arm's length (Buckley and Casson, 1976). However, technology may accumulate with the firm not so much because of the characteristics of the market for technology once it has been created as because of the conditions under which it is most easily generated and used in production. Technology is then difficult and costly to transfer or exchange between firms precisely because it tends to be associated with the research and production experience accumulated within a particular firm, rather than vice versa. Armour and Teece (1980) take a step in this direction in recognizing from a transaction costs perspective that vertical integration may increase R&D and the rate of technological change.

It seems reasonable to suppose that the accumulation of technology and the growth of production within the firm will affect the transaction costs of exchange. The transaction cost theorist has instead tended to start from exchange in a market, which gives way to more consciously organized control where it is relatively inefficient. Coase (1937) stressed the market conditions which lead to a reorganization or an extension in the organization of the firm. However, the nature and extent of a firm's transactions and co-operative arrangements with other firms, as well as its market share, also depend upon its innovative capacity *vis-à-vis* other firms. As paths of technological development become established within each firm this is likely to affect the conditions of technology transfer between them, which has been the focus of much of the internalization literature.

A similar criticism can be made of the conventional structure–conduct–performance paradigm of industrial organization theory, which is essentially static and does not deal with industrial dynamics or evolution (Carlsson, 1987). Once again, the firm appears as a passive reactor to changes in market structure. This is rather unfortunate, since early analysis of the growth of the firm in the 1950s (such as Penrose, 1959) had appeared to fit in nicely with treatments of imperfect competition, and the emergence of the study of industrial economics. Indeed, as noted above, Hymer's theory of the growth of the MNC was based precisely on this combination of an active firm increasing the extent of its market power, and colluding with others to raise what Bain (1956) termed barriers to entry or new competition.

However, there are problems with the market power theory of the firm if it is used as a general explanation of the growth of international production, especially in the context of the technological competition that exists today between the firms of the major industrialized countries. In most industries the level of expenditure on research and development has been rising in recent years. Countries have become increasingly concerned about their technological competitiveness, while firms have been under steadily more pressure to maintain and build upon their major sources of innovative strength. It is necessary for all theories of the dynamics of international production to come to terms with this. The implication of the market power view is that profitability is usually seen as being raised through a restriction of output and of the number of firms competing. In fact the steady generation of ownership advantages through technological accumulation, rather than serving as a barrier to potential new entrants, may increase competition amongst firms already in the international oligopoly, causing them to expand their own research and production. Research-intensive lines of activity are not generally known for their lack of competition in world markets; quite the reverse.

In an industry with rapid technological accumulation the high profitability associated with the existence of strong ownership advantages is not due to a restriction of output, a lack of competition, and a high degree of industrial concentration as a feature of market structure. It is rather accounted for by the greater scope that innovation provides for productivity improvements, and with them the faster growth of output. Competition is more intense in terms of the creation of new products and processes.

Yet the market power theory of the firm as used by Hymer may be relevant to certain types of MNC activity, even if it does not provide a general explanation of MNC growth. Firms are more likely to seek out co-operative agreements or collusion with other firms where they are in a weak position *vis-à-vis* other firms in their industry, or where competition is very intense. Where they are relatively weak the licensing of technology is liable to run in just one direction, while where they are a leading member of an international oligopoly cross-licensing arrangements are to be expected. Increasing overlaps between firms in their technological development (as technological interrelatedness rises) is also likely to lead to an increase in cross-licensing as well as greater technological competition. There may therefore be new areas of business co-operation within an essentially competitive environment. Collusion between MNCs is quite possible, but it is generally to improve the relationship between their international production networks rather than being an explanation of them.

Analysing trends in technological competition (and co-operation) between MNCs in the future is likely to be of considerable interest. One question which has been raised is the extent to which the recent upsurge in the internationalization of production is leading to an increasing locational concentration of research activity. This in turn has effects on the competitiveness of both firms and countries. Work on international industrial dynamics of this kind is still at a relatively early stage, but similar work on cumulative patterns of technological change is already attracting increasing attention in other fields. Further explorations of the relationship between technological innovation and the production of MNCs, hopefully, will make a distinctive and important contribution. As Dunning has recently suggested:

> It is to be hoped that a next generation of scholars will give more attention to issues of innovation and entrepreneurship as they impinge upon the internationalisation of business. We believe that if a new breakthrough in our understanding of foreign production occurs, it will be in this direction.
>
> (1988b: 36)

NOTES

1 Alan Rugman (1980) invoked internalization as a general theory of the MNC-cum-FDI, while Robert Aliber (1970, 1971) made international currency valuation the cornerstone of what he seemed to think of as a general theory of FDI-cum-MNC.

2 That Cowling and Sugden do not seem to identify themselves with the Hymer tradition need not be of concern here.

3 Dunning (1983a, 1988a) refers to these as ownership advantages of an asset kind, and ownership advantages of a transaction cost-minimizing kind, or, following Teece (1983), ownership advantages of a governance cost-minimizing kind.

4 Although the distinction between appropriability and co-ordination remains an important conceptual one, in practice where the firm controls complementary assets it may be difficult to differentiate between the two. The significance of this division is discussed further by Teece (1990).

5 They are monopolistic only if they are based entirely on product differentiation. If firms have advantages that are related to production – scale economies, patented technology, or high start-up costs – then they need not have monopolistic control of (segments of) the final product market. Their monopoly power is a result of collusion, which is made easier by such barriers to entry, but is exercised jointly rather than individually. It might still be said that each firm has a quasi-monopolistic position in the everyday sense that each

exercises a monopoly over the use of its own patented technology or large-scale plants (Jenkins, 1987). However, if they do not sell the use of such technology or plants in an external market then they are not monopoly sellers; hence the term *quasi-* monopoly. The market they actually serve is oligopolistic, even if it is divided by collusive agreement.

REFERENCES

Aliber, R.Z. (1970) 'A theory of direct foreign investment', in C.P Kindleberger (ed.) *The International Corporation: a Symposium*, Cambridge, Mass.: MIT Press.
—— (1971) 'The multinational enterprise in a multiple currency world', in J.H. Dunning (ed.) *The Multinational Enterprise*, London: Allen & Unwin.
Armour, H.O., and Teece, D.J. (1980) 'Vertical integration and technological innovation', *Review of Economics and Statistics* 62.
Armstrong, P., Glyn, A., and Harrison, J. (1984) *Capitalism since World War II*, London: Fontana.
Atkinson, A.B., and Stiglitz, J.E. (1969) 'A new view of technological change', *Economic Journal* 79, 3.
Bain, J.S. (1956) *Barriers to New Competition: their Character and Consequences in Manufacturing Industries*, Cambridge, Mass.: Harvard University Press.
Baran, P.A., and Sweezy, P.M. (1966) *Monopoly Capital*, New York: Monthly Review Press.
Bornschier, V., and Chase-Dunn, C. (1985) *Transnational Corporations and Underdevelopment*, London: Greenwood.
Buckley, P.J. (1983), 'New theories of international business: some unresolved issues', in M.C. Casson (ed.) *The Growth of International Business*, London: Allen & Unwin.
—— (1985) 'The economic analysis of the multinational enterprise: Reading versus Japan?', *Hitotsubashi Journal of Economics* 26, 2.
—— (1988) 'The limits of explanation: testing the internalisation theory of the multinational enterprise', *Journal of International Business Studies* 19, 2.
Buckley, P.J., and Casson, M.C. (1976) *The Future of the Multinational Enterprise*, London: Macmillan.
—— (1981) 'The optimal timing of a foreign direct investment', *Economic Journal* 91, 1.
—— (1985), *The Economic Theory of the Multinational Enterprise: Selected Papers*, London: Macmillan.
Cantwell, J.A. (1987a) *A Dynamic Model of the Post-war Growth of International Economic Activity in Europe and the US*, University of Reading Discussion Papers in International Investment and Business Studies, No. 104.
—— (1987b) *Technological Competition and Intra-Industry Production in the Industrialised World*, University of Reading Discussion Papers in International Investment and Business Studies, No. 106.
—— (1987c) 'The reorganisation of European industries after integration: selected evidence on the role of multinational enterprise activities', *Journal of Common Market Studies* 26, reprinted in J.H. Dunning and P. Robson (eds.) *Multinationals and the European Community*, Oxford: Blackwell, 1988.

—— (1989a) 'The changing form of multinational enterprise expansion in the twentieth century', in A. Teichova, M. Levy-Leboyer and H. Nussbaum (eds.) *Historical Studies in International Corporate Business*, Cambridge: Cambridge University Press.

—— (1989b) *Technological Innovation and Multinational Corporations*, Oxford: Blackwell.

Cantwell, J.A., Corley, T.A.B., and Dunning, J.H. (1986) 'An exploration of some historical antecedents to the modern theory of international production', in G. Jones and P. Hertner (eds.) *Multinationals: Theory and History*, Farnborough: Gower.

Cantwell, J.A., and Sanna Randaccio, F. (1989) *Multinationality and Growth amongst the World's largest Firms*, University of Reading Discussion Papers in International Investment and Business Studies, No. 134.

Cantwell, J.A. and Tolentino, P.E.E. (1987) 'Technological Accumulation and Third World Multinationals', paper presented at the annual meeting of the European International Business Association, Antwerp, December.

Carlsson, B. (1987) 'Reflections on 'industrial dynamics': the challenges ahead', *International Journal of Industrial Organisation*, 5, 2.

Casson, M.C. (1981) 'Foreword', in A.M. Rugman, *Inside the Multinationals: the Economics of Internal Markets*, London: Croom Helm.

—— (1982) 'The theory of foreign direct investment', in J. Black and J.H. Dunning (eds.) *International Capital Movements*, London: Macmillan.

—— (1986a) 'General theories of the multinational enterprise: a critical examination', in G. Jones and P.Hertner (eds.) *Multinationals: Theory and History*, Farnborough: Gower.

—— (1986b) 'The international division of labour', in M.C. Casson *et al.* (1986).

—— (1987) *The Firm and the Market: Studies in Multinational Enterprise and the Scope of the Firm*, Oxford: Blackwell.

Casson, M.C., Barry, D., Foreman-Peck, J., Hannart, J.F., Horner, D., Read, R.A. and Wolf, B.M. (1986) *Multinationals and World Trade: Vertical Integration and the Division of Labour in World Industries*, London: Allen & Unwin.

Caves, R.E. (1982) *Multinational Enterprise and Economic Analysis*, Cambridge: Cambridge University Press.

Coase, R.H. (1937) 'The nature of the firm', *Economica* 4, 4.

Cowling, K., and Sugden, R. (1987) *Transnational Monopoly Capitalism*, Brighton: Wheatsheaf.

Dunning, J.H. (1977) 'Trade, location of economic activity, and the multinational enterprise: a search for an eclectic approach', in B. Ohlin, P.-O. Hesselborn and P.M. Wijkman (eds.) *The International Allocation of Economic Activity*, London: Macmillan.

—— (1981), *International Production and the Multinational Enterprise*, London: Allen & Unwin.

—— (1982) 'Explaining the international direct investment position of countries: towards a dynamic or developmental approach', in J. Black and J.H. Dunning (eds.) *International Capital Movements*, London: Macmillan.

—— (1983a) 'Market power of the firm and international transfer of technology', *International Journal of Industrial Organisation* 1, 1.

—— (1983b) 'Changes in the level and structure of international production: the last 100 years', in M.C. Casson (ed.) *The Growth of International Business*, London: Allen & Unwin.

—— (1986) 'The investment development cycle and Third World multinationals', in K.M. Khan (ed.) *Multinationals of the South: New Actors in the International Economy*, London: Pinter.

—— (1988a) 'The eclectic paradigm of international production: an update and some possible extensions', *Journal of International Business Studies* 19, 1.

—— (1988b) 'The theory of international production', *International Trade Journal* 3.

Dunning, J.H., and Cantwell, J.A. (1990) 'The changing role of multinational enterprises in the international creation, transfer and diffusion of technology', in F. Arcangeli, P.A. David and G. Dosi (eds.) *Technology Diffusion and Economic Growth: International and National Policy Perspectives*, Oxford: Oxford University Press.

Emmanuel, A. (1982) *Appropriate or Underdeveloped Technology?* Chichester: Wiley.

Flowers, E.B. (1976) 'Oligopolistic reactions in European and Canadian direct investment in the US'. *Journal of International Business Studies* 7, 2.

Giddy, I.H. (1978) 'The demise of the product cycle model in international business theory', *Columbia Journal of World Business* 13, 1.

Graham, E.M. (1975) 'Oligopolistic Imitation and European Direct Investment', Ph.D. dissertation, Harvard Graduate School of Business Administration.

—— (1978) 'Transatlantic investment by multinational firms: a rivalistic phenomenon?', *Journal of Post-Keynesian Economics*, 1, 1.

—— (1985) 'Intra-industry direct investment, market structure, firm rivalry and technological performance', in A. Erdilek (ed.) *Multinationals as Mutual Invaders: Intra-industry Direct Foreign Investment*, London: Croom Helm.

Gray, H.P. (1982) 'Macroeconomic theories of foreign direct investment: an assessment', in A.M. Rugman (ed.) *New Theories of the Multinational Enterprise*, London: Croom Helm.

Hirsch, S. (1967) *The Location of Industry and International Competitiveness*, Oxford: Oxford University Press.

Hufbauer, G.C. (1965) *Synthetic Materials and the Theory of International Trade*, London: Duckworth.

—— (1970) 'The impact of national characteristics and technology on the commodity composition of trade in manufactured goods', in R. Vernon (ed.), *The Technology Factor in International Trade*, New York: Columbia University Press.

Hymer, S. (1975) 'The multinational corporation and the law of uneven development', in H. Radice (ed.) *International Firms and Modern Imperialism*, Harmondsworth: Penguin.

—— (1976) *The International Operations of National Firms: a Study of Direct Foreign Investment*, Cambridge, Mass.: MIT Press.

Hymer, S., and Rowthorn, R.(1970) 'Multinational corporations and international oligopoly: the non-American challenge', in C.P. Kindleberger (ed.) *The International Corporation: a Symposium*, Cambridge, Mass.: MIT Press.

Jenkins, R. (1984) *Transnational Corporations and Industrial Transformation in Latin America*, London: Macmillan.

—— (1987), *Transnational Corporations and Uneven Development: the Internationalisation of Capital and the Third World*, London: Methuen.

Johnson, H.G. (1958) *International Trade and Economic Growth*, London: Allen & Unwin.

Kay, N. (1983) 'Multinational enterprise: a review article', *Scottish Journal of Political Economy* 30, 3.

Kindleberger, C.P. (1969) *American Business Abroad: Six Lectures on Direct Investment*, New Haven, Conn.: Yale University Press.

Knickerbocker, F.T. (1973) *Oligopolistic Reaction and the Multinational Enterprise*, Cambridge, Mass.: Harvard University Press.

Kojima, K. (1978) *Direct Foreign Investment: a Japanese Model of Multinational Business Operations*, London: Croom Helm.

Kojima, K., and Ozawa, T.(1985) 'Toward a theory of industrial restructuring and dynamic comparative advantage', *Hitotsubashi Journal of Economics* 26, 2.

Lall, S. (1976) 'Theories of direct foreign private investment and multinational behaviour', *Economic and Political Weekly* 11, 31-3.

Leontief, W.W. (1954) 'Domestic production and foreign trade: the American capital position reexamined', *Economia Internazionale* 7, 1.

Linder, S.B. (1961) *An Essay on Trade and Transformation*, New York: Wiley.

Nelson, R.R., and Winter, S.J. (1977) 'In search of a useful theory of innovation', *Research Policy* 5, 1.

—— (1982) *An Evolutionary Theory of Economic Change*, Cambridge, Mass.: Harvard University Press.

Newfarmer, R.S., ed. (1985) *Profits, Progress, and Poverty: Case Studies of International Industries in Latin America*, Notre Dame, Ind.: University of Notre Dame Press.

Nicholas, S.J. (1983) 'Agency contracts, institutional modes, and the transition to foreign direct investment by British manufacturing multinationals before 1935', *Journal of Economic History* 43.

—— (1985) 'The theory of multinational enterprise as a transactional mode', in P. Hertner and G. Jones (eds.) *Multinationals: Theory and History*, Farnborough: Gower.

—— (1986) *Multinationals, Transaction Costs and Choice of Institutional Form*, University of Reading Discussion Papers in International Investment and Business Studies, No. 97.

Ozawa, T. (1974) *Japan's Technological Challenge to the West, 1950-1974: Motivation and Accomplishment*, Cambridge, Mass.: MIT Press.

—— (1979) *Multinationalism, Japanese Style: the Political Economy of Outward Dependency*, Princeton, N.J.: Princeton University Press.

—— (1982) 'A newer type of foreign investment in Third World resource development', *Rivista Internazionale di Scienze Economiche e Commerciali* 29, 12.

—— (1990) 'Europe 1992 and Japanese multinationals: transplanting a subcontracting system in the expanded market', in B. Bürgenmeier and J.L. Mucchielli (eds.), *Multinationals and Europe 1992*, London: Routledge.

Pasinetti, L.L. (1981) 'International economic relations', chapter 11 in *Structural Change and Economic Growth: A Theoretical Essay on the Dynamics of the Wealth of Nations*, Cambridge: Cambridge University Press.

Pavitt, K. (1987) 'International patterns of technological accumulation', in N. Hood and J.E. Vahne (eds.) *Strategies in Global Competition*, London: Croom Helm.

Penrose, E.T. (1959) *The Theory of the Growth of the Firm*, Oxford: Blackwell.

62   John Cantwell

Pitelis, C.N. (1987) *Corporate Capital: Control, Ownership, Saving and Crisis*, Cambridge: Cambridge University Press.

Posner, M.V. (1961) 'Technical change and international trade', *Oxford Economic Papers* 13.

Rosenberg, N. (1976) *Perspectives on Technology*, Cambridge: Cambridge University Press.

—— (1982) *Inside the Black Box: Technology and Economics*, Cambridge: Cambridge University Press.

Rothschild, K. (1947) 'Price theory and oligopoly', *Economic Journal* 57.

Rugman, A.M. (1979) *International Diversification and the Multinational Enterprise*, Lexington, Mass.: Lexington Books.

—— (1980) 'Internalization as a general theory of foreign direct investment: a reappraisal of the literature', *Weltwirtschaftliches Archiv* 116, 2.

—— (1981) *Inside the Multinationals: the Economics of Internal Markets*, London: Croom Helm.

Sanna Randaccio, F. (1980) 'European Direct Investments in US Manufacturing', M.Litt. thesis, University of Oxford.

Savary, J. (1984) *French Multinationals*, London: Pinter.

Steindl, J. (1952) *Maturity and Stagnation in American Capitalism*, London: Oxford University Press.

Stiglitz, J.E. (1987) 'Learning to learn, localised learning and technological progress', in P. Dasgupta and P. Stoneman (eds.) *Economic Policy and Technological Performance*, Cambridge: Cambridge University Press.

Stopford, J.M., and Turner, L. (1986) *Britain and the Multinationals*, Chichester: Wiley.

Sugden, R. (1983) *Why Transnational Corporations?*, Warwick Economic Research papers, No. 222.

Teece, D.J. (1977) 'Technology transfer by multinational firms: the resource costs of transferring technological know-how', *Economic Journal* 87, 2.

—— (1983) 'Technological and organizational factors in the theory of the multinational enterprise', in M.C. Casson (ed.) *The Growth of International Business*, London: Allen & Unwin.

—— (1990) 'Capturing value from technological innovation: integration, strategic partnering and licensing decisions', in F. Arcangeli, P.A. David and G. Dosi (eds.) *Modern Patterns in Introducing and Adopting Innovations*, Oxford: Oxford University Press.

Tolentino, P.E.E. (1987)'The Global Shift in International Production and the Growth of Multinational Enterprises from the Developing Countries: the Philippines', Ph.D. thesis, University of Reading.

Usher, A.P. (1929) *A History of Mechanical Inventions*, Cambridge, Mass.: Harvard University Press.

Vernon, R. (1966) 'International investment and international trade in the product cycle', *Quarterly Journal of Economics* 80, 2.

—— (1971) *Sovereignty at Bay*, Harmondsworth: Penguin.

—— (1974) 'The location of economic activity', in J.H. Dunning (ed.) *Economic Analysis and the Multinational Enterprise*, London: Allen & Unwin.

—— (1979) 'The product cycle hypothesis in a new international environment', *Oxford Bulletin of Economics and Statistics* 41, 4.

Warren, B. (1980) *Imperialism: Pioneer of Capitalism*, London: Verso.

Wells, L.T., ed. (1972) *The Product Life Cycle and International Trade*, Boston, Mass.: Harvard University Press.
Williamson, O.E. (1975) *Markets and Hierarchies: Analysis and Antitrust Implications*, New York: Free Press.

3 A reassessment of Hymer's contribution to the theory of the transnational corporation

Mohammad Yamin

There are two major theoretical landmarks in the development of ideas on the TNCs. First is the seminal contribution of Hymer (1960). The second is the systematic incorporation of the concept of internalization in the explanation of the emergence and growth of TNCs. This chapter concentrates on a reassessment of Hymer's contribution. It points out that Hymer's work incorporated two rather than one explanations of what he called 'international operations' of national firms. Briefly, one explanation stressed the possession of advantages by firms and the other the removal of conflicts between them. Naturally these explanations of international operations are related and are from the same intellectual stable. Nevertheless there are significant differences between them which cannot be overlooked.

For a variety of reasons Hymer's 'advantage' theory proved highly influential, while his 'removal of conflict' theory has been virtually ignored. In this chapter we offer a number of reasons for this and at the same time suggest that the 'removal of conflict' theory may prove to be of some relevance in the context of recent developments in the international economy and also in the context of theoretical debates. A related point that is argued in this chapter is that, contrary to what is often supposed, there is a degree of continuity between Hymer's original thesis and his later work. Thus it is usually suggested that Hymer's later work represents a radical departure from his original contribution. It will be argued that in an important way this is misleading.

Finally some suggestions are offered in an attempt to clarify the relationship between the so-called 'structural' and transactional market failures that are thought to distinguish Hymer's contributions from the internalization theory. Our main point is that while Hymer's theory would have benefited from a more systematic consideration of transaction costs it is also the case that he did not totally ignore them. Furthermore we argue that, in any case, transaction costs can actually reinforce the 'Hymerian' view that monopoly/market power rather than efficiency factors give rise to the TNCs.

HYMER'S ORIGINAL CONTRIBUTION

Hymer's thesis (1960, published 1976) can be thought of as having made two lasting contributions. These were two ideas that are now commonly accepted and have in fact laid the foundations of all subsequent developments in the theory of DFI and the TNCs. The first was that DFI could not be explained as if it were portfolio investment – that is, inter-country movements of capital responding to differential rates of return on capital (interest rates). Hymer showed that even as an explanation of portfolio investment the interest differential theory was not very robust (e.g. the addition of risk and uncertainty would render the direction of capital flows indeterminate). More importantly, however, when the interest differential theory was applied to DFI a number of inconsistencies arose. For instance, firms that were undertaking direct *investment* were also *borrowing* abroad. As Hymer remarked, if DFI is motivated by higher interest rates abroad the practice of borrowing substantially abroad seems strange. Another inconsistency noted by Hymer was that DFI has a persistent industrial distribution and this distribution is more or less the same in all countries where DFI takes place. It is not clear that capital movements motivated by interest rate differentials should have such an industrial distribution. On the contrary, one would expect portfolio investment to flow, over time, to all activities and industries but only in a limited number of countries.

Hymer's second and even more fundamental contribution was to argue for the association between market failure and DFI. Virtually without exception every subsequent attempt to explain DFI and the TNCs has at its centre some sort of market failure; whilst some post-Hymer explanations have focused on conventional departures from perfect competition such as product differentiation and other aspects of entry barriers, internalization theories are (some would argue) based on a radically different concept of market failure.

Two explanations of international operations

Hymer argued that the important theoretical shortcoming of the interest differential theory was that it did not explain control. For Hymer DFI was one form of what he called 'international operations',[1] by which he meant the various ways (full or partial equity ownership, licensing, formal cartels or tacit collusion) in which firms of one nationality can control the decision-making of another. Movements of capital associated with DFI were thus not a response to higher interest rates in 'host' countries but took place in order to finance international operations. In order to explain DFI it was therefore necessary to explain why firms found it profitable to control firms in other countries.

Hymer was specifically concerned with the international operations of *national* firms; his interest was mainly in explaining the initial act of international operation rather than the growth of the multinational corporation; the scope of his theory is thus narrower than internalization theories or Dunning's eclectic theory (see chapters 4 and 5). The primacy of the national firm in his analysis reflected the view that there were significant barriers to international operations and thus advantages for national firms in their home market. The costs of international operations were of two kinds: (1) fixed and non-recurring – different language, lack of familiarity with the customs, politics and economies of foreign countries; (2) recurring costs – discrimination by national governments, consumers and suppliers and, perhaps most important of all, exchange rate risks.

Given that there were costs associated with international operations, why – or, perhaps more appropriately, under what circumstances – would some firms still find it profitable to control firms in other countries? Hymer argued that the *major*[2] need for control arose for two reasons: the possession of advantages and the removal of conflict.

Possession of advantages as a cause of DFI

Hymer observed that firms are very unequal in their ability to operate in a particular industry. In other words, a firm may possess an advantage over its rivals in a particular industry, and the possession of this advantage may cause it to have extensive international operations of one kind or another. Hymer was greatly influenced by Bain's analysis of the advantages of incumbent firms as compared with potential entrants in industries with significant entry barriers. However, he argued that the advantages a firm may have over firms in another country may be very different from those it may have over firms in its own country. On the one hand, the advantage over firms in another country may be weaker because the firm would be subject to the various costs of international operations. On the other hand, and because of the imperfect integration of the international economy and the nationally segmented nature of factor markets, its advantage over foreign competitors might be stronger compared with its advantage over other firms in its own market, e.g. American firms will have easier access to the US capital market; skilled American workers might be willing to work for the subsidiary of an American firm but not for a domestically owned firm in the foreign country. Thus foreign firms might be denied access to the general fund of skill and ability available in abundance in the USA.

Beyond these general considerations he did not examine in any detail the kinds of advantages that firms may use to operate internationally. He noted that 'there are as many kinds of advantages as there are functions in making and selling a product' (1976: 41). However, he did not focus on any particular advantage. Nor did he consider whether all advantages were equally suitable as a basis for DFI or other forms of international operations. These tasks were left to later scholars.[3]

Hymer's main concern was to show that the possession of advantages can explain the need to control the activities of firms in other countries. Quite simply, a firm with a particular advantage may find it profitable to exploit it in other countries. Whether this exploitation takes the form of a subsidiary or of letting/leasing the advantage to domestic enterprises would depend on the degree of imperfection in the market for the advantage. In particular, as long as there are many buyers of the advantage, licensing or other arm's-length methods would be viable and it would be possible for the firm to appropriate the full rent from the asset. But when there are only a few buyers and sellers of the advantage a situation of bilateral monopoly/oligopoly is encountered and it can easily be shown that integration is one way of maximizing joint profits. The same result may be achieved by various forms of collusion between the firms. In explaining the preference for DFI Hymer did stress structural interdependence but, as will be pointed out in more detail below, he was not completely oblivious to what are now called 'transaction cost' considerations.

Removal of conflict as a cause of DFI

Hymer pointed out that enterprises in different countries are frequently connected to each other through markets. They compete by selling in the same markets or one firm may sell to another. In such a situation profits may be increased if one firm controls all the enterprises rather than having separate firms in each country. In other words, it is profitable to substitute centralized decision-making for decentralized decision-making. Whether or not this takes place depends on whether markets are perfect. In particular, if there is duopolistic or oligopolistic interdependence between the firms involved in horizontal relationships, some form of collusion will increase joint profits, and once again integration or merger is possibly the most effective form of collusion. However, if there are many firms, or if entry is easy, then there is not much point in trying to control the market, and international operations will not take place. A similar analysis will apply if the interdependence between firms is vertical. Again as long as there are only a few buyers and sellers integration or any other effective form of co-operation between the firms will increase joint profits.

In neither the horizontal nor the vertical case is it necessary for one of the firms to possess an advantage over the others, although they are likely to be leading members of their respective national oligopolies. The only consideration is whether the increased profits from co-operation/collusion are more than sufficient to offset the costs of international operations. The important point is that international operation is no longer synonymous with the exploitation of some form of firm-specific asset under the firm's own control.

It is perhaps significant that the only case histories of international operations that Hymer looked at in any detail would come under the 'removal of conflict' rather than the 'possession of advantage' category. One example, which he took from Dunning's early study of American investment in Britain (1958) was the tobacco industry – the conflict between American Tobacco and the British tobacco firms who had formed themselves into the Imperial Tobacco Company (this was itself a defensive response to the acquisition by American Tobacco of a British firm). Following a period of cut-throat competition both in the British and in other markets, a market-sharing agreement was reached according to which Imperial Tobacco obtained a monopoly in Britain and Ireland. The US and dependent markets were to be supplied by American Tobacco. A new company under joint ownership (British-American Tobacco) was set up to handle the rest of the export business.

The other and constrasting example was the meat packing industry. Both American and British firms had established meat-packing plants in Latin American countries. Bitter competition ensued, but unlike the tobacco case there was no successful resolution of the conflict between US and British meat packers. Both sets of firms continued to operate independently in Latin American markets. These examples also serve to highlight a significant feature of the theory of international operations: because oligopolistic interdependence was so central to Hymer's analysis he was acutely aware of the uncertainties that are inherent in oligopolistic situations. Thus, as he emphatically pointed out, his theory could not predict the *extent* of international operations because neither the form nor the success of the methods chosen for the resolution of conflict could be predicted. This point is relevant in the context of recent criticisms of Hymer for his neglect of transaction costs (see below).

THE CONTINUITY IN HYMER'S CONTRIBUTION

As we noted at the beginning it is usually supposed that there is a definite intellectual break and discontinuity in Hymer's contribution to the literature on TNCs. For example, Casson (1987: 5) has observed that 'by the time of its [Hymer's thesis] publication Hymer had become a publicly committed Marxist and had modified his views of the MNE quite considerably as a result'. This is somewhat misleadng. It is true, of course, that Hymer's views had undergone a considerable radicalization, but in my opinion this radicalization had resulted primarily in a change of focus rather than method.

Whereas in his thesis and other early work Hymer was primarily interested in the multinational firm as an institution, in his later, more 'radical' writings he was primarily interested in broader, systemic issues. He was more concerned with analysing not the operations of multinational firms *per se* and in isolation but the workings of the world economy, in which multinationals were becoming increasingly prominent. But the *theory* of the multinational enterprise that was, implicitly, incorporated into his broader analysis was a generalization of his 'removal of conflict' view of international operations.

In this context one of his last papers, 'The internationalisation of capital' (1979, originally published 1972), is particularly interesting. Despite its title the paper does not concern itself with the internationalizations of the various circuits of capital. In this sense Hymer's contribution is very different from what may be called the more orthodox Marxist analyses of TNCs and internationalization of capital (Palloix, 1975; Jenkins, 1987). Hymer's conception of the internationalization of capital reflected a gradual development of a community of interest amongst capitalists of different nationalities. And he believed that the TNCs were the focal point of this community of interest. He said that:

> the international flow of private capital, through the multinational corporations or alongside it, gives individual wealth holders a stake in the international capitalist system as a whole, in proportion as their income comes less and less from their home country and more and more from the world economy at large.
>
> (1979: 82–3)

Developing this theme, Hymer observed that if the owner of a small family firm allows it to be taken over by a multinational he will be giving up a profitable but inflexible investment in the national firm in return for shares in the multinational, traded on the world market and guaranteed by all the forces that lie behind the international law of private property. He added further that:

> He [the owner of the national firm] is no longer locked into his industry or his country; the viability of his concern is ensured by its connection to the multinational firm. Furthermore his need for Swiss bank accounts and other ways of escaping the control of his national government is diminished because now his capital receives the special priveleges of foreign capital.
>
> (1979: 85)

In as much as multinationals competed with each other the competition was very restrained:

> The large firms of the world are all competing for these various sources of future growth but in an oligopolistic rather than in a cutthroat way. They recognize their mutual interdependence and strive to share in the pie without destroying it. As they do so they come to be less and less dependent on their home country's economy for their profits, and more and more dependent on the world economy. Conflicts between firms on the basis of nationality are thereby transformed into international oligopolistic market sharing and collusion.
>
> (1979: 82)

Thus for Hymer himself, at least to judge by his subsequent work, the 'removal of conflict' had as much relevance to understanding TNCs as the possession of advantages. Of course, the difference between these two views of TNCs should not be exaggerated. There is much that is shared in common by the two explanations of international operations put foreward by Hymer. The following passage, which, it can argued, represents the intellectual core of Hymer's theory, applies to both explanations:

> The theory of international operations is part of the theory of the firm. It is concerned with the various relationships between enterprises in one country and enterprises of another. More particularly, it is concerned with the conditions under which an enterprise of one country will be controlled by a firm of another country or enterprises in several countries will be controlled by the same firm. It is a problem of determining the extent of vertical and horizontal integration of firms. The tools used to analyse international operations are the same, essentially, as those used to analyse the firm in its operations. But there are two important differences: the operations are international and firms are national.
>
> (1976: 27–8)

Nevertheless there *are* significant differences between the two explanations and it is something of a puzzle why the 'possession of advantage' theory proved extremely influential whilst until very recently the removal of conflict theory was completely ignored. In textbook exposition Hymer's theory is simply equated with the notion of the possession of advantages. Thus, for example, Hood and Young note, 'early theorists of DFI [therefore] focused . . . on ownership advantages which the MNE were believed to have acquired within [this] imperfectly competitive environment' (1979: 45–6). Cowling and Sugden (1987) whose own explanation of TNCs is very similar to Hymer's 'resolution of conflict' theory, are actually unaware of this and refer to the monopolistic advantage theory of Hymer, which they regard as inadequate (see also chapter 2). Casson (1987) and Dunning and Rugman (1985) have noted Hymer's argument that multinationals can come about as a result of collusion between firms to increase global profits, but they provide no explanation as to why this aspect of his analysis has been ignored. Both Casson (1987) and Dunning and Rugman (1985) are more concerned to show that Hymer's emphasis on 'structural' imperfections and his neglect of transactional imperfections are the cause of the inadequacies of his theory and his preoccupation with market power rather than efficiency consequences of TNCs. We will return to this discussion later in the chapter. First, however, we will examine some of the reasons why only his 'possession of advantage theory' became very influential.

THE RISE AND 'FALL' OF THE 'ADVANTAGE' THEORY OF DFI

We can offer three basic reasons for the subsequent and highly selective treatment and interpretation of Hymer's original thesis. First, and perhaps somewhat paradoxically, is the incomplete nature of his contribution *vis-à-vis* the 'possession of advantage' theory. Second are parallel and reinforcing developments in adjacent fields of economic analysis, and finally certain structural features of the international economic environment.

As for the incomplete nature of his contribution, we have already pointed out that Hymer did not concentrate on any particular advantage, nor did he consider whether all advantages were equally suitable as a basis for international operations. A related point is that Hymer did not sufficiently examine the role of exporting in the utilization of advantages, or how the inter-industry pattern of international operations and export intensity may be related to the extent and distribution of different sorts of advantages between firms and industries. His work had opened a new perspective on the study of DFI and other forms of international operations, a perspective which suggested a rich array of questions. The body of literature (for a survey see, *inter alia*, Hood and Young, 1979, or Caves, 1982) that addressed these issues regarded the possession of advantages as almost a logically necessary precondition for DFI. And as long as the 'possession of advantage' approach was capable of generating exciting research on the theoretical and empirical aspects of DFI and TNCs the role and the necessity of advantages in the theory were unlikely to be questioned.

Second, developments in trade theory, and in particular the emergence of the neotechnology and technology gap explanations of the direction and pattern of trade, particularly of trade in manufactured products, were emphasizing similar factors to those suggested by the advantage theory of direct investment. Thus, as Dunning (1981) has pointed out, the neotechnology and the scale economy models introduced new explanatory variables which focused 'not on the specific resource endowment of countries but on the exclusive possession of certain assets by enterprises' (p. 23). Vernon's (1966) original product cycle model was in fact an attempt to integrate insights from the neotechnology trade theories and the ownership advantage theory of DFI. We believe that Vernon's model in fact significantly bolstered the advantage theory of DFI because it furnished a plausible solution to a problem that Hymer's theory could not resolve: why should multinationals (at that time) be predominantly American rather than of other nationalities?. Hymer himself had posed a similar question: 'why do firms of different countries have unequal ability?' (p. 72). But beyond suggesting that firms which have advantages are likely to be from advanced countries rather than from less developed countries he did not explain the distribution of DFI amongst firms of different nationalities. In retrospect Vernon's product cycle model may be seen in part as an attempt to explain the preponderance of US TNCs at the time.

According to Vernon the US economy possessed a number of unique characteristics which helped to explain the dominance of its firms in the international economy. These characteristics – relative abundance of capital, a very large market and a high level of *per capita* income – created opportunities for product innovations of a kind that would, in time, find a ready market in other developed and eventually less developed countries. Vernon implied that US innovations reflected conditions that the 'normal' process of economic growth would create in many other countries. The question still remains as to why entrepreneurs in other countries should not respond to the opportunities for new products and services in the US market by developing exports to it. Vernon regarded this as unlikely because he believed firms have a national rather than an international horizon so far as their innovative activity is concerned.

This brings us to the third factor. Hymer (and Vernon) were writing at a time and about a world in which the international integration of the world economy was relatively undeveloped. In fact, according to Hymer, it was precisely this lack of international integration that was the basis of the barriers to international operations and hence of the costs and disadvantages of 'foreignness'. Similar considerations underlay Vernon's notion of a nationally limited technological or innovative horizon. In an imperfectly integrated world economy the concept of monopolistic advantage as a prerequisite of international operations has strong theoretical appeal. However, with increasing international integration and the reduction in the cost of international operations this relevance may be progressively undermined, as the possession of advantage may no longer be necessary in order to offset such costs.[4]

On the other hand, with increasing international integration, precisely because the costs of international operations are now much lower, and more and more firms are therefore likely to encounter each other in various markets, 'removal of conflict' may become a highly relevant framework of analysis. An important aspect of internationalization is that multinational firms are increasingly truly global rather than purely multi-domestic, a distinction introduced by Porter (1986). For such firms the costs specifically incurred in international operations may be quite insignificant, as in addition to the general reduction of the costs of communication and administrative control available to all firms, global firms may have acquired the capacity to 'learn in advance' the conditions in different countries (Buckley, 1985). In fact a close reading of Hymer suggests that he would probably have agreed with this assessment (that for global firms the costs of international operations are negligible). For him the most important cost of such operations came about from exchange rate risks. However, he also pointed out that:

> If a company is *truly international* so that its liabilities each year in any currency were proportionate to its income in that currency it would be no more concerned about changes in the exchange rates than American firms are concerned with the devaluation of the dollar when they decide to invest in America.
>
> (1976: 36; emphasis added)

However, even though for a global firm the possession of advantages may no longer be crucial, the proper handling of its relationship with other equally global firms remains critical. In fact as such firms encounter each other more regularly and in many more markets than in the earlier, multi-domestic phase of their development the handling of potential inter-firm conflict is of much greater importance. Thus Porter and Fuller (1986) have suggested that for global firms the proper handling of 'coalition' activity is of first-order strategic importance. In a similar vein Buckley and Casson (1987) have analysed co-operation in international business. The prominence or frequency of co-operative or coalition activity cannot, of course, be taken as a confirmation of the Hymer type of analysis (and an acceptence of his presumption of an essentially collusive rather than a competitive world economy). Buckley and Casson (1987) are in fact interested in the possible efficiency of co-operative behaviour. More generally, others have pointed out that with the development of multinational firms the world economy has become more rather than less competitive, as it makes possible a much greater mobility of capital than was possible before (Clifton, 1977; Yamin, 1988).

Nevertheless the point remains that in an increasingly integrated world the handling of inter-firm relations does become a central concern of TNCs, and therefore Hymer's 'removal of conflict' view of international business must be regarded at least as a serious contender for a relevant theoretical perspective.

There is another reason why 'removal of conflict' may prove a more enduring contribution of Hymer's than the possession of advantages. The latter was never a unified theory of international operations or of DFI. It could only explain horizontal DFI. In fact for a long time vertical DFI was ignored. Virtually all those writers who were applying or developing Hymer's 'possession of advantage' theory simply ignored vertical DFI. The 'removal of conflict' theory has no such limitation, as it can handle both types of inter-firm relations and interdependence. In this respect it is rather similar to the internalization framework. Finally, the credibility of the advantage theory of DFI suffered further as a result of the theoretical onslaught by a number of writers in the internalization school. Among the most effective critiques are Hennart (1982) and Buckley (1983, 1985). Buckley, for example, has noted that the concept of firm-specific advantage is essentially a short-term concept and is treated as a given rather than as a product of a dynamic investment programme.

'STRUCTURAL' VERSUS 'TRANSACTIONAL' MARKET FAILURES

A number of authors have criticized Hymer and those who have followed his approach to the analysis of international operations of emphasizing so-called structural market failures (i.e. essentially Bain-type entry barriers) and collusive behaviour and ignoring transaction costs (Casson, 1987; Dunning and Rugman, 1985; Teece, 1985). Casson, for example, remarks that Hymer ignores the transaction costs incurred in connection with defining property rights and negotiating, monitoring and enforcing contracts (1987: 6). The first point is that this contrast is somewhat exaggerated.

Explaining the reasons why a firm utilizes its own advantage in preference to licensing, Hymer notes:

> The firm is a practical institutional device which substitutes for the market. The firm *internalizes* or supersedes the market. A fruitful approach to our problem is to ask why the market is an inferior method of exploiting the advantage; that is, we look for imperfections in the market. . . . Impurities in the market [by which Hymer means the existence of oligopolistic interdependence] are not the only kind of imperfections which are relevant here. In a world of *uncertainty* there may be a conflict of evaluation which makes co-operation difficult. . . .
> Aside from causing a conflict of evaluation, uncertainty *makes it difficult for buyers and sellers to achieve a satisfactory contract*. If a contract

provides rigid provisions, changing conditions will hurt one party and benefit the other. . . . A reluctance to license may also arise from the inherent danger of losing the advantage. The licensee may discover a process which substitutes for the advantage.

(1976: 48–51; emphasis added)

Thus even in his thesis Hymer was certainly *aware* of what we now call transactional difficulties that undermine contractual agreements.[5] Nevertheless it is correct to say that for him 'market impurities' were much the more significant. However, this, we must presume, reflected his judgement as to the relative importance of different sorts of impediments to arm's-length transactions. In this respect not much has changed, as it is still essentially a matter of judgement as to which type of market failure is more important.

Second, as we have noted, Hymer was acutely aware that the outcome of oligopolistic interdependence is inherently uncertain; that collusion may take several different forms and may even fail (recall the meat-packing example). However, his explanation of which particular outcome may dominate was at best incomplete. In this context we agree with Casson's argument that Hymer's explanation of international operations does suffer from an inadequate emphasis on transaction costs:

collusion can be effected through alternative arrangements – notably a cartel – and without a theory of transaction costs Hymer could not explain why in certain industries and at certain times an MNE will prevail and, in other industries and other times, an international cartel.

(1987: 7)

But if the only role of transaction costs was to provide a more complete theory of collusion there would have been little controversy or debate surrounding it. The controversy has arisen because it is claimed that it is the quest for *efficiency* in the face of transaction costs rather than the exercise of market power which has been the main determinant of the forms of industrial organization, including the transnational corporation (Williamson, 1981, 1985). To sustain this argument one thing that is necessary is to assume that transaction market imperfections occur naturally or are at least exogenous to firms. This is explicitly stated by Rugman (1981) and Dunning and Rugman (1985). Whether this assumption is theoretically defensible has been examined elsewhere (Yamin and Nixson, 1988) and will not be pursued here.[6]

Third, another relevant issue is that if the existence of transaction costs is a prerequisite for the possession and exercise of market power then it may not be possible to disentangle efficiency and market power factors in organizational design (e.g. the development of TNCs) merely by demonstrating that such organizations have developed in order to minimize transaction costs. This is precisely the view recently put forward by Malcomson (1984). He has argued that market power is predicated on the existence of (*a*) transaction costs and (*b*) anything that results in markets not clearing. For example, in the labour market employers may be able to exert power over their employees because of the transaction cost workers face in finding another job, as much of their skill may be transaction-specific and non-transferable, and because of the possibility of excess supply in the market. In the absence of these conditions the employer's threat to lay workers off may be of no significance. Similar considerations may apply in the relationship between a firm and its subcontractors. Thus a firm has power over its subcontractors to the extent that they have invested in transaction-specific assets and because they may not easily find an independent marketing outlet.

That such power may not be used and that, in any case, the power relation may be symmetrical or at least bilateral is not really at issue. The point is that the possibility that a particular organizational form or even the firm itself represents the resolution of conflict in favour of one set of agents cannot be ruled out (cf. Marglin, 1974, 1984). The demonstration, therefore, that a particular organizational form such as the TNC has emerged in order to minimize transaction costs does not prove that it is efficient. As Cowling and Sugden (1987) have remarked, 'the possibility of cost reductions when moving from market to non-market transactions is not itself sufficient to yield Pareto improvements. This is guaranteed by the voluntary exchange principle' (p. 10; see also chapter 8).

A point that is usually made by internalization theorists is that, if the quest for market power was the basis of vertical/horizontal integration, then it would be observed everywhere, and because it in fact occurs only selectively the market power explanation is not valid. However, as argued above, this is not correct, as market power is also a function of transaction costs and therefore market power-induced integration would also occur selectively in situations that give rise to significant transaction costs (i.e. the existence of transaction-specific assets).

Following this line of reasoning, it may be that those theories of the TNC that stress collusion and market power such as the work of Hymer and more recently that of Cowling and Sugden (1987) may actually be strengthened by transaction cost considerations rather than undermined by them. Thus Sugden (1983) and Cowling and Sugden (1987) point out that multinationals arise in order to improve the bargaining power of firms in the labour market. By locating production in different countries firms reduce the possibility and effectiveness of collective action by all their workers. In other words, multinationals arise in order to 'divide and rule'. See also Ietto-Gillies(1988). However, this argument is incomplete, as all firms would have the incentive to weaken the bargaining power of labour – but, clearly, not all firms are multinationals, even though multinationality is not as exclusive a status as it was at the time of Hymer's original contribution. However, it may well be that a combination of 'divide and rule' *and* transaction costs will prove a fruitful theoretical approach (see also chapter 9).

CONCLUDING REMARKS

This chapter has argued than Hymer's contribution to the literature on TNCs consists of two major strands and that for a number of reasons one of these strands, the 'removal of conflict', has been virtually ignored. Recognition of this is relevant in the context of the debate on the role of ownership-specific advantages in the theory of TNCs. Some writers such as Buckley (1985), Casson (1987) and Rugman (1981) have argued that ownership-specific advantages, a concept which has its roots in Hymer's 'advantages' theory of international operations, are in fact not necessary to explain the existence of TNCs. A similar argument is put forward by Cowling and Sugden (1987), who have built a theory of transnational monopoly capitalism which is very close to Hymer's 'removal of conflict' explanation and in fact constitutes a development of it. This aspect of Hymer's original contribution thus remains highly relevant in the context of current developments in the theory of TNCs.

Furthermore we agree that Hymer's insights are somewhat incomplete and that a more systematic consideration of transaction costs would have put his 'removal of conflict' theory on a more rigorous footing. However, we also believe that the contrast between 'structural' and 'transactional' market imperfections can be exaggerated and that, in any case, the transaction cost approach cannot necessarily discriminate between market power and efficiency considerations.

NOTES

1 Hymer's definition of international operations is very similar to Dunning's concept of international production (1981, 1988).

2 The minor need for control arose from the motive of (international) diversification (Hymer, 1976: 40).

3 The work of such authors as Johnson (1970), Caves (1971, 1974), Hirsch(1976) and Lall (1980) are the more influential examples of the various theoretical and empirical attempts to specify the nature of the advantages most likely to be exploited via DFI.

4 Clearly, ownership advantages will play a role in explaining why some TNCs

grow faster than others (Casson 1987). More generally the relative strength of individual TNCs is defined by a particular configuration of technological, marketing and managerial prowess, and the *outcome* collusion between TNCs will reflect the distribution of such prowess between them.

5 In a subsequent paper (Hymer, 1968), which had apparently remained unknown until Mark Casson's recent discovery of it, Hymer explicitly acknowledges the contribution of Coase. But whilst he adopts a Coasian explanation of the determinants of the scale of the firm he does point out that he is considering the matter only 'from the firm's point of view' (Hymer, 1968: 7). As such, of course, it is non-problematic to state that 'the firm reaches its optimal size when marginal scale advantages are just overtaken by marginal management costs (ibid., p. 8). This is just a description of how firms make decisions. There is no necessary implication that these decision are also socially optimal.

6 Of course even in the context of collusion an efficiency gain may result, as *ceteris paribus*, a merger may be a Pareto improvement, compared with other forms of collusion. By minimizing transaction costs a merger produces a gain for the members of the cartel, leaving other parties (e.g. consumers) no worse off. The problem is that the *ceteris paribus* assumption may be implausible if agents seek monopoly positions (and is this not a natural consequence of 'opportunism'?), as they would then seek to shape the environment in which they operate. Once again, therefore, the assumption of 'naturally' occurring market imperfections must be questioned.

REFERENCES

Buckley, P. (1983) 'New theories of international business: some unresolved issues', in M. Casson, (ed.) *The Growth of International Business*, London: Allen & Unwin.

—— (1985) 'A critical review of the theories of the multinational enterprise', in P. Buckley and M. Casson, *The Economic Theory of the Multinational Enterprise: Selected Papers*, London: Macmillan.

Buckley, P., and Casson, M. (1987) 'A theory of cooperation in international business', in F. Contractor and P. Lorange (eds.) *Cooperative Strategies in International Business*, Lexington, Mass.: Lexington Books.

Casson, M. (1987) *The Firm and the Market: Studies in Multinational Enterprise and the Scope of the Firm*, Oxford: Blackwell.

Caves, R. (1971) 'International corporations: the industrial economics of direct foreign investment', *Economica*, February.

—— (1974) 'Causes of direct foreign investment: foreign firms' share in Canadian and United Kingdom manufacturing industries', *Review of Economics and Statistics*, August.

—— (1982) *Multinational Enterprise and Economic Analysis*, Cambridge: Cambridge University Press.

Clifton, J. (1977) 'Competition and the evolution of the capitalist mode of production', *Cambridge Journal of Economics* 2.

Cowling, K. and Sugden, R. (1987) *Transnational Monopoly Capitalism*, Brighton: Wheatsheaf.

Dunning, J. (1958) *American Investment in British Manufacturing Industry*, London: Allen & Unwin.

—— (1981) *International Production and the Multinational Enterprise*, London: Allen & Unwin.

—— (1988) 'The eclectic paradigm of international production: an update and a reply to its critics', *Journal of International Business Studies*, Spring.

Dunning, J. and Rugman, A. (1985) 'The influence of Hymer's dissertation on the theory of foreign direct investment', *American Economic Review*, May.

Hennart, J. (1982) *A Theory of Multinational Enterprise*, Ann Arbor, Mich.: University of Michigan Press.

Hirsch, S. (1976) 'An international trade and investment theory of the firm', *Oxford Economic Papers*, July.

Hood, N., and Young, S. (1979) *The Economics of Multinational Enterprise*, London: Longman.

Hymer, S. (1976, originally written in 1960) The International Operations of National Firms: a Study of Foreign Direct Investment, Ph.D. dissertation, Massachusetts Institute of Technology: MIT Press.

—— 1968) 'The large multinational "corporation": an analysis of some motives for international integration of business', *Revue Economique* 6, translated from the French by Nathalie Vacherot with an introduction by Mark Casson.

—— (1979) 'The internationalisation of capital', in R.B. Cohen, N. Fotton, M. Nikos, and J. van Liere, with N. Donnis (eds.) *The Multinational Corporation: a Radical Approach. Papers by Stephen Hymer*, Cambridge: Cambridge University Press.

Ietto-Gilles, G. (1988) 'Internationalisation of production: an analysis based on labour', *British Review on Economic Issues*, autumn.

Jenkins, R. (1987) *Transnational Corporations and Uneven Development: the Internationalisation of Capital and the Third World*, London: Methuen.

Johnson, H. (1970) 'The efficiency and welfare implications of the multinational corporation', in C. Kindleberger (ed.) *The International Corporation: a Symposium*, Cambridge, Mass.: MIT Press.

Lall, S. (1980) 'Monopolistic advantages and foreign investment by US manufacturing industry', *Oxford Economic Papers*, March.

Malcomson, J. (1984) 'Efficient labour organisation: incentives, power and the transaction costs approach', in F. Stephen (ed.) *Firms, Organizations and Labour: Approaches to the Economics of Work Organization*, London: Macmillan.

Marglin, S. (1974) 'What do bosses do? The origins and functions of hierarchy in capitalist production', *Review of Radical Political Economics*, summer.

—— (1984) 'Knowledge and power', in F.Stephen (ed.) *Firms, Organization and Labour: Approaches to the Economics of Work Organization*, London: Macmillan.

Palloix, C. (1975) 'The internationalisation of capital and the circuit of social capital', in H. Radice (ed.) *International Firms and Modern Imperialism*, Harmondsworth: Penguin.

Porter, M., ed. (1986), *Competition in Global Industries*, Cambridge, Mass.: Harvard Business School.

Porter, M., and Fuller, M. (1986) 'Coalitions and global strategy', in M. Porter (ed.) *Competition in Global Industries*, Boston, Mass.: Harvard Business School Press.

Rugman, A. (1981) *Inside the Multinational: the Economics of Internal Markets*, London: Croom Helm.

Sugden, R. (1983) *Why Transnational Corporations?* Warwick Economic Research Papers, No. 222, Coventry: University of Warwick.

Teece, D. (1985) 'Multinational enterprise, internal governance and industrial organization', *American Economic Review*, May.

Vernon, R. (1966) 'International investment and international trade in the product cycle', *Quarterly Journal of Economics*, May.

Williamson, O. (1981) 'The modern corporation: origins, evolution, attributes', *Journal of Economic Literature*, December.

—— (1985) *The Economic Institutions of Capitalism: Firms, Markets, Relational Contracting*, New York: Free Press.

Yamin, M. (1988) 'Aspects of the involvement of transnational corporations in the restructuring of the world economy', *Manchester Papers on Development*, July.

Yamin, M., and Nixson, F. (1988) 'Transnational corporations and the control of restrictive business practices: theoretical issues and empirical evidence', *International Review of Applied Economics*, January.

ACKNOWLEDGEMENTS

I am grateful to Christos Pitelis, Roger Sugden and Willy Seal for comments on this chapter. The usual *caveat* applies.

4 The transaction cost theory of the multinational enterprise

Jean-François Hennart

This chapter critically reviews what many scholars (e.g. Kay, 1983) see as the dominant explanation of the multinational enterprise (MNE), the transaction cost or internalization approach.[1] It argues that transaction cost theory constitutes a general theory of economic organization which can explain the choice between hierarchical co-ordination and other forms of organization, such as spot markets and contracts, and hence provides a key element in our understanding of the reasons for the existence and the development of MNEs. The first section shows that the transacton cost model is a unifying paradigm that can explain the most common forms of foreign direct investment. The second discusses the ability of the paradigm to account not only for pure market or hierarchical forms but also for the rich variety of institutions which combine, in various proportions, these two 'pure institutional types'. In the third section I look at organization costs within firms.

TRANSACTION COSTS AS A GENERAL THEORY OF THE MULTINATIONAL ENTERPRISE

In a chapter in *Multinational Enterprise in Historical Perspective* D.K. Fieldhouse (1986: 25) writes that:

> Historical research has shown that the tidy logic of growth of firms theory, the main intellectual foundation for the concept of the MNC [multinational corporation], simply does not fit the unruly variety of corporate motivation. It is critical that most early theorizing was based on recent American experience, mainly in manufacturing and petroleum, and even this was not uniform. Still more variable were the historical reasons for US and European investment in overseas mining, plantations, and utilities. In none of these last did FDI [foreign direct investment] commonly or necessarily flow from the growth patterns of

metropolitan firms. In many of them capitalists established new corporate enterprises without a previous home base, specifically to produce a commodity which could only be obtained elsewhere, or to exploit an evident overseas need for public services, such as railways or telecommunications in Latin America. Motives for FDI were therefore infinitely more complex than any unitary theory of the MNC could possibly comprehend, and had no necessary connection with the internalization concept.

Are motives for the MNE so disparate that a general theory of the MNE cannot be constructed? This section demonstrates that transaction cost theory can in fact account for the wide variety of the types of foreign direct investment cited by Fieldhouse. As a starting point, it is useful to reflect on the nature of the MNE.

Structural and natural market imperfections

The existence of MNEs puzzles traditional microeconomists. Operating overseas usually costs more than operating at home, because a foreigner does not have the same contacts and knowledge of local customs and business practices as indigenous competitors. Hence it is difficult to understand why firms based in one country would be exploiting their advantages by undertaking production in another country. Why not sell or rent these advantages to local entrepreneurs, who could then combine them with local factors of production at lower costs than those experienced by foreign direct investors?

The answer to this paradox is that the market for the advantages may be so imperfect that the firm is willing to incur the additional costs of operating in a foreign environment. This idea that MNEs owe their existence to 'market imperfections' was first put forth by Hymer (1960, published 1976), Kindleberger (1969) and Caves (1971).[2] The market imperfections they had in mind were 'structural' imperfections of the monopolistic type, i.e. they arose from exclusive control of proprietary technology, privileged access to inputs, scale economies, control of distribution systems, and product differentiation (Bain, 1956; Dunning and Rugman, 1985). Hymer noted that US firms expanded abroad in order to exploit their superior technology. That technology often had few substitutes and the number of potential licensees in any given foreign market was also often limited. Hence foreign direct investment (FDI) was chosen to reduce the costs of bilateral monopoly. Because of bilateral monopoly, the seller (the licensor) and the buyer of technology (the licensee) would haggle with each other, and would find it difficult to enforce price discrimination schemes across countries (Hymer,

1976: 49–50). A merger between the licensor and the licensee could maximize their joint income by forcing them to take into account the gains and the losses they would have inflicted on each other; it would force them to internalize 'pecuniary' externalities. FDI thus led to a gain for the two interdependent agents now joined within an MNE, but not necessarily for society, since it redistributed income towards the MNE and away from its customers.[3] This led Hymer towards a generally negative view of MNEs, which he considered 'an instrument for restraining competition between firms of different nations' (Hymer, 1970: 443).

The insight of transaction cost theories of the MNE, simultaneously and independently developed in the 1970s by McManus (1972), Buckley and Casson (1976), Brown (1976) and Hennart (1977, 1982), is that 'market imperfections' are inherent attributes of markets, and MNEs are institutions for bypassing these imperfections. Markets experience 'natural' imperfections, i.e. imperfections that are due to the fact that the implicit neoclassical assumptions of perfect knowledge and perfect enforcement are not realized (Teece, 1981; Dunning and Rugman, 1985).[4]

The dominant mode of organization in markets is the price system. If knowledge were perfect and individuals perfectly honest, market transaction costs would be zero. The three tasks that must be performed by any system of organization – to inform agents of the needs of others, to reward them for productive behaviour, and to curb bargaining – would be costlessly performed by prices. Prices would convey information to all interacting parties on the social consequences of their actions, and would provide the information needed for optimum joint decisions. Prices would constitute a decentralized information system. Through prices each agent would be fully appraised of everyone else's needs, and incited to adapt to those needs so as to maximize social welfare. With a large number of buyers and sellers, prices would be exogenous, thus curbing bargaining. Prices would also reward agents in proportion to their output (measured at market prices): an agent who took the day off would see his income correspondingly reduced.

In practice, markets are never fully efficient, and market transaction costs (the sum of information, enforcement and bargaining costs) are positive. This is because agents have 'bounded rationality' and a tendency to opportunism (Williamson, 1975). With bounded rationality, the value of the goods and services exchanged will never be perfectly measured; hence prices will provide flawed signals, and a price system will not maximize the social product. Agents will generate non-pecuniary externalities. Positive measurement costs joined with opportunism will also make it possible for agents to cheat – i.e. given positive detection costs, they will be able to alter the terms of trade to their advantage within a given range without loss of revenue. Lastly, imperfect information will also segment the market, thus making prices endogenous, and bargaining profitable.

If it is very costly to measure the value of goods and services, and opportunities for bargaining and dishonesty are therefore high, it may pay to eliminate these opportunities by aligning the interests of the parties, i.e. by reducing the incentives they have to cheat. This can be achieved by breaking the connection between output and performance. The price system can be replaced by a mode of organization in which buyers and sellers no longer profit from their ability to change the terms of trade in their favour, but instead are rewarded for following the directives of a central party directing the exchange. These directives, which can better reflect the overall costs and benefits of the activity, will supersede flawed market prices. Such a system of organization is called hierarchy (Hennart, 1982, 1986c).

MNEs use hierarchy as a way of eliminating market transaction costs. By transforming independent agents into employees, they reduce their incentive to cheat. MNEs make it possible to organize some interactions which cannot be organized by markets, bringing gains of trade to the interacting parties and resulting in a net gain for society. Thus, while Hymer and Kindleberger see FDI as a method of maximizing monopoly power, or, in other words, as a way of internalizing pecuniary externalities, for transaction cost theorists FDI is undertaken to reduce transaction costs and internalize non-pecuniary externalities.

The distinction between pecuniary and non-pecuniary externalities is subtle but important. Pecuniary externalities arise from structural imperfections in markets characterized by monopoly or monopsony, while non-pecuniary externalities can be explained by natural market imperfections. For transaction cost theorists, FDI does not require that the investing firm possess monopolistic advantages. It requires only that some markets be such that hierarchical co-ordination incurs lower costs than co-ordination through prices. When US steelmakers invest in the mining of Liberian iron ore they do not exploit abroad a monopolistic advantage in a superior proprietary technology. In fact many steel firms have so little competence in the mining of iron ore that they have their captive mines managed by specialist firms (Cleveland Cliffs and Hanna Mining, for example). FDI can more generally be explained as the internalization of markets: steel firms invest abroad to internalize the market for iron ore, the same way horizontal direct investments by manufacturing firms internalize the market for technological know-how.

The following pages develop the idea that MNEs are economic institutions which internalize the non-pecuniary externalities resulting from 'natural' market imperfections. By focusing on 'natural' market imperfections the transaction costs approach throws light on a much wider range of motives for FDI strategies than can be explained by concentrating on 'structural' market imperfections.[5] Transaction cost economics can also be used to explain the conditions under which firms will internalize pecuniary externalities, and this point will be briefly addressed below (pp. 96–8).

Types and forms of foreign direct investment

As Dunning (1977, 1979, 1981) has shown, two conditions must be realized for the MNE to arise: (1) locating facilities abroad must be desirable and (2) a firm must find it profitable to own the foreign facilities. A firm eager to sell overseas must decide whether to produce at home and export to the foreign market, or to locate production overseas. The decision is based on a comparison of delivered cost, and is a function of the relative production cost of a domestic and foreign location, of transport costs, and of tariff and non-tariff barriers to trade.[9] A second decision is whether the firm will organize its interdependence with foreigners through market or hierarchical means. Transaction cost theory informs this second decision.

If the firm decides to produce at home and export to foreign markets, it must chose between integrating forward into distribution, thus internalizing the market for distribution services, and contracting with independent agents and distributors (see Fig. 4.1, where the hierarchical solution has been italicized). If it chooses to produce abroad, it can either sell or rent its advantages to local entrepreneurs (through franchising, licensing or management contracts) or exploit them itself by integrating horizontally into foreign manufacturing. The same analysis can be used for a firm that requires inputs from abroad (Fig. 4.2). It can either internalize the market for the input it needs (integrate vertically backwards) or obtain it by spot purchases or long-term contracts.

Figures 4.1–2 show that the expansion of firms abroad can take very diverse forms, from setting up sales subsidiaries to developing mines and plantations. Yet, once a foreign location is optimal, whether a firm will own foreign facilities – and hence become an MNE – can be explained by focusing on one simple question: when will markets for intermediate inputs be subject to such high transaction costs that hierarchical co-ordination is more efficient? The question is addressed in the following pages, focusing first on horizontal, then on vertical investments.

Horizontal investments

Knowledge

Most applications of transaction cost theory to the MNE have explored the

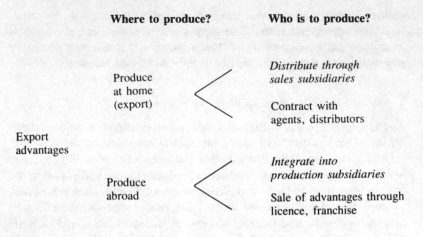

Figure 4.1

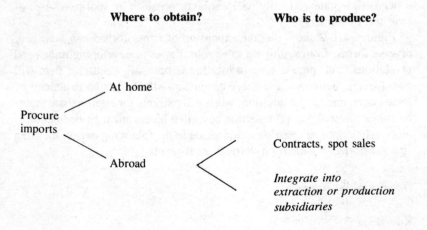

Figure 4.2

internalization of one particular type of input – knowledge (Buckley and Casson, 1976; Magee, 1977; Casson, 1979; Rugman, 1981; Teece, 1981; Caves, 1982; Hennart, 1977, 1982). Arrow's paradox serves as the starting point: the information buyer does not, by definition, know the exact characteristics of what he is buying; if the seller were to provide that information, he would, by revealing the information, be transferring it free of charge to the buyer (Arrow, 1962). The basic problem of the transfer of knowledge is therefore one of information asymmetry.

The patent system offers one solution to this problem. By giving the owner of information a monopoly in its use, patents encourage him to disclose his knowledge, thus reducing information costs and increasing the efficiency of the market for knowledge. However, the efficiency of a patent system crucially depends on the power and the willingness of public authorities to establish and enforce monopoly rights in knowledge. By taking out a patent the inventor is disclosing it to potential buyers, but also to potential imitators. It is therefore crucial that the inventor be protected against infringement. An inventor who fears that his rights will not be protected will keep his invention secret and will exploit it himself, i.e. he will internalize the market for his know-how. On the other hand, when patent rights are well protected, the knowledge holder will be able to sell or rent (license) the rights to his know-how to domestic and foreign manufacturers. The degree to which patents provide protection depends on technological factors (such as the extent to which knowledge can be clearly defined and described on paper and the possibility of designing around the patent), and on government policies, such as the length of the patent grant and the level of penalties for infringement. Licensing will be more prevalent whenever patent rights are easy to establish and to defend, while horizontal investments will be chosen to transfer knowledge which is difficult to codify into patents and easy to copy (Caves *et al.*, 1982; Hennart, 1982). Since governments vary in the extent to which they provide patent protection, the efficiency of transferring knowledge through licensing will also depend on the country being entered.

A considerable amount of evidence reveals systematic differences across countries and industries in the choice made between licensing and horizontal investment. Table 4.1, for example, gives the percentage of licensed production relative to total UK foreign production (the sum of sales by foreign licensees of UK firms and sales of foreign subsidiaries of UK concerns), an index of the extent to which technology was transferred through contract. This ratio varies from a high of 71 per cent in the shipbuilding industry to a low of 4 per cent in the food, drink and tobacco industry. Davidson and McFetridge (1982) have shown that the choice between licensing and FDI can be explained by the relative efficiency of the market for

Table 4.1 Share of UK licensed sales in total foreign production (licensed sales + FDI sales), 1983 (%)

Sector	Share
Food, drink and tobacco	4.0
Chemicals and allied industries	25.8
Metal manufactures	12.3
Mechanical and instrument engineering	21.5
Electrical engineering	7.6
Shipbuilding	71.1
Motor vehicles	45.1
Textile, leather, clothing, footwear	5.0
Paper, painting and publishing	13.6
Rubber	34.8
Other manufacturing	21.2
All manufacturing	17.5

Source: author's calculation from Buckley and Prescott (1989).

knowledge. They studied 1,382 cases of technology transfer undertaken by thirty-two US MNEs and found that the probability of licensing an innovation was greater the older the technology, the more peripheral it was to the innovator's business, the smaller the investment in R&D necessary to develop it, and the greater the innovator's experience in international licensing.

Goodwill

Horizontal investments also arise from the internalization of another intangible, reputation (goodwill). Trademarks are to reputation what patents are to knowledge: they are the legal instrument establishing property rights in reputation. The ability of a firm to exploit its reputation depends on the extent to which trademarks are protected from unauthorized imitation (counterfeiting). A firm can either capitalize on its reputation by itself producing goods and services bearing its trademark, or it can rent the use of its trademark to others through franchising. The efficiency of franchising depends on the extent to which trademarks are protected from counterfeiting, since no one will rent what can be acquired free. Franchising is also subject to free-riding. If consumers are mobile, the trademark becomes a public good to all those who are using it, in the sense that the quality of goods and services supplied by anyone using the trademark will affect all those who share in the trademark.[7] A trademark user can maximize his income by reducing the quality of the good he produces and sells under the trademark. If detection of such behaviour is costly, a cheater will be able to capture much of the savings from reduced quality, while the losses in franchise sales that will result from his behaviour will be shared by all those who use the trademark. Consequently, franchisers write contracts that carefully stipulate minimum quality standards and spend significant resources enforcing them.

Another way of reducing a franchiser's incentive to free-ride is to transform him into an employee. As an employee the trademark user is paid a straight salary, unrelated to the outlet's profits, and gains nothing from reducing quality. But breaking the link between output and reward also has an unfortunate, if unavoidable, side effect: the trademark user, now an employee, has little motivation to exert any effort which cannot be specified and measured by his employer. Hence the choice between franchising independent owners and establishing company-owned outlets will depend on the comparison of two types of cost: that of monitoring the work effort of employees *v.* that of specifying and enforcing a minimum level of quality by contract. These considerations explain why franchising is commonly used for the international exchange of goodwill in fast food, the hotel industry and car hire. In these activities drawing up and enforcing contractual quality standards is relatively easy, whereas the dispersion of outlets raises the cost of monitoring employees. The reverse seems to be true in banking, insurance, advertising and management consultancy. In these activities minimum quality levels are difficult to stipulate by contract in a manner that is enforceable in court, while the relatively small number of outlets necessary to reach customers reduces the level of monitoring costs (Hennart, 1982: 89–93).

The relative levels of market transaction costs and internal organization costs may also vary within a given industry. In the fast food industry, high-volume outlets in concentrated locations, which are easy to monitor, tend to be operated by the trademark owner, while small, dispersed outlets are franchised (Hennart, 1982; Brickly and Dark, 1987). A similar pattern has been uncovered by Dunning and McQueen (1981) in the international hotel industry. Worldwide, more than half the rooms in hotels operated by multinational corporations are run under franchise or management contracts, but the proportion is much greater (82 per cent) in developing countries, where political risk and cultural distance raise the cost of managing hotels over that of franchising them to local operators.

Vertical investments

Backward integration

One early and persistent type of FDI has been that undertaken by firms based in developed countries to obtain minerals and agricultural products necessary for their downstream activities. The investments of integrated oil companies into the extraction of crude oil, those of steel firms in iron ore, and those of rubber manufacturers into natural rubber plantations are but a few examples (Wilkins, 1970, 1974). Transaction cost theory suggests that such 'backward integration' will be chosen whenever markets for raw materials and intermediate inputs are characterized by high transaction costs. These costs arise when (1) the number of parties to the exchange is small (small-number conditions) or (2) when parties differ in the amount of information they have on the transaction (information asymmetry).

Small-number conditions. Small-number conditions result from economies of scale, from high transport costs, and from the presence of physical asset specificity. Asset specificity arises when one or both parties to the transaction invest in equipment specially designed to carry out the transaction, and which has lower value in other uses (Williamson, 1985). When these conditions are present, spot markets are likely to fail, because a party making transaction-specific investments, and for whom the costs of switching partners are consequently high, will fear that the more flexible party will opportunistically renegotiate the terms of trade. One possible way for parties to protect themselves is to write a contract fixing the terms and conditions of the trade over a period of time corresponding to the life of the plant. However this approach generally fails when the environment is uncertain, for reasons developed below (pp. 101–2). Vertical integration will then be desirable, because it transforms one of the parties into an employee of the other. As an employee the erstwhile trader is no longer rewarded for his opportunism but instead for obeying the directives of his boss. Vertical integration makes it possible to reduce opportunism by aligning the incentives of both parties (Williamson, 1979).

This theoretical framework provides a convincing explanation of the pattern of vertical integration found in many domestic industries, for example that between coal mines and electric power plants (Joskow, 1985), between automobile assemblers and parts manufacturers (Monteverde and Teece, 1982; Walker and Weber, 1984), between aerospace firms and their component suppliers (Masten, 1984), and between wood processing and timber growing (Globerman and Schwindt, 1986). The same logic can be applied to foreign backward investments, since they are vertical investments that cross borders.

The aluminium industry provides an interesting example. There are three stages in the production of aluminium: bauxite is mined, then shipped to alumina plants, where it is refined into alumina, and alumina is then smelted into aluminium in smelters. About 90 per cent of the total volume of bauxite shipments in the free world consists of intra-firm transfers. The reason is that most buyers of bauxite find themselves facing a small number of potential sellers, and vice versa, a result of high economies of scale and barriers to entry at both the mining and the refining stages, and of high asset specificity in bauxite refining. The high degree of asset specificity derives from cost savings that can be obtained when refineries are built to process a single type of bauxite. Since bauxites are heterogeneous, each refinery must obtain its bauxite from one or a small number of mines, and switching costs are high. To organize such a bilateral relationship through spot markets would be hazardous, because, after investments have been made, the owner of the mine could exploit the owner of the alumina plant (or vice versa) by unilaterally changing the price of bauxite. Using contracts also entails serious risks, for reasons that are discussed at pp. 101–2. Vertical integration is thus the preferred solution (Stuckey, 1983).

By contrast, in the case of alluvial tin, co-ordination between stages is efficiently performed by spot markets. There is no asset specificity in the smelting of alluvial tin ores, since these ores are very homogenous (they are nearly pure tin). Tin ores are also of high value, so their transport costs are low relative to their value, and they can be transported long distances. The result is an efficient market for tin ores, eliminating the need for vertical integration between mining and smelting.[8] Tin ores obtained from lode mining, however, tend to carry various impurities, and the smelters handling these ores must be specifically designed to treat those impurities. Consequently, the lode sector of the tin industry is characterized by greater vertical integration (Hennart, 1986a, 1988a).

The considerations outlined above explain the need of MNEs to own suppliers of other intermediate inputs, such as parts or sub-assemblies. In most cases MNEs will own their foreign suppliers when the components they manufacture are specific to the purchaser, while independent suppliers will be used for standard parts, which are sold in a relatively broad market.[9]

Information asymmetry. Another reason for vertical backward investments is quality control. Quality control problems arise in situations of information asymmetry. If a buyer cannot distinguish *ex ante* between good and bad quality, he will tend to reduce his offer price to reflect this risk. A seller of high-quality products may not be able to persuade a buyer that the goods he offers are of high quality, and will therefore avoid the market. Markets will fail in the sense that they will be used to sell goods of increasingly lower quality (Akerlof, 1970). Hence sellers and buyers have incentives to integrate.

The banana industry offers an interesting example of this motive for vertical integration. Bananas are certainly an unsophisticated product, so it is surprising that vertically integrated MNEs dominate their international trade.[10] But bananas are highly perishable, as they spoil twenty-one days after cutting. Their quality also depends on careful handling and proper ripening conditions. Careless handling and ripening are difficult to detect *ex ante*: damage incurred at the cutting and shipping stages will be revealed only when the banana reaches the supermarket. Hence it is difficult to achieve consistent high quality if grower, shipper and distributor are separate concerns (Read, 1986; Litvak and Maule, 1977). Consistent quality is better assured by vertical integration because it reduces the incentive to cheat at each stage (Casson, 1982).

Forward integration

Forward vertical integration by domestic firms into foreign distribution is probably the most common form of FDI. This form of investment can be explained by the same general factors that lead to backward investments, i.e. the reluctance of parties to the exchange to make transaction-specific investments under market conditions and the problems of quality control (Chandler, 1977; Williamson, 1981; Hennart, 1982; Nicholas, 1983).

Small-number conditions. To distribute a product efficiently requires investments both in physical assets (warehouses, stocks, transport networks, repair facilities, offices or shops, and in knowledge. The distributor must learn how to demonstrate and service the product, how to price it, and how to adapt it to local tastes and conditions of use. These investments vary in size and especially in their specificity. In some cases, they are 'general purpose' and can be used to sell products from a number of manufacturers; in others, they are specific to a single supplier and have little or no value in other uses.

As in the case of backward vertical integration, there are two main, often reinforcing reasons why the market for distribution services is often narrow. First, distribution is often subject to high economies of scale or scope. Vertical integration then solves the resulting bargaining stalemates. Second, effective distribution sometimes requires substantial manufacturer-specific investments. These investments can be physical or intellectual, but they are specific to a particular manufacturer, and have limited or no value in the distribution of products of other manufacturers. One example is the time the distributor spends learning how to demonstrate and repair a new product, and to adapt it to special needs. A distributor may be reluctant to make such investments, fearing that, after they are made, the manufacturer will opportunistically renegotiate the margins by threatening to sign a new contract with another distributor. This fear may cause the distributor to commit fewer resources to distribution than would be optimal (Nicholas, 1983).

A manufacturer can persuade a distributor to make manufacturer-specific investments by offering exclusive distribution rights. Here again, the more uncertain the environment, and the longer the period of time needed for the distributor to recover his transaction-specific investments, the greater the chance that such a long-term contract will break down. In these cases, vertical integration may be the most efficient option. Integration into distribution will thus be observed in the distribution of products requiring specialized facilities or specific demonstration and repair.

Quality control. Another problem inherent in subcontracting distribution is that of quality control. The problem is similar to that experienced in franchising and arises when the distributor can affect the quality of the goods and services as perceived by the consumer. In this case, manufacturers will integrate into distribution if they cannot easily define and enforce contractual rules to prevent the distributor from debasing quality but can cheaply and effectively monitor the behaviour of employees (Caves and Murphy, 1976; Hennart, 1982).

The observed pattern of vertical integration into distribution reflects a trade-off between the need to have distributors make the requisite level of investment and keep quality at an agreed level on one hand, and the cost of operating company-owned distribution facilities on the other. That cost rises if there are scope economies in distribution and if it is difficult to monitor the behaviour of employees. Here, again, there is a striking parallel between domestic and international integration. Williamson (1981) has shown how the extent of domestic forward integration by US manufacturers varied at the turn of the century from none in the case of hardware, jewellery, liquor and dry goods, to full integration into both wholesaling and retailing in the case of new, complex, high-priced machines requiring specialized demonstration and repair. Vertical forward integration by MNEs abroad had then a similar pattern: no integration for dry goods, integration into wholesaling for products that required specialized handling, and integration into retailing in the case of new, sophisticated products which required demonstration, installation and after-sales service (Chandler, 1959, 1977; Wilkins, 1970; Hennart, 1982; Nicholas, 1983). In short, the observed pattern of vertical forward integration abroad, as well as that of backward vertical integration, is consistent with the view that MNEs expand abroad to bring activities in-house which are subject to high market transaction costs.

Free-standing firms

Up to now this survey has discussed the familiar forms of FDI we observe today. Many pre-1914 European investments were, however, of a very different type. In contrast to today's MNEs, which venture abroad from a domestic base, many pre-1914 foreign investments were 'free-standing'

(Wilkins, 1988). 'Free-standing' firms maintained a head office in the major capital-exporting countries of the time (principally the United Kingdom and the Netherlands but also France, Belgium and Germany), but all their productive assets were located overseas. The widespread use of this form of investment is seen in a partial list of pre-1914 British free-standing companies operating outside the UK, the US and Canada which contains more than 2,500 entries (US Federal Trade Commission, 1916). To this figure must be added the very large number of British free-standing firms in the United States and Canada, as well as a substantial number of free-standing companies registered in Paris and Brussels and operating worldwide.[11]

As noted at the beginning of this chapter, Fieldhouse argues that the existence of this type of FDI cannot be explained by internalization theory because the development of these free-standing firms did not 'flow from the growth patterns of metropolitan firms'. For Fieldhouse, today's MNEs exploit abroad advantages which they have acquired in their domestic market. In the case of free-standing firms there was no 'firm' competence to draw on: the home office was usually made up of a part-time corporate secretary and a board of part-time directors. In short, the head office of such companies was 'little more than a brass nameplate somewhere in the City' (Nicholas, 1982: 606). Wilkins (1989) sees in this lack of home-office capabilities the reason for the widespread failure of British free-standing companies in the United States. Free-standing firms had no firm-specific advantages acquired in the domestic market which they could exploit abroad.

Transaction cost economics suggests some reasons for the existence of free-standing firms, for their industrial distribution, and for their uneven rate of survival. As explained above, FDI should be seen not only as the process by which firms exploit firm-specific advantages abroad, but more generally as a way to reduce the costs of organizing transnational interdependencies through markets. The general approach followed earlier to explain vertical and horizontal FDI also applies here: free-standing firms arose to bypass international capital markets when loan transactions would have been subject to high transaction costs.

Capital can be transferred on international markets through bank loans and corporate bonds. This mode of transfer gives the lender no right to the residual value of the venture (the value of the firm net of contractual payments to inputs), and no 'general and discretionary right' to direct the behaviour of the borrower. Lending involves making funds available to the debtor, to be paid back later with interest. The risk is that the debtor might be unable to meet his obligations, either because he has deliberately spent the funds for other purposes with no intention of repaying, or because he has been unsuccessful in his investments. To protect himself against this eventuality the lender can screen borrowers carefully, and lend only to those with a good reputation and track record. The lender can also ask the borrower to give him title to some collateral whose value to the borrower exceeds the value of the loan. Sometimes the assets created with the borrowed funds have good collateral value and can serve to secure the loan, as when an airline invests in aeroplanes. Investments in mining, agriculture or R&D projects yield little collateral, because capital sunk into unsuccessful mines or R&D does not yield salable assets.

Entrepreneurs who cannot show a good track record, who have no contacts, or who cannot provide collateral by contributing their own funds to the venture, are unlikely to obtain finance. One solution in that case may be to internalize the market for loanable funds, i.e. to have the lenders become full or part owners of the borrower's business (or vice versa). Internalization may reduce transaction costs in the market for capital for three main reasons. Equity links give the lenders much greater control over the use of their funds, as equity owners have the right to review decisions *ex ante* and they have easier access to internal documents.[12] By contrast, a lender is strictly limited in the quantity, quality and timeliness of the information he can obtain on his client. Equity control is also more flexible than debt contracts, because it allows greater discretion to preserve the value of a going concern when problems occur (Williamson, 1988). Lastly, borrowers on markets have an incentive, if they have no personal funds at stake, to misrepresent projects and to take excessive risks, since they stand to capture all the profits net of interest payments and repayment of principal, while lenders are likely to shoulder all the risks (Jensen and Meckling, 1976). Transforming borrowers into employees whose reward is independent of the projects undertaken reduces this incentive.

As in the case of horizontal investments, described above, two conditions must be met for free-standing firms to arise. First, there must be a gain from transferring capital from the home base of the free-standing firm to the foreign country where investment takes place. Second, capital must be more efficiently transferred through equity links than through international capital markets. This implies that free-standing firms should have undertaken projects which would have been more costly to finance through international bank loans or the international bond market. These would have been investments that had little collateral value, and for which little information was available to lenders, because they were undertaken in foreign countries and by individuals little known to the domestic public. Through free-standing firms, lenders could monitor the use of their funds and exercise managerial control over the venture, a degree of control presumably much greater than that enjoyed by holders of foreign bonds.[13]

The argument that the choice between debt and equity is determined by the characteristics of the project to be financed is still controversial, and its extension to international capital transfers speculative.[14] Nevertheless, a number of features of free-standing firms suggest that the argument has some plausibility. Free-standing companies were created in capital-rich countries to bring additional funds to enterprises located in capital-poor countries which could not obtain local financing. This was clearly the pattern in Malaysia, where the Western banks, following the British tradition, provided only short-term credit (Drake, 1980; Mackenzie, 1954). Rubber plantations and tin-mining and smelting firms found that local sources of capital were insufficient to finance their expansion, and they found it advantageous to access the London capital market. They were then taken over or reorganized as British-based free-standing companies (Drabble, 1973; Hennart, 1987; Van Helten and Jones, 1989). The evidence also shows that free-standing firms were particularly active in sectors such as mining and plantations, where debt financing is usually difficult to obtain in the early stages.[15] Free-standing firms seem also to have survived longer in countries with underdeveloped capital markets. By the 1920s they had disappeared in the United States, whereas they survived in Malaysia and in Nigeria until the 1960s (Wilkins, 1988; Hennart, 1986b, 1987).

Table 4.2 The transaction cost theory of the multinational enterprise

Type of MNE	Market internalized
Horizontal integration by R&D-intensive firms	Technological and managerial know-how
Horizontal integration by advertising-intensive firms	Reputation; managerial skills in quality control and marketing
Vertical integration into distribution	Distribution and marketing services
Vertical integration into raw materials and components	Raw materials and components
Free-standing firms	Capital

The aim thus far has been to show that, contrary to what is sometimes asserted, transaction cost theory can account for all the major types of MNEs. As shown in Table 4.2, different types of MNE result from the internalization of various types of markets (naturally, in many cases the MNE will be simultaneously internalizing a number of markets). Hence transaction cost theory is a powerful tool for revealing the fundamental features of MNEs which are hidden behind the wide diversity of their forms.

Transaction cost theory and structural market imperfections

Although the analysis to this point has focused on MNEs as internalizers of *non-pecuniary* externalities, transaction cost theory is also useful in explaining when and how MNEs internalize *pecuniary* externalities. Recall that pecuniary externalities are those that competitors impose on each other through the impact of their actions on the prices they face. One particular instance is competition. Consider an homogenous good produced by single-plant monopolists located in a number of different countries. Competition between these producers will reduce their income. Competitors can, however, maximize their joint income if they agree to segment the markets and to concentrate production in the lowest-cost plant. For Hymer, the MNE is the vehicle through which such collusion is organized.

For transaction cost theorists, this argument provides only a partial explanation for the existence of MNEs. MNEs also arise to internalize non-pecuniary externalities. Moreover, Hymer's argument is incomplete. FDI is not the only method available of reaching collusion. Competitors can also co-ordinate their behaviour through contract by taking part in a cartel (Casson, 1985). Hence the desire for collusion does not necessarily lead to MNEs. The transaction cost approach is useful in analysing the circumstances under which this will be the case. The main problem with a cartel is that of free-riding: all members would like to sell more in the high-price market, but by doing so they lower prices. Consolidating all firms into an MNE eliminates the incentive to cheat but raises management costs and may be opposed by host governments. This suggests that, absent legal restrictions on cartels, the propensity to internalize pecuniary externalities by cartel rather than by internalization will be greater the easier it is to detect cheating and the lower the need to adapt to changing conditions. Hence cartels should be more prevalent in industries producing homogenous products and characterized by slow growth and static technology (Casson, 1985).

Pecuniary externalities are also generated in the licensing process. Consider a patent owner licensing one producer in each country. Because of differences in the elasticity of demand, the optimal price for the product is likely to vary across markets. Maximization of rents (and hence of royalties received by the licensor) requires that licensees be prevented from invading each other's markets. In some cases, high transport costs, tariffs or government regulations segment markets. When barriers to trade are low, the licensor must explicitly forbid licensees from exporting products to other markets. In practice, such territorial restrictions are often illegal. A firm which integrates into foreign manufacture is, however, better able to prevent competition between plants producing the licensed product because it needs no explicit contract to eliminate competition between its sub-units (Casson, 1979). Hence transaction cost theory explains when the internalization of pecuniary externalities will be achieved by the establishment of an MNE rather than by contractual means.

TRANSACTION COSTS AS A GENERAL THEORY OF INSTITUTIONAL FORMS

Although the dichotomy between markets and hierarchies has useful heuristic properties, it fails to account for the large number of hybrid institutional forms used in international business. It is in this area that transaction cost theory has perhaps made the most progress in the last decade.

Equity joint ventures

One hybrid or 'intermediate' form that is gaining increasing attention is the equity joint venture. Transaction cost theory can explain the circumstances under which this institutional form will be chosen in preference to its alternatives, contracts or mergers and acquisitions. Equity joint ventures, like contracts, are arrangements undertaken to combine the services of assets held by two or more parties. Joint ventures differ from contracts in that in the case of contracts a single party takes full title to the residual value of the firm, while in joint ventures the parties providing inputs are paid for some or all of their contribution out of the profits earned by the venture. Hence a party supplying inputs by contract who delivers inferior inputs gets to keep the full amount earned in this way, while a joint venture partner who does the same will shoulder part of the cost of his dishonesty, since he is paid for his deliveries from the profits of the venture. Supplying the venture with inferior inputs lowers the profits of the venture and imposes a loss on the joint venturers which is proportional to their equity stake. Joint ventures are therefore more efficient than contracts when the market for the inputs to be combined is subject to high transaction costs, because joint ventures align the interests of the interacting parties better. Note that the markets for the intermediate inputs supplied by *both* parties must both be subject to high transaction costs, for otherwise the party with the more marketable input could gain by transferring this input by contract to the party with the less marketable input. Fig 4.3 (Hennart, 1988b) illustrates this point. Assume that the production of a particular good or service requires the combination of two types of knowledge, *a* and *b*, held by firms A and B, respectively. If *a* can be easily licensed, but not *b*, *a* and *b* will be combined by B, with A licensing *a* to B. If the reverse is true, B will license *b* to A. For a joint venture to be the chosen method of combining *a* and *b*, the market exchange of both *a* and *b* must be subject to high transaction costs.

Firm A

	Marketable know-how	Non-marketable know-how
Firm B Marketable know-how	Indeterminate	B licenses A
Non-marketable know-how	A licenses B	A joint venture with B

Figure 4.3

The presence of two failing markets is not sufficient for joint ventures to emerge. Inputs which are difficult to exchange on the market could be combined if either firm bought out the other, or if they merged. A further condition for the existence of joint ventures must therefore be that mergers and acquisitions of the firms owning the complementary assets are more costly than pooling the services of the assets in a joint venture. Besides the obvious case when governments restrict mergers and acquisitions, joint ventures will be preferred when the assets that yield the desired services are a small and inseparable part of the total assets held by both potential partners or when a merger or a total acquisition would significantly increase management costs (Hennart, 1988b; Buckley and Casson, 1987).[16]

Even though joint ventures constitute an efficient way to combine poorly marketable inputs held by two or more firms, they also have offsetting costs. The incentive that suppliers of inputs have to cheat is not totally eliminated, since each joint venture partner can claim only a fraction of the residual value of the business. Each partner may therefore still find it advantageous to maximize his gain at the expense of the venture by, for example, supplying fewer inputs than was contractually agreed when the venture was formed. This contrasts with full equity control, where the parent, having full rights to the residual value of the venture, is incited to maximize it. As a result, the efficiency of a joint venture hinges on the convergence of the goals of the parties to the agreement, or, failing this, on the degree to which opportunism by the partners can be controlled by contractual means. Whenever partners have conflicting goals which cannot be reconciled by contract, their actions will lower the profits available for sharing, and the joint venture mode of organization will prove to be very costly for one or both parties.

This transaction cost model of the joint venture is consistent with the findings of the pioneering studies of Franko (1971) and Stopford and Wells (1972). These authors examined the choice made by US MNEs between wholly owned subsidiaries and joint ventures and concluded that MNEs resisted entering into joint ventures in two situations: first, when they already held or could acquire on the market or through contract the assets necessary to operate abroad; and, second, when the market for the assets they were contributing to the venture was characterized by high transaction costs. Hence parent companies supplying their affiliates (or buying from them) intermediate products which had no market price were likely to insist on full ownership. Similarly, parents which exploited types of knowledge and goodwill which were difficult to protect through contracts were less likely to joint-venture. On the other hand, parents tended to choose joint ventures when they needed complementary resources they could not easily acquire on the market. The need to joint-venture was particularly strong when the foreign affiliate represented a diversification move for the parent, and hence the parent needed industry-specific knowledge or distribution facilities; when the MNE had little knowledge of the market entered, and hence needed country-specific knowledge; or when the MNE needed resources controlled by local firms. Similar findings are reported by Stopford and Haberich (1978) in the case of British MNEs, and by Yoshino (1976), Yoshihara (1984) and Tsurumi (1976) in the case of Japanese MNEs.

Three recent econometric studies support this analysis of the rationale for joint ventures. Gatignon and Anderson (1988) found that the probability of US parents fully owning their overseas subsidiaries varied positively with the ratios of R&D to sales and of advertising to sales of the industries of the parents, and with the firm's international experience (as proxied by the number of previous foreign investments). Joint ventures were more likely in countries with cultures radically different from the US, controlling for legal restrictions on incoming investment and political risk. A study by Gomes-Casseres (1989), using the same database of pre-1975 affiliates of US MNEs, also showed that advertising intensity, international experience, a high percentage of intra-system sales within the MNE, and familiarity with the host country tended to lead to full ownership. Affiliates which were in an industry different from the parent's and which operated in resource-intensive industries were more likely to be joint ventures. Research and development intensity was insignificant, but an interaction term between diversification and research and development intensity had a significantly negative coefficient, indicating that when the subsidiary was outside the parent's core business R&D intensity encouraged joint ventures, whereas, when the subsidiary was active in the parent's main product line, R&D

intensity led to full ownership of subsidiaries.[17] Hennart (1990a) looked at the choice made by Japanese MNEs between partial and full ownership of their US subsidiaries. As in the case of US MNEs, Japanese investors were more likely to enter joint ventures when they had little experience of the US market or when their US subsidiary was either in a different industry from that of the parent or in a natural resource industry, indicating the need for country and industry-specific knowledge and for access to natural resources. Unlike the other two studies, the research and development and advertising intensities of the Japanese parents had, however, no inpact on the choice between full and partial ownership of their subsidiaries.[18] Although research continues in this area, taken together, these studies provide broad support for a transaction cost view of joint ventures.

Contracts

Another common hybrid form is the contract. As mentioned on pp. 90–1, contracts are efficient modes of organization under small-number conditions when the environment is relatively predictable. Contracts reduce enforcement costs by specifying *ex ante* the terms and conditions of the trade and the compensation to be paid in the case of breach, relying on third parties (the courts or private arbitrators) to determine whether a violation has taken place, to decide on the compensation to be paid in each case, and to enforce payment of such compensation. Through contracts parties are protected against opportunistic behaviour over a stated period. Contracts suffer, however, from a number of limitations. They are more costly than spot markets, for, while a large number of traders typically share the costs of running spot markets, the cost of writing contracts must be paid by the contracting parties themselves. The additional cost of writing a contract can be justified only if a trade is long-lived. Furthermore, contracts are more risky than vertical integration because they rely on enforcement by third parties. The aggrieved party has limited control over the amount and form of the compensation he will receive for breach. Breach must be proved to third parties. But while fraudulent behaviour is clear to those involved, it is difficult to prove in court, limiting the effectiveness of contract protection.

The most severe drawback of contracts is that they often fail under conditions of high uncertainty. As the degree of uncertainty increases, specifying *ex ante* all possible contingencies and the contractual changes to be made in each case becomes an increasingly difficult task. Yet leaving contracts incomplete makes it possible for parties to exploit each other. Hence contracts can be expected for recurrent trades in small-number conditions when the environment is relatively predictable.

Stuckey's (1983) description of contractual failures in the bauxite market illustrates the contractual problems that arise when the environment changes in unpredictable ways. Because bauxite mining and refining both require significant investments of long economic life,[19] contracts cover very long periods – typically twenty to twenty-five years. Over such a long time span contracts cannot effectively protect the parties against changes in the environment which affect their profit stream. The long-term contracts signed in the 1960s by Japanese bauxite purchasers specified prices which were denominated in dollars, with adjustments based on the quality of the bauxite actually shipped. Shortly after they were signed, economic conditions changed dramatically. The end of the Bretton Woods system of fixed exchange rates radically altered the profitability of the contracts by changing the local currency equivalent of the dollar prices, while the two oil shocks made the Japanese aluminium industry, which relied for its electricity on oil-fired power plants, increasingly uncompetitive. This led to acrimonious bargaining, and to a shift from contracts to vertical integration. Similar problems arose in the iron ore industry following the slump in demand in the 1970s (Franz *et al.*, 1986).

New forms of investment and counter-trade

The transaction cost analysis of contracts also throws light on two other issues which are yet poorly understood: the 'new forms' of investment, and counter-trade. The term 'counter-trade' describes a variety of trade practices developed in the 1960s by Soviet-bloc countries to trade with Western firms and which have spread to developing countries. They currently represent about 15 per cent of world trade. Counter-trade has been generally described as a form of barter. As such, its increasing popularity among developing countries has been seen as a puzzling return to archaic practices (de Miramon, 1985). However, a careful look at the structure of three common forms of counter-trade contracts (counter-purchase, buy-backs and offsets) shows that they do not include barter clauses (i.e. the swapping of goods for other goods) but that they consist instead of two separate money-for-goods contracts, with imports made conditional on the exporter purchasing goods and services from the importer. Hence the essence of most counter-trade contracts is not barter but reciprocity (Hennart, 1989b). Reciprocity has been shown by Williamson (1985) to improve the enforceability of contracts by equalizing the exposure of the parties to the risk of breach. This puts counter-trade in a new perspective: the majority of counter-trade obligations are not imposed to save foreign exchange, but rather to increase the enforceability of contracts. The need to impose counter-trade will be strongest in countries which have banned or severely restricted both inward and outward FDI (Murrell, 1982; Kogut, 1986; Mirus and Yeung, 1986; Hennart, 1989b). The limited amount of empirical evidence available on counter-trade is consistent with the view that some forms of counter-trade are a substitute for FDI (Murrell,1982; Casson and Chukujama, 1989; Hennart, 1989b, 1990b).

Transaction cost theorists see counter-trade as an attempt to increase the enforceability of contracts in situations where the most desirable alternative, FDI, is not a viable option. The theory predicts that these reciprocal contractual forms will perform better than simple contracts, but that they can never be perfect substitutes for FDI. Through FDI suppliers of inputs get paid for their contribution from the profits of the venture. If they under-supply inputs, they will make offsetting losses. Their incentives for opportunism are therefore proportional to their share of equity. When opportunities for opportunism are large because markets for inputs are subject to high information costs and/or to small-number conditions, obtaining inputs through FDI is efficient because it reduces transaction costs.

This analysis helps clarify the debate on the 'new forms of investment'. The term describes the wide range of contractual substitutes for FDI (such as licensing, franchising, turnkey contracts, production sharing and management contracts) used by developing countries to obtain the inputs held by MNEs (such as technology, management skills and access to foreign markets) while avoiding the political costs of FDI (Oman, 1984; Dunning and Cantwell, 1984; Buckley, 1985). Rather than obtaining the inputs as a bundle and giving the residual value of the venture to the foreign investor (the FDI solution), the 'new forms' solution consists in leaving the residual in local hands, and in purchasing the needed inputs from foreigners by contract. Some scholars see the trend towards these new forms as inevitable, and applaud them as providing a solution to the conflicts between MNEs and host countries. Their discussions have overlooked the fact that one of the attributes of equity control is to align incentives between seller and buyer of inputs, and that this property cannot be fully emulated by contractual arrangements, no matter how sophisticated. Hence there are cases where the mandated replacement of FDI by contracts is likely to reduce eficiency in the transfer of MNE capabilities to host countries (Hennart, 1989a).

To better understand why, consider Fig. 4.4. Efficient production overseas requires the combination of inputs held by A, a host-country firm, and B, a foreign firm. Some of the intermediate inputs supplied by host-country firm A are sold in relatively efficient markets (for example, commodity chemicals) while others (such as the tacit knowledge of local conditions) face relatively inefficient markets. The same is true for home-country firm B. Some of its know-how is easy to license, while some other types are poorly protected, and therefore non-marketable. When the know-how

Host-country factors
held by A

	Marketable	Non-marketable
Marketable know-how	Indeterminate (1)	B licenses A (2)
Non-marketable know-how	B invests in host country (3)	A joint ventures with B in host country (4)

Home-country factors held by B

Figure 4.4

held by B is easy to license, but the input contributed by A is difficult to measure, the arrangement that minimizes transaction costs consists in A taking a licence from B, and holding title to the residual (cell 2). This is because A is both more incited and better able to cheat in the transfer of its input to B than B is in the licensing of its know-how to A. Giving a right to the residual to the party most likely to cheat reduces total transaction costs. (For a more general treatment see Grossman and Hart, 1986; Yeung and Mirus, 1989). The 'new forms' are in this case an efficient way of obtaining foreign inputs. If, on the other hand, the inputs held by B are difficult to transact on markets, but A's inputs are sold on efficient markets, then efficiency demands that B should keep full title to the profits, that it should become a direct investor, buying A's input on the market (cell 3). Imposing the use of 'new forms' is inefficient in this case, for it increases the level of total transaction costs incurred in combining inputs.

THE BENEFITS AND COSTS OF HIERARCHY

The transaction cost theory of the MNE is very young, since its birth can be dated to the publication of McManus's (1972) pioneering essay. Therefore it is not surprising that a considerable amount of both theoretical and empirical work remains to be done.

More attention needs to be paid to organization costs within firms (Kay, 1983; see also chapter 6). High transaction costs in international markets are not a sufficient condition for the existence of MNEs, since there will be cases where firms, in their attempts to internalize market failures, will incur higher organization costs than markets. Even if organization costs within firms fell below those in markets, they could still be high enough as to absorb all the gains from exchange and co-ordination, and no economic interaction would then take place, either within firms or in markets. To be complete, a transaction cost theory of economic organization should therefore consider *simultaneously* the costs of conducting market exchange (market transactions costs) and those of effecting exchange within the firm (internal organization costs), and show how firms can reduce organization costs. In other words, alongside a theory of why markets fail we need a theory of why firms succeed.

Some scholars have argued that firms are superior to markets because they replace failing external markets with internal ones. Although some firms do use prices for some types of internal co-ordination, this concept of 'internal markets' fails to capture the fundamental reason why firms displace markets. Most employees are guided and rewarded not by market prices but by directives voiced by their superiors, formalized through company rules, or internalized through indoctrination. Even in the relationship between head office and foreign subsidiaries, interdependencies and measurement problems limit the use of internal prices as a control mechanism (Shapiro, 1984: 19; Robbins and Stobaugh, 1973: 511). If firms can be more efficient than markets when the latter fail, it must be not because they replicate what markets do, but rather because they use a method of organization which is radically different from that used in markets (Hennart, 1982, 1986c).

As argued earlier, firms can succeed when markets fail because they use a system of organization, hierarchy, with a very different incentive structure: in a hierarchy parties to the exchange are no longer rewarded by their ability to change the market terms of trade in their favour but, instead, are paid for carrying out the directives of a central party, the boss. What makes firms, in some circumstances, more efficient than markets is the fact that they eliminate market transaction costs by breaking the connection between output and performance. This has, however, one unavoidable consequence: it tends to reduce an individual's incentive to exert initiative and effort. The agent's tendency to slack in his effort, to shirk, was tightly constrained in a price system. Now that reward is no longer proportional to output, employee behaviour will have to be monitored. The firm will have to replace price constraints by behaviour constraints. Employees will also have less incentive to collect information carefully, since they do not directly benefit from it, but instead pass it on to the boss. The costs of hierarchical organization, which we can call 'internal organization costs', are those of preventing employees from shirking, and those of inciting employees to collect information and transmit it faithfully to their superiors.

Firms will therefore replace markets when the costs of controlling shirking and of insuring effective information collection and transfer will be lower than those of measuring goods and services and curbing cheating. The firm does not avoid the market when it internalizes: it merely shifts the transaction from the market for goods and services to that for labour. Internalization will take place when transaction costs in the product market are higher than those experienced in the labour market.

The higher the costs of monitoring performance the greater the costs of hierarchy. Because the level of shirking and information loss may, in some activities, grow more than proportionately with the relaxation of price constraints and their replacement by behaviour constraints, the firm may selectively reintroduce price constraints for some activities. Firms will pay employees through piecework, and they will set up some activities as profit centres and reward their managers for maximizing the profits of the sub-units. Hence what distinguishes the firm from the market is the mix of constraints used: firms are institutions which use primarily behaviour constraints, while markets use mostly price constraints.[20] Nevertheless, it is because firms use hierarchy, i.e. because they replace price by behaviour constraints, that they can experience, in certain transactions, lower organization costs than markets.

The preceding analysis offers some interesting implications for research. Keeping market transaction costs constant, whether a particular transaction will be internalized by the firm or not will depend on the costs incurred by firms in monitoring employees. These costs are likely to vary across activities, across time periods, across countries and across firms.

Monitoring is easy on machine-paced processes, where an employee's behaviour provides a good clue to his performance. Monitoring employees will be costly, on the other hand, for tasks which are not programmable but require judgement and on-the-the spot decisions, and for which employees need to be dispersed over space. As noted above, this explains why some activities are franchised while others are operated with employees, and why trademark owners usually operate easily accessible units themselves but franchise dispersed ones. The same considerations should explain which services can be exploited abroad through FDI, and the extent of vertical integration into distribution. Much more research is needed in this area.

Changes through time in the cost of monitoring employees may also explain differences in the international transmission of knowledge. During the first part of the nineteenth century England had a technological advantage comparable to that enjoyed by US firms in the two decades following World War II. Yet while the US exploited its technological advantage through FDI, the mode by which British know-how was transferred in the first half of the nineteenth century was through the migration of skilled artisans, who exploited that know-how themselves by setting up production overseas. This difference in transfer modes can be explained by the fact that the costs of both market and inter-firm exchange were so high in the nineteenth century as to make internalization within the individual the only feasible alternative (Hennart, 1982: 128–30).

Monitoring employees is also likely to be more costly the greater the cultural differences between the MNE home and host countries.[21] Everything else constant, the greater the cultural gap, the less likely it is that the firm will internalize the transaction. Davidson and McFetridge (1985) found, for example, that the probability that US firms would internalize knowledge (as opposed to licensing it) increased if the target country was geographically and culturally close to the United States. Buckley and Davies (1981) estimated the share of foreign subsidiary sales to total foreign sales of British firms (the sum of foreign subsidiary sales of British MNEs and sales by licensees of British firms). This measure of the extent to which British firms used hierarchical rather than market transfer of knowledge was higher in the former sterling area countries, which are culturally close to the UK, than in non-sterling area countries. The extent of management problems that derive from cultural differences is also likely to vary with the mode chosen to enter foreign markets. A firm that enters a foreign market through acquisition inherits the corporate culture of the acquired firm, and must mesh it with its own. By contrast, a green-field entry reduces the cost of cultural adaptation by allowing the investor to impose his corporate style from the outset. A joint venture also reduces cultural shock by making it possible to delegate the management of the venture to the local partner. These hypotheses were generally confirmed by Kogut and Singh (1988), who found that, everything else constant, foreign direct investors in the US from countries with a culture very different from that of the United States tended to use green-field joint ventures more often than full or majority acquisitions.

Firms in a given country and in a given industry may also differ in the costs they incur in monitoring employees. These differences would lead to diverging levels of internalization for given levels of market transaction costs. Whether these divergences are significant (whether there are 'firm effects' in internalization) is a fascinating area for future research.

Lastly, the model sketched above provides an answer to a puzzle in the transaction cost theory of the MNE. The theory as it stands predicts that an inefficient market will be internalized, but it does not predict by whom. Recall our example of the steel firm integrating into foreign iron ore mines. Transaction cost theory explains why these two activities ought to be integrated, but not why steel firms have integrated into iron ore mining rather than the reverse. As a step towards solving this puzzle, consider the following. Assume that production of a good requires combining the services of labour in two countries, France and Germany, and that the output of those services is mobile, but that their sale involves high transaction costs.[22] One example might be the design of a car which requires combining the output of two design teams located in two countries. Each design team is organized as a firm, firm F in France and firm G in Germany. Since we have assumed that high transaction costs prevent one team from contracting for the output of the other team, a merger of firms F and G will be necessary for the car to be designed. Whether F will take over G or G will take over F can be shown to depend on the level of the costs experienced by firms of each country in controlling shirking by employees of the other country. Hence if firm G is more skilful at monitoring employees than firm F, it will find it profitable to take over firm F, and become the employer of F's design team, or, in other words, it will become the foreign direct investor. If, on the other hand, F is relatively more adept at management than G, it will be F which will become the investor. If both firms experience similar costs in monitoring employees in foreign countries, they may decide to monitor each other by forming a joint venture. Hence the foreign direct investor will be the interacting party who has the better management skills, and therefore experiences lower costs in controlling shirking by the other party (Grossman and Hart, 1986; Yeung and Mirus, 1989).[23] This explains why the pattern of vertical integration in the banana industry has been of American shippers and wholesalers integrating into Central American plantations, and not of Central American growers integrating into US distribution. It also explains why Middle East petroleum producers have been slow at integrating into European distribution in order to recreate the vertical links betwen crude oil production and refining that had been established by Western oil companies but broken with the nationalization of their Middle East holdings.[24]

CONCLUSION

The goal of this chapter has been to show that the transaction cost approach provides a general theory of the MNE which gives a convincing explanation of the multiple forms taken by this increasingly important economic institution.[25] Transaction costs theory looks at the MNE as one of many possible ways of organizing economic activity and explains why and when this particular organizational form will be chosen in preference to its various alternatives. This broad comparative-institutional view accounts for its success in explaining hybrid organizational forms, such as contracts and joint ventures. This broad view also sheds light on the modes of organization used in firms by comparing them with those used in markets.[26]

Up to now, transaction cost researchers have mostly been concerned with factors that determine market transaction costs, and have built a theory of the MNE from differences in their level across transactions (and, at a higher level of aggregation, industries). These scholars have begun to analyse factors that lead to differences across activities in the internal organization costs experienced by MNEs. A complete theory of the MNE, which requires the simultaneous consideration of *both* types of cost, market transaction costs as well as internal organization costs, is slowly emerging, providing a rich set of insights and testable propositions that will advance theory, policy and practice.

NOTES

1   In this survey the terms 'internalization theory' and 'transaction cost theory' will be used interchangeably to describe the body of theory which sees the MNE as resulting from the internalization of externalities, mostly, but not exclusively, of a non-pecuniary kind. The difference between pecuniary and non-pecuniary externalities is discussed below.

2   Hymer's work is discussed more extensively in chapter 3.

3   Discriminatory pricing may be necessary for knowledge to be generated if there are increasing returns to scale. See Casson (1979).

4   Dunning and Rugman (1985) call these 'transaction cost market imperfections'. The term 'imperfection' is somewhat misleading in so far as it suggests comparison with an ideal neoclassical market which would experience zero transaction costs. In reality the comparison is between markets and a variety of other institutions (including firms), each experiencing positive transaction costs.

5   As Casson (1987) notes, structural and natural imperfections, though conceptually distinct, are related, because market structure affects the level of transaction costs, while transaction costs in turn affect market structure.

6   Note that the imposition of tariffs is not *per se* a sufficient reason for FDI, unless MNEs can minimize tariff payments by undervaluing intra-firm trade.

7   If consumers are not mobile, a franchiser who would reduce quality would bear the full monetary consequences of his action.

8   There are some cases of vertical integration between mines and smelters in the lode sector, but they reflect political motives. For further details see Hennart (1986a, 1988a).

9   Fiscal considerations may also be relevant here. Vertical integration transforms arm's-length trades into internal ones. This makes it possible to alter the nominal price at which transactions take place without affecting revenues. By altering nominal prices the MNE has the possibility of shifting accounting profits to low tax jurisdictions, of reducing *ad valorem* tariff duties, and of repatriating earnings disguised as expenditures. This possibility is limited by the presence of world prices for the goods shipped and by the sophistication of tax authorities.

10   In 1980 60 per cent of the banana export trade was handled by three vertically integrated MNEs (Casson, 1986: 51).

11   At the turn of the century, free-standing firms dominated the Russian petroleum

industry, the Indian jute and tea industries, the Chilean nitrate industry and the Malayan tin and rubber industries, among others.

12   In large corporations this right is exercised through the board of directors.

13   Buying shares in free-standing firms was preferable to buying shares in foreign firms for four main reasons: first, free-standing firms were registered in capital-exporting countries; second, their managers were home-country nationals, usually well known and respected; third, their shares were denominated in local, not foreign currency; fourth, they were traded on liquid markets. Note that the advantage of equity investment over bonds was that the equity holder had the potential for control. This does not mean that all owners exercised control. While large equity owners intervened directly in the management of free-standing firms, small investors usually found it more expedient to sell their shares when they disagreed with the firm's management.

14   The existence of non-voting shares would seem to contradict the argument. I am indebted to Bernard Yeung for bringing this to my attention.

15   Even today new mining ventures not sponsored by large companies cannot generally obtain bank financing until they have achieved profitable production. The most common form of financing is equity (private placement to a small group of investors or public offerings on the over-the-counter market – the so-called penny stocks) (Mikesell and Whitney, 1987).

16   This approach makes no distinction between a partial acquisition and a greenfield joint venture.

17   In addition, Gomes-Casseres found that a high level of GNP *per capita* in host countries and government restrictions on inward FDI encouraged joint ventures.

18   Note that Hennart used the parent's R&D and advertising intensity while Gomes-Casseres and Gatignon and Anderson used the R&D and advertising intensities of the industry of the parent. Hennart tried various measures of the R&D intensity of the industry of the Japanese parents, but they were all statistically insignificant.

19   An efficiently sized bauxite mine costs half a billion US dollars and a refinery between 500 million and a billion.

20   One can make the parallel assumption that the opportunities for fraud rise more than proportionally when one substitutes price for behaviour constraints. Hence the presence of behaviour constraints in market transactions (i.e. contracts).

21   This is true whether the firm operates the subsidiary through expatriates or through local personnel: the cross-cultural contact, with its potential for misunderstandings and deception (Root, 1987), must be made in all cases, whether between HQ and the subsidiary manager, between the subsidiary manager and his or her employees, or between the employees and local suppliers or customers.

22   If design services from either of the two firms can be transacted on the market at low transaction costs, licensing will be used to combine factors, and internalization will not be required. See Fig. 4.3.

23   The problem is more complex than this simplified example would suggest. Here we have assumed that the output of each design team suffers from high transaction costs, but that these costs are equal. In other words, the cost to F of ascertaining the quality of G's blueprints is the same as the cost to G of ascertaining the quality of F's blueprints. If this is not the case, who will employ whom will also depend on the relative level of transaction cost in the sale

of the intermediate inputs supplied by F and G, as previously discussed (see Fig. 4.3).

24 Alongside increasing managerial sophistication in some Arab countries (notably Kuwait), asymmetries between European countries and Middle Eastern countries in restrictions on inward FDI are also a factor.

25 The analysis presented here has been mostly static. For a critique of static theory see Buckley (1983). For dynamic versions of transaction cost theory see, for example, Buckley and Casson (1981), Nicholas (1983), Hill and Kim (1988), and Yeung and Mirus (1989).

26 The comparative advantage of transaction cost theory is that it can use the same language to explain the efficiency characteristics of both organizations. Its limitation is its narrow focus on efficiency as the sole determinant of organizational form.

REFERENCES

Ackerlof, G. (1970) 'The market for "lemons": qualitative uncertainty and the market mechanism', *Quarterly Journal of Economics* 74: 448–500.

Arrow, K. (1962) 'Economic welfare and the allocation of resources for invention', in K. Arrow (ed.) *The Rate and Direction of Inventive Activity*, Princeton, N.J.: Princeton University Press, 609–25.

Bain, J. (1956) *Barriers to new Competition*, Cambridge, Mass.: Harvard University Press.

Brickly, James, and Dark, Frederick (1987) 'The choice of organizational form: the case of franchising', *Journal of Financial Economics* 18: 401–20.

Brown, W.B. (1976) 'Islands of conscious power: MNCs in the theory of the firm', *MSU Business Topics* 24: 37–45.

Buckley, Peter (1983) 'New theories of international business', in Mark Casson (ed.) *The Growth of International Business*, London: Allen & Unwin.

—— (1985) 'New forms of international industrial cooperation', in P. Buckley and M. Casson (eds.) *The Economic Theory of the Multinational Enterprise*, New York: St Martin's.

Buckley, Peter, and Casson, Mark (1976) *The Future of the Multinational Enterprise*, London: Macmillan.

—— (1981) 'The optimal timing of a foreign direct investment', *Economic Journal* 91: 75–87.

—— (1987) 'A theory of cooperation in international business', in Farok Contractor and Peter Lorange (eds.) *Cooperative Strategies in International Business*, Lexington, Mass.: Lexington Books.

Buckley, Peter, and Davies, H. (1981) 'Foreign licensing in overseas operations: theory and evidence from the UK', in R. Hawkins and A.T. Prasad (eds.) *Research in International Business and Finance*, Greenwich, Conn.: JAI Press.

Buckley, Peter, and Prescott, K. (1989) 'The structure of British industry's sales in foreign markets', *Managerial and Decision Economics* 10: 189–208.

Casson, Mark (1979) *Alternatives to the Multinational Enterprise*, London: Macmillan.

—— (1982) 'Transaction costs and the theory of the MNE', in A. Rugman (ed.) *New Theories of the Multinational Enterprise*, New York: St Martin's Press.

—— (1985) 'Multinational monopolies and international cartels', in P.J. Buckley and M.C. Casson (eds.) *The Economic Theory of the Multinational Enterprise: Selected Papers*, London: Macmillan, 60–97.

—— (1986) 'Introduction', in M.Casson *et al.*, *Multinationals and World Trade: Vertical Integration and the Division of Labour in World Industries*, London: Allen & Unwin.

—— (1987) *The Firm and the Market*, Cambridge, Mass.: MIT Press.

Casson, Mark and Chukujama, F. (1989) 'Countertrade: Theory and Evidence', unpublished manuscript, University of Reading.

Caves, R. (1971) 'International corporations: the industrial economics of direct foreign investment', *Economica* 38: 1–27.

—— (1982) *Multinational Enterprise and Economic Analysis*, New York: Cambridge University Press.

Caves, R., and Murphy, W. (1976) 'Franchising: firms, markets, and intangible assets', *Southern Economic Journal* 52: 572–86.

Caves, R., Crookell, H. and Killing, P. (1982) 'The imperfect market for technology licences', *Oxford Bulletin of Economics and Statistics*.

Chandler, Alfred (1959) 'The beginnings of "Big Business" in America', *Business History Review* 33: 1–31.

—— (1977) *The Visible Hand*, Cambridge, Mass.: Belknap Press.

Davidson, William H., and McFetridge, D. (1982) *International Technology Transactions and the Theory of the Firm*, Working Paper No. 106, Amos Tuck School of Business Administration.

—— (1985) 'International technology transfer mode', *Journal of International Business Studies*, summer, 5–21.

Drabble, J.H. (1973) *Rubber in Malaya: the Genesis of the Industry*, Kuala Lumpur: Oxford University Press.

Drake, P.J. (1980) *Money, Finance, and Development*, New York: Wiley.

Dunning, John H. (1977) 'Trade, location of economic activity, and the multinational enterprise: a search for an eclectic approach', in B. Ohlin, P.O. Hesselborn and P.M. Wijkman (eds.) *The International Allocation of Economic Activity*, New York: Holmes & Meier.

—— (1979) 'Explaining changing patterns of international production: in defence of the eclectic theory', *Oxford Bulletin of Economics and Statistics* 41: 269–95.

—— (1981) *International Production and the Multinational Enterprise*, London: Allen & Unwin.

Dunning, John, and Cantwell, John (1984) 'The "New Forms" of International Involvement of British Firms in the Third World', unpublished manuscript, University of Reading.

Dunning, John, and McQueen, Matthew (1981) 'The eclectic theory of international production: a case study of the international hotel industry', *Managerial and Decision Economics*, 2: 197–210.

Dunning, John, and Rugman , Alan (1985) 'The influence of Hymer's dissertation on the theory of foreign direct investment', *American Economic Review* 75: 228–32.

Fieldhouse, D.K. (1986) 'The multinational: a critique of a concept', in A. Teichova, M. Levy-Leboyer and H. Nussbaum (eds.) *Multinational Enterprise in Historical Perspective*, Cambridge: Cambridge University Press.

Franko, L. (1971) *Joint Venture Survival in Multinational Corporations*, New York: Praeger.

Franz, J., Stenberg, B., and Strongman, J. (1986) *Iron Ore: Global Prospects for the Industry, 1985-95*, Washington, D.C.: World Bank.

Gatignon, H., and Anderson, E. (1988) 'The multinational corporation degree of control over subsidiaries: an empirical test of a transaction cost explanation', *Journal of Law, Economics, and Organization* 4, 2: 305-36.

Globerman, S., and Schwindt, R. (1986) 'The organization of vertically related transactions in the Canadian forest products industries', *Journal of Economic Behavior and Organization* 7: 199-212.

Gomes-Casseres, B. (1989) 'Ownership structures of foreign subsidiaries: theory and evidence', *Journal of Economic Behavior and Organization* 11: 1-25.

Grossman, Sanford, and Hart, Oliver (1986) 'The costs and benefits of ownership: a theory of vertical and lateral integration', *Journal of Political Economy* 691-719.

Hennart, Jean-François (1977) 'A Theory of Foreign Direct Investment', Ph.D dissertation, University of Maryland.

—— (1982) *A Theory of Multinational Enterprise*, Ann Arbor, Mich.: University of Michigan Press.

—— (1986a) 'The tin industry', in M. Casson *et al.*, *Multinationals and World Trade*, London: Allen and Unwin.

—— (1986b) 'Internalization in practice: foreign direct investment in Malaysian tin mining', *Journal of International Business Studies* 17, 2: 131-43.

—— (1986c) 'What is internalization?', *Weltwirtschaftliches Archiv* 791-804.

—— (1987) 'Transaction costs and multinational enterprise: the case of tin', *Business and Economic History* 16: 147-9.

—— (1988a) 'Vertical integration in the aluminium and tin industries', *Journal of Economic Behavior and Organization* 9, 3: 281-300.

—— (1988b) 'A transaction costs theory of equity joint ventures', *Strategic Management Journal* 9, 4: 361-74.

—— (1989a) 'Can the new forms of investment substitute for the old forms? A transaction costs perspective', *Journal of International Business Studies* 20, 2: 211-33.

—— (1989b) 'The transaction cost rationale for countertrade', *Journal of Law, Economics, and Organization* 5, 1: 127-53.

—— (1990a) 'The transaction cost theory of joint ventures: an empirical study of Japanese subsidiaries in the United States', *Management Science* (forthcoming).

—— (1990b) 'Some empirical dimensions of countertrade', *Journal of International Business Studies*, (forthcoming).

Hill, Charles, and Kim, W. Chan (1988) 'Searching for a dynamic theory of the multinational enterprise: a transaction cost model', *Strategic Management Journal* 9: 93-104.

Hymer, Stephen (1960) 'The International Operations of National Firms', Ph.D. dissertation, Massachusetts Institute of Technology, published in 1976 by MIT Press.

—— (1970) 'The efficiency (contradictions) of multinational corporations', *American Economic Review*, 60, 2: 441-8.

Jensen, Michael, and Meekling, William (1976) 'Theory of the firm: managerial behavior, agency costs, and capital structure', *Journal of Financial Economics* 3: 305-60.

Joskow, Paul (1985) 'Vertical integration and long-term contracts: the case of coal-burning electric generating plants', *Journal of Law, Economics and Organiza-tion* 1.

Kay, Neil (1983) 'Multinational enterprise: a review article', *Scottish Journal of Political Economy* 30, 3: 304-12.

Kindleberger, C.P. (1969) *American Business Abroad*, New Haven, Conn.: Yale University Press.

Kogut, B. (1986) 'On designing contracts to guarantee enforceability: theory and evidence from East-West trade', *Journal of International Business Studies* 17: 47-62.

Kogut, B., and Singh, H. (1988) 'The effect of national culture on the choice of entry mode', *Journal of International Business Studies* 19, 3: 411-32.

Litvak, Isaiah and Maule, Christopher (1977) 'Transnational corporations and vertical integration: the banana case', *Journal of World Trade Law* 11, 6: 537-49.

Mackenzie, C. (1954) *Realms of Silver: One Hundred Years of Banking in the East*, London: Routledge.

Magee, S. (1977) 'Information and the multinational corporation: an appro-priability theory of direct foreign investment', in J.N. Bhagwhati (ed.) *The New International Economic Order*, Cambridge, Mass.: MIT Press.

Masten, Scott (1984) 'The organization of production: evidence from the aerospace industry', *Journal of Law and Economics* 27: 403.

McManus, J. (1972) 'The theory of the multinational firm', in Gilles Paquet (ed.) *The Multinational Firm and the Nation State*, Don Mills, Ont.: Collier-Macmillan.

Mikesell, Raymond, and Whitney, John (1987) *The World Mining Industry*, Boston, Mass.: Allen & Unwin.

de Miramon, J. (1985) 'Countertrade: an illusory solution', *OECD Observer* 134: 24-9.

Mirus, R., and Yeung, B. (1986) 'Economic incentives for countertrade', *Journal of International Business Studies* 17, 13: 27-39.

Monteverde, Kirk, and Teece, David (1982) 'Supplier switching costs and vertical integration in the automobile industry', *Bell Journal of Economics* 13: 206-13.

Murrell, P. (1982) 'Product quality, market signaling, and the development of East-West trade'. *Economic Inquiry* 20: 589-603.

Nicholas, S.J. (1982) 'British multinational investment before 1939', *Journal of European Economic History* 11: 605-30.

—— (1983) 'Agency contracts, institutional modes, and the transition to foreign direct investment by British manufacturing multinationals before 1935', *Journal of Economic History* 43: 675-86.

Oman, C. (1984) *New Forms of International Investment in Developing Countries*, Paris: OECD.

Read, Robert (1986) 'The banana industry: oligopoly and barriers to entry', in Mark Casson *et al.* (eds.) *Multinationals and World Trade*, London: Allen & Unwin.

Robbins, S., and Stobaugh, R. (1973) *Money in the Multinational Enterprise*, New York; Basic books.

Root, Franklin (1987) *Entry Strategies for International Markets*, Lexington, Mass.: Lexington Books

Rugman, Alan M. (1981) *Inside the Multinationals: the Economics of Internal*

Markets, New York: Columbia University Press.

Shapiro, A. (1984) 'The evaluation and control of foreign affiliates', *Midland Corporate Finance Journal*, spring: 13–25.

Stopford, J., and Haberich, K. (1978) 'Ownership and control of foreign operations', in Michel Ghertman and James Leontiades (eds.) *European Research in International Business*, New York: North Holland.

Stopford, J., and Wells, L. (1972) *Managing the Multinational Enterprise*, New York: Basic Books.

Stuckey, J. (1983) *Vertical Integration and Joint Ventures in the Aluminium Industry*, Cambridge, Mass.: Harvard University Press.

Teece, David (1981) 'The multinational enterprise: market failure and market power considerations', *Sloan Management Review* 22, 3: 3–17.

Tsurumi, Y. (1976) *The Japanese are Coming*, Cambridge: Ballinger.

US Federal Trade Commission (1916) *Report on Cooperation in American Export Trade*, Washington, D.C.: Government Printing Office.

Van Helten, Jean-Jacques, and Jones, Geoffrey (1989) 'British business in Malaysia and Singapore since the 1870s' in R.P.T. Davenport-Hines and Geoffrey Jones (eds.) *British Business in Asia since 1860*, Cambridge: Cambridge University Press.

Walker, G., and Weber, D. (1984) 'A transaction cost approach to make-or-buy decisions', *Administrative Science Quarterly* 29: 373–91.

Wilkins, Mira (1970) *The Emergence of Multinational Enterprise: American Business abroad from the Colonial Era to 1914*, Cambridge, Mass.: Harvard University Press.

—— (1974) *The Maturing of Multinational Enterprise: American Business abroad from 1914 to 1970*, Cambridge, Mass.: Harvard University Press.

—— (1988) 'The free-standing company, 1817–1914', *Economic History Review* 61, 2: 259–82.

—— (1989) *The History of Foreign Investment in the United States to 1914*, Cambridge, Mass.: Harvard University Press.

Williamson, Oliver E. (1975) *Markets and Hierarchies: Analysis and Antitrust Implications*, New York: Free Press.

—— (1979) 'Transaction cost economics: the governance of contractual relations', *Journal of Law and Economics* 22, 2.

—— (1981) 'The modern corporation: origins, evolution, attributes', *Journal of Economic Literature* 19, 4: 1537–68.

—— (1985) *The Economic Institutions of Capitalism: Firms, Markets, Relational Contracting*, New York: Free Press.

—— (1988) 'Corporate finance and corporate governance', *Journal of Finance* 63, 3: 567–98.

Yeung, Bernard, and Mirus, Rolf (1989) 'On the Mode of International Expansion: the Role of Agency Costs in an Expanded Framework', unpublished manuscript.

Yoshihara, H. (1984) 'Multinational growth of Japanese multinational enterprises in the postwar period', in A. Okuchi and T. Inoue (eds.) *Overseas Business Activities*, Tokyo: University of Tokyo Press.

Yoshino, M. (1976) *Japanese Multinational Enterprises*, Cambridge, Mass.: Harvard University Press.

ACKNOWLEDGEMENTS

I wish to thank Jean Boddewyn, Peter Buckley, Mark Casson, Geoffrey Jones, Christos Pitelis, Roger Sugden, Mira Wilkins, Bernard Yeung and especially Kathleen Saul for many valuable suggestions.

5 The eclectic paradigm of international production: a personal perspective

John H. Dunning

SOME INTRODUCTORY REMARKS

In one respect, at least, it is inappropriate that the present author should be contributing to a volume entitled *The Nature of the Transnational Firm*. This is because the eclectic paradigm of international production is not (and has never purported to be) an explanation of the trans- or multinational *firm*. Its focus of interest has always been directed to explaining the level and pattern of the foreign value-added activities of *firms*, and/or of countries.

There is, of course, much common ground between the theory of international production, defined as the production financed by foreign direct investment, and explanations of the extension of the territorial boundaries of the firm, but the one major difference is that some variables which are *exogenous* to the latter set of explanations become *endogenous* when the subject of interest is groups of firms or countries.

It is perhaps worth observing that it has been only in the last fifteen years or so that scholars have been preoccupied with explaining the existence and growth of the multinational enterprise, as opposed to the act of foreign direct investment. Stephen Hymer's thesis, for example, was entitled 'The International Operations of *Firms*', and might well have been subtitled 'The Industrial Economics of Foreign Direct Investment'. It is true that he viewed the act of foreign direct investment as a market-replacing activity, but, in seeking to explain the growth of US direct investment in Europe and Canada, he drew as much upon *industry*- as *firm*-specific concepts and variables. Eight years after he completed his thesis, in an article published in a French journal Hymer (1968) gave more explicit attention to the international firm *qua* firm, and it is quite clear that in the intervening period he had acquainted himself with the writings of Ronald Coase (1937) and Maurice Bye (1958).

The most influential theory of foreign direct investment, up to the early 1970s at least, was the product cycle theory, first put forward by Ray Vernon in a seminal article in 1966, although for a fuller exposition of the theory the reader is invited to read the (somewhat neglected) monographs by Gary Hufbauer (1965) and Seev Hirsh (1967), both of whom were Vernon's students. Vernon, like myself, has always been interested in explaining foreign production as a form of international economic involvement, on a par with, but different from, international trade. Though virtually all trade is conducted by firms, I am sure that no trade theorist would wish to argue that the penetration of foreign markets by domestic firms or of domestic markets by foreign firms could be explained by firms internalizing markets. So why, I wonder, when there is a shift in the location of production by international firms, should one have to play a new intellectual ball game?

I think one answer relates to the role of the firm in traditional trade theory. Quite simply, there wasn't one. To all intents and purposes the firm was a black box. By the extremely restrictive assumptions underlying neoclassical trade theory, and as described in most international economics textbooks, markets – and markets alone – determine the structure of cross-border resource allocation. *Inter alia* this is because the transaction costs of using the market as an exchange and co-ordinating mechanism are assumed to be zero. Each firm produces only a single product (or, more correctly, engages in only one economic activity) from one particular location. It can possess no lasting competitive advantages over other firms producing in the same country. Trade under such circumstances is determined by factors exogenous to firms. Firms are simply production units, the function of which is to transform inputs into more valued outputs. Their actions are completely constrained by circumstances beyond their control. The fact that firms are able to penetrate foreign markets is entirely explained by their being able to secure location-bound resources on better terms than can firms located in the countries to which they export, and has nothing to do with any specific advantage which they enjoy *vis-à-vis* their competitors. It would serve no purpose for a firm to set up a branch facility in a foreign country, because it would be in no better position to supply the market in that country than a local firm. Indeed, if it chose to produce the same goods, it would most likely be disadvantaged compared with firms from its home country.

But what happens when the assumption of the immobility of factors of production is broken down, or technology is no longer presumed to be costless and instantaneously transferable across national boundaries? According to Vernon, foreign production is likely to replace exports whenever the cost of combining the intermediate products produced in the home market, but which are transferable across national boundaries at low or zero cost, can be used more efficiently (i.e. at lower cost) with the resources of a foreign country than with those of the home country. In such circumstances, foreign production represents a change in the location, but not the ownership nor the character, of economic activity. The important assumption is that the intermediate products, to which the firm has privileged access (its so-called ownership advantages) and which made the exports possible in the first place, are the privileged property of the exporting firm; otherwise a foreign firm might have acquired and made use of them at least as effectively as the exporting firm could. The question of the obstacles (or barriers) to such acquisition were not discussed by Vernon (who, in the early 1960s at least, was not aware of Hymer's thesis); indeed, at that time, Vernon appeared uninterested in organizational issues.

In the meantime, other studies concentrated almost entirely on the industrial organization aspects of foreign direct investment. Here the question explored by Horst (1972a, b), Caves (1971, 1974a, b), Bauman (1975) and other scholars (whose work is summarized by Clegg, 1987) was 'How is it possible for the affiliates of foreign-owned *firms* to compete with indigenous firms on their own territory?' Again the emphasis was *firms*, and on industry-specific characteristics. It was observed, for example, that the subsidiaries of multinational firms tended to concentrate their activities in sectors with a number of distinctive characteristics, and that there were reasons to suppose that the ownership advantages of such firms reflected the structure of resource endowments and markets of their countries of origin. Thus US-owned firms were more prone to possess advantages based on the supply of high-income goods and capital- or technology-intensive producer products, because these were intangible assets which the US economy was in a comparatively favoured position to supply.

Scholars paid little attention to why US firms chose to exploit their competitive advantages in foreign countries by setting up or acquiring production facilities rather than by other means, eg. licensing, franchise agreements, etc.

So, by the mid-1970s, there were two main approaches to understanding foreign production. The first essentially used the tools of locational economics to explain both the origin and the exploitation of competitive advantages of firms. The other drew upon the work of industrial organiza-tion economists, notably Bain (1956), in order to explain differences between the advantages possessed by indigenous and foreign firms (*firms*, note) in explaining why foreign-owned affiliates were concentrated in some industries but not in others. This approach was not interested in locational issues at all, nor with the origin of the advantages possessed by foreign firms. Moreover, these advantages were assumed to exist prior to the foreign investment being made, and to have nothing to do with the undertaking of foreign production *per se*. Richard Caves, however, did distinguish between advantages associated with being part of a multi-plant complex, and introduced surplus entrepreneurial capacity as a potential ownership advantage for a foreign investor, which clearly was translated into an actual advantage only if and when the foreign investment was made.

This, indeed, was the starting point for scholars to switch their focus to the multinational firm as a market-replacing institution. It also coincided with more attention being paid to explaining the sequential growth of foreign production, in contrast to the initial act of investment, which was the predominant interest of economists of the Hymer–Kindleberger tradition.

There were other reasons, too, for this redirection of emphasis. Increasingly the uniqueness of foreign direct investment was identified, not only in terms of the resources it provided, but in the way in which those resources were used. Researchers began to observe differences between the organization of activity among multinational firms and between such firms and those of their non-multinational competitors. Partly it was felt that these differences reflected the fact that they were multi-plant firms, and that common ownership brought its own separate or distinctive characteristics,[1] and partly because that multinationality itself affected the response of firms to changes in their economic environment (Kogut, 1985). Questions of advantages which accrued to firms as a result of their foreign activities became of central interest, rather than advantages stemming from the possession of particular property rights which enabled them to penetrate foreign markets in the first place, or to optimize the geographical distribution of their production facilities. Multinationals could exist simply because the cost of engaging in cross-border transactions, through the market, was higher than where these transactions were organized within the same firm. The greater the cross-border market failure which could be efficiently internalized by multinational hierarchies, then, *ceteris paribus*, the more likely would foreign production occur.

Throughout the last decade, the internalization theory has been the leading explanation of why a firm should choose to engage in foreign investment rather than organize its cross-border activities in a different way. It is difficult to quarrel with the theory if that is all it is seeking to explain.[2] But when the theory also purports to explain the level, structure and location of *all* international production, then, immediately, it opens itself to criticism – unless, as Rugman would seem to claim in his various contributions (e.g. 1980, 1986), it takes on board all kinds of market imperfections, in which case the theory loses much of its incisiveness.

THE ORIGINS OF THE ECLECTIC PARADIGM

My own perception of the determinants of international production dates back to the time I wrote my first book, *American Investment in British Manufacturing Industry* (1958). Earlier research by Rostas (1948), Frankel (1955) and some UK study teams which visited the United States in the early post-war period had shown that labour productivity in US manufacturing industry, was on average, was two and a half times higher than in UK industry. The question which this fact posed in my mind was 'Was that difference in productivity due to the superior indigenous resources of the US economy, i.e. those traditionally explained by trade and location theories, or was it due to the better way US firms, *qua* firms, organized and managed the resources at their disposal?' My hypothesis was that if it was entirely due to the latter, then American-owned subsidiaries in the UK should perform at least as well as their parent companies, and fare considerably better than their UK-owned competitors. This I called the ownership-specific effect (not firm-specific effect, note), as the productivity differences were assumed to depend on the country of ownership of the firm. If, however, US subsidiaries in the UK performed no better than their indigenous competitors, and hence much less well then their parent companies, I hypothesized that it would be due to the location-specific (and non-transferable) characteristics of the US economy. This I called the location-specific component of any productivity differential.

As might have been expected, I discovered that US affiliates were not as productive as their parent companies but were more productive than their local competitors, which suggested that Anglo-American productivity differences, when measured at a *country* level, were partly explainable by location and partly by ownership-specific characteristics. However, my study omitted to ask a follow-up question: 'To what extent is the origin of the ownership advantages of US firms itself home-country-specific?' Nor did it attempt to distinguish between the advantages which arose as a result of the direct investment in the UK and those which the US firm possessed prior to engaging in foreign production.[3]

I took up the theme of ownership and location specific advantages again in two papers in the early 1970s. The first (Dunning, 1972) concerned the likely impact of Britain's entry into the European Economic Community (EC). In it I suggested that, while the removal of tariff barriers had consequences for the location of economic activity within the Community, it would also be likely to affect the competitive position of firms of different national origins differently and, in consequence, the ownership of economic activity in the Community.[4]

The second paper (Dunning, 1973) was an attempt to review the various attempts which had been made to explain the activities of firms outside their national boundaries over the past decade. In that paper I tried to integrate the industrial organizational and locational approaches to understanding foreign production. I argued (like Hymer) that, while the first was necessary to explain why foreign firms could compete successfully with domestic firms in supplying the latter's own markets, the second was relevant to explaining why these firms chose to supply their markets from a foreign, rather than a domestic, base.

In 1975 I was asked to present a paper at a Nobel Symposium on the International Location of Economic Activity, which was held in Stockholm in June 1976. This symposium was organized by Bertil Ohlin and attended by leading international economists, economic geographers and regional scientists. For the most part the seminar was oriented towards country-specific factors influencing the changing distribution of international economic activity, but the starting point of my paper was that a country's economic space could be considered in two ways. The first was the value of output produced within its national boundaries independently of the ownership of that production. The second was the output produced by its own firms, including that part produced outside its national boundaries. I distinguished between the competitive advantage of countries and firms, which I have been at pains to stress in several of my writings.[5]

In explaining the activity of firms outside their national boundaries I extended the ownership and locational advantages identified in my earlier writings to include another set of choices available to firms, which related to the way the firms organized the use of their ownership and locational advantages. In other words, I acknowledged that, to explain international production, one had also to explain why firms opted to use their ownership advantages for further value-added activities, rather than sell these advantages (or their rights) to foreign firms. I further accepted that the way in which a firm responded to exogenous locational costs and benefits might also affect its long-run competitive position. I finally distinguished between those ownership advantages which arose as a direct result of a firm engaging in international production and those which it might possess prior to its becoming a multinational. These former advantages, in particular, I argued, could not be separately sold to independent foreign firms to exploit. They could be realized only through vertical or horizontal integration, or, putting it another way, by the common ownership of related activities along a particular value-added chain or across two or more value-added chains.

I would be the first to admit that, in my work on internalization advantages, I was considerably influenced by my colleagues Peter Buckley and Mark Casson of the University of Reading, who were in the process of writing *The Future of the Multinational Enterprise*, although my first exposure to the concept of internalization, as applied to the multinational firm, came in 1972 when I read an article by J.C. McManus in Guy Paquet's edited volume *The Multinational Firm and the Nation State*. A year later, on a visit to Uppsala in Sweden, I had conversations with Nils Lundgren, a Swedish economist who was thinking along the same lines in his attempt to explain the growth of Swedish foreign direct investment.[6] Nevertheless,

I regarded this new insight as a useful addition to my own approach to explaining the determinants of the foreign production, and not as a replacement of it – a view I still hold today.

Over the past fourteen years I have benefited enormously from the comments of friends and colleagues on the eclectic theory (or paradigm, as I now prefer to call it)[7] of international production. I accept that in my earlier work I did tend to look at internalization advantages more as those which arose from the way ownership advantages were exploited than as a market replacement activity which conferred its own hierarchical advantages. While, as set out in a paper published in the *Journal of International Business Studies* (Dunning, 1988c), I still prefer to think of ownership advantages as any kind of income-generating assets which make it possible for firms to engage in foreign production, I readily acknowledge that these may arise as a direct consequence of market-replacing activities. But, even here, I believe that a firm's ability to benefit from such an activity must be related to the assets which it possesses prior to the act of internalization.

The economies of common governance arise because a firm integrates its existing activities with new activities. For example, a firm which is currently producing in country A and believes it will benefit from diversifying its risks if it produces in country B will gain from such diversification only if it produces in *both* country A and country B! A firm which benefits from the cross-border economies of scope or scale will do so only if the new investment is in addition to its existing investment. A firm which makes a foreign acquisition to obtain new and up-to-date technology presumably does so because it believes it can use that technology along with its existing assets to strengthen its competitive position.[8] This may seem an obvious point, but to me, at any rate, the distinction between benefits which accrue from the gains to be had from internalizing the market of an existing asset and those which arise from co-ordinating existing assets with new assets, *vis-à-vis* some alternative use which might be made of those assets, is an important one.

To some extent, I accept that these are semantic points. Much more important is the debate as to whether the extent to which ownership advantages in the eclectic paradigm are assumed to be exogenous or endogenous variables. If the former, then, of course, the main question of interest surrounds their use or, in some cases, their mode of acquisition. Or is it that only those ownership advantages which directly arise from market-replacing activities are endogenous? I must say, I find (some of) the internalization literature very ambiguous on this point.

But, again, much depends upon the perspective and the time frame. From the viewpoint of explaining why some countries are net outward direct investors[9] and others are not, other factors exogenous to firms but endogenous to countries must be accommodated. Also, in explaining the changing competitive position of firms, it is perfectly clear that this may have as much to do with the creation of new ownership-specific advantages as with the changing characteristics of markets or hierarchies.

I will return to this latter point later, but it does seem that at least some internalization economists acknowledge that a firm's propensity to engage in foreign investment may change as factors other than market-replacing or locational advantages change. Once that is admitted, it must surely be accepted that it is not unreasonable to hypothesize that today's level and structure of international production may be influenced by the past ownership advantages, or changes in those advantages, of the firms undertaking the production.

Let me now reiterate the main ingredients of the eclectic paradigm.[10] The subject to be explained is the extent and pattern of international production. The paradigm avers that, at any given moment of time, this will be determined by the configuration of three sets of forces. (1) the (net) competitive advantages which firms of one nationality have over those of another nationality in supplying any particular market or set of markets. These advantages may arise either from the firm's privileged possession of a set of income-generating assets,[11] or by their ability to co-ordinate existing assets with other assets across national boundaries in a way which benefits them relative to their competitors or potential competitors who are not able or willing to undertake such production. (2) The extent to which firms perceive it to be profitable to internalize the markets for these assets, and by so doing add value to their output. (3) The extent to which firms choose to locate these value-adding activities outside their national boundaries.

The eclectic paradigm further argues that the significance of each of these advantages and the configuration between them will vary between industries (or types of value-added activities), regions or countries (the geographical dimension) and between firms. Thus there are likely to be country-specific differences in the ownership advantages of (say) Korean firms compared with (say) Canadian firms. The extent of market failure influencing whether or not the market for technology is internalized is likely to be different in (say) the wood and pulp industry from (say) the semiconductor industry; while the relationship to the comparative locational advantages of Thailand and Taiwan as a manufacturing base for motor vehicles might be differently regarded by (say) the Toyota from (say) the Honda Corporation.

The eclectic paradigm is to be regarded more as a framework for analysing the determinants of international production than a predictive theory of the multinational firm. I have frequently argued that no single theory can be expected to encompass all kinds of foreign production satisfactorily, simply because the motivations for and expectations of, such production vary so much. The variables necessary to explain import-substituting investment are likely to be different from those which explain resource-oriented investment, and both are likely to be different from those which explain rationalized investment.

SOME CRITICISM OF THE PARADIGM

Let me now turn to the criticisms of the eclectic paradigm, some of which are covered by other contributors to this volume.

A shopping list of variables?

First, it is claimed that the variables identified by the paradigm are so numerous that its predictive value is almost nil. This is accepted up to a point. But, as we have said, the purpose of the paradigm is not to offer a full explanation of all kinds of international production, but rather to point to a methodology and to a generic set of variables which contain the ingredients necessary for any specific explanation of particular types of foreign value-added activity.

In any case, the same criticism can be directed towards other general theories of international production. The kinds of market failure relevant to explaining resource-based investment are totally different from those explaining rationalized investment. Partial theories do not suffer from this same deficiency; however, unlike the general theories, they can explain only some kinds of foreign direct investment. The product cycle theory has little relevance to resource-based foreign investment. Knickerbocker's (1973) follow-my-leader or oligopolistic interaction approach is entirely dependent on a particular type of market structure. Kojima's normative macroeconomic theory (1978, 1982) cannot easily encompass intra-industry investment. Aliber's theory (1970, 1971) is only relevant for explaining foreign investment in different currency areas. And so on.

Interdependence of OLI variables?

Second, it is suggested that it is misleading to give the impression that the triumvirate of variables which make up the eclectic paradigm are independent of each other. For example, a firm's response to its exogenous locational variables might itself influence its ownership advantages, including its ability and willingness to internalize markets. A particular R&D strategy intended to strengthen a firm's competitive position may require modification to the siting of its existing innovatory facilities, while a change in a firm's organizational structure may directly affect its ability to penetrate the markets of its competitors. Over time the separate identity of the variables becomes even more difficult to justify.

Nevertheless, conceptually, I believe there is something to be said for separating those reasons for international production which are due primarily to the competitive position of firms of a particular ownership from those to do with the resource endowments and markets of the countries in which they operate. The policy implications of a decline in inward investment which results from a reduction in the attractiveness of a country's location-bound resources are very different from those which reflect the strengthening competitive position of its indigenous, relative to foreign-owned, firms. An increase in outward investment due to the integration of markets allowing better exploitation of the economies of common governance (such as is encouraging more pan-European direct investment) flags a very different message to governments of home countries than investment driven out by unattractive conditions in the domestic market, as was the case in India for most of the 1970s and early 1980s, South Africa and the Philippines in the mid-1980s and Sweden in the mid and late 1980s.

No role for strategy: a static approach?

Third, it is argued that the eclectic paradigm takes no account of differences in the strategic response of firms to any given configuration of OLI variables. This criticism may be coupled with another that suggests the paradigm is couched in static (or comparatively static) terms and offers little guidance as to the *path* or *process* of the internalization of firms (or of countries). In recent papers (Dunning, 1989, 1990b), I have begun to take on board this criticism (which incidentally may be applied to the internalization theory of the multinational enterprise). My reasoning is as follows. At a given moment of time, the pattern of international production represents a point on a set of trajectories towards (or, for that matter, away from) the internationalization of production by firms. That trajectory itself is set by the continuous and iterative interaction between the OLI configuration over a succession of time periods and the strategy of firms in response to these configurations, which, in turn, will influence the OLI configuration in subsequent time periods. Let OLI_{t_0} be the OLI configuration in time t_0, OLI_{t_1} the OLI configuration in time t_1, S_{t-n} the past (i.e. pre-t_0) strategies of firms still being worked out, and $\Delta S_{t_0 \rightarrow t_1}$ any change in the strategic response of firms to that configuration between time t_0 and t_1. Then, *ceteris paribus*,

$$\text{OLI}_{t_1} = f\left(\text{OLI}_{t_0} \; S_{t-n} \; \Delta \; S_{t_0} \to {}_{t_1}\right) \tag{1}$$

If we extend the analysis to a second time period, t_2, then

$$\text{OLI}_{t_2} = f\left(\text{OLI}_{t_1} \; S_{t-n} \; \Delta \; S_{t_1} \to {}_{t_2}\right) \tag{2}$$

This analysis further suggests that S_{t-n} and $S_{t_0} \to {}_{t_2}$ determines the path of the movement from OLI_{t_0} to OLI_{t_2}.

Strategic response is, of course, just one of the many endogenous variables which might affect the OLI configuration of firms (mainly by its impact on O and I advantages). Others include technological or organizational innovations, changes in the composition of senior management or of labour productivity, new marketing techniques, mergers, acquisitions, and so on. No less significant are exogenous changes, such as changes in population, raw material prices, exchange rates, government policies towards outward or inward direct investment, and so on. If we take all endogenous variables other than strategy to be *EN* and all exogenous variables to be *EX* and we assume that changes in *EN* and *EX* do not affect the firms' strategies, then we can rewrite equation 1 as:

$$\text{OLI}_{t_1} = f\left(\text{OLI}_{t_0} \; S_{t-n} \; \Delta \; S_{t_0} \to {}_{t_1}\right) \Delta \; EN \; {}_{t_0} \to {}_{t_1} \; \Delta \; EX \; {}_{t_0} \to {}_{t_1}\right) \tag{3}$$

Equation 2 can be similarly reconstructed, and it is easy to incorporate any change in strategy which embraces the response to $\Delta \; EN$ and $\Delta \; EX$ if it occurs before t_1 is reached by adding * to $\Delta \; S_{t_0} \to {}_{t_2}$ in the equation.

Of course, it may be argued that this drives a coach and horses through the generality of the eclectic paradigm, as the nature of the interaction between the values of most exogenous and endogenous variables likely to affect international production and the strategies of firms are difficult to predict. Yet, from the time of Vernon (1966) onwards, economists and business analysts have been trying to do just that. Vernon, for example, suggests that both the strategy of firms and the locational advantages of at least some value-added activities associated with the production of a product change as that product moves through its cycle. As the product becomes more widely demanded, as foreign governments are tempted to impose import restrictions to encourage local production, and as the fear of competitors (or the threat of entry by new competitors) usurping one's own foreign markets becomes more pronounced, then the ownership (or potential ownership) advantages of firms and the attractions of a foreign location become altered in a way which leads to more foreign direct investment. Thus a firm's O and L position affecting its investment in time $t + 1$ (e.g.

the mature stage of the product cycle) is affected both by its OL configuration in the early, i.e. the innovating, stage of the cycle, and by the changes in the exogenous variables, e.g. demand by the foreign customers, and endogenous variables, e.g. the presence (or absence) of economies of plant size, and any changes in the strategy of firms consequential upon these eventualities.

Later scholars introduced a time and strategy-related dimension more explicitly into their analysis. Again, reinterpreting Knickerbocker's analysis in terms of the OLI paradigm, we may say that firms are prompted to go overseas, in part at least, because they consider their O advantages are (or could become) threatened if they do not follow their competitors' lead, or because their advantages would be less without their presence.[12] In other words, the strategy followed by firms in response to a given OLI configuration in time t_0 is governed by their desire to protect or influence that configuration in t_1. (This incidentally does not necessarily mean that all firms will engage in more foreign direct investment.)

Most studies on the internationalization process, which has traditionally been the province of marketing or organizational scholars, implicitly or explicitly assume not only that I or L advantages change as a firm enlarges its foreign markets or gains experience of them but that the action it takes will be influenced by the response to the OLI configuration and the likely action of other firms and governments on that configuration, both in the presence and in the absence of their own investments.

The investment development cycle

It is thus possible to formalize the introduction of strategy and changes in endogenous and exogenous variables into the OLI paradigm, and, in some cases at least, to offer some broad predictions of the outcome of such changes over time. This indeed is precisely what the concept of the investment development cycle or path seeks to do (Dunning, 1981, 1988a). The basic hypothesis is that, as a country develops, the configuration of the OLI advantages facing foreign-owned firms which might invest in that country, and of its own firms which might invest overseas, undergoes change, and that it is possible to identify the conditions making for the change as well as its effect on the trajectory of development. The concept also suggests the ways in which the interaction between foreign and domestic firms might itself influence the country's investment path, but only recently has this aspect been incorporated into the literature cycle (Tolentino, 1990).

The investment development path identifies several stages of development a country may pass through. The first stage is one of pre-industrialization, in which a country is presumed to have no inward or outward investment, in the first case because it has insufficient locational attractions and in the second because its own firms possess no ownership advantages. Depending on its resources, government policy, the organization of activity and the strategy of firms, the OLI configuration changes so as to first attract inward investment in resource-based sectors, in the traditional and labour-intensive manufacturing sectors, in trade and distribution, and transport and communications, construction, and perhaps some tourism.

Depending very much on the extent to which the country is able to create a satisfactory legal system, commercial infrastructure and business culture, and to provide both domestic and foreign firms with the transport and communications facilities and human resources they need; and depending on government policy towards inward direct investment (cf. Japan, which largely disallowed such investment in the 1960s, with Germany, which adopted an open-door policy towards it), its locational attractions will increase; and because foreign firms are likely to have more experience in manufacturing the goods and services now likely to be demanded (and have probably penetrated the local market by imports in any case) inward investment will continue to grow. Gradually it and any investment by indigenous firms will affect both supply and demand conditions for the products supplied by foreign firms and their desire to internalize their markets for the competitive advantages. To begin with, L and O advantages are likely to complement each other. Thus as supply capabilities improve they give rise to agglomerative or cluster-type economies and increases in labour productivity. The introduction of new machinery and production methods is likely to lead to lower real labour costs and scale economies. The latter are also made possible by growing markets.

The improvement in the locational advantages of a country may also help indigenous firms to develop their own competitive advantages. The growth of Japanese outward investment and more recently that of several developing countries is entirely consistent with a reconfiguration of the OLI advantages of indigenous firms brought about by the development process. Once again, the values of both exogenous and endogenous variables change to affect each of these components. In this early stage, the role of government is especially important. In an unpublished paper, Ozawa (1989) shows the absolutely critical role of the Japanese government in influencing the ability of Japanese firms to generate competitive advantages relative to their competitors and to locate their value-added activities outside Japan. It has also affected the strategy of the Japanese companies themselves.

As countries move along their development path, the OLI configuration facing outward and inward investors continues to change. Some foreign (and domestic) firms which earlier found the country attractive to invest in, because of its low labour costs or plentiful natural resources, no longer do so. In other cases, locational advantages have become more attractive as a technological infrastructure and a pool of skilled labour is built up. This, in turn, makes it possible for domestic firms to develop their own O advantages and begin exporting capital.

Eventually, as countries reach some degree of economic maturity, the OLI configuration facing their own firms may be such that their propensity to engage in outward direct investment exceeds that of foreign-based firms to engage in inward investment. Again, whether or not this happens rests on the strategy both of firms and of governments for generating the competitive (and especially the innovatory) advantages of their own firms and to make their own locations attractive to domestic and foreign investors. The literature is replete with examples of how the kind of variable is likely to influence the OLI configuration over time and the determinants of the value of these variables. Predictions for individual countries are difficult because they involve predicting the behaviour of governments. Different countries at the same stage of their development paths seem to display different propensities to engage in outward and inward investment. Others may display similar propensities for different reasons. Thus in the late 1980s both Sweden and Japan are significant net outward investors, but whereas the Japanese push outwards represents a positive restructuring to make way for the upgrading of its domestic industry, in the Swedish case it is more symptomatic of the falling competitiveness of the domestic economy.

I have dwelt at some length on the investment development path, becaue it does introduce (albeit at a macro-level) a dynamic element into the theory of international production. Moreover, it confirms that the equations set out above do seem to make sense. The configuration of OLI variables affecting (say) Japanese firms in the world economy in 1988 is a function of the OLI configuration facing them in (say) 1968 and the changes in the endogenous and exogenous variables which have affected their behaviour in the intervening period. Of these, there is strong evidence that the way in which these two sets of variables interact is itself an important factor determining the movement towards a new OLI configuration. We also believe that the concept outlined is very relevant in explaining the growth of outward investment from Third World countries, especially from Korea, Singapore, Taiwan and Mexico.

The Kojima criticism of the eclectic paradigm

We next turn to the criticism of Kiyoshi Kojima (1982) to the eclectic paradigm. To Kojima my approach, and that of the Reading economists as a group, is purely a microeconomic phenomenon. Indeed, he seems to assume that the internalization and eclectic paradigms are trying to explain the same phenomena. They are not. As far as I am aware, no one from the internalization school has sought to explain the changing propensity of countries to invest or be invested in over time.[13]

Nevertheless, Kojima is right in supposing our macroeconomic perspective is different from his. Let me give an analogy. Suppose the subject for explanation is the trade in goods. Kojima would be interested in answering the question 'Why does one country export certain types of goods and import other kinds of goods?' whereas I would be concerned with explaining whether a particular country was a net importer or exporter of particular types of goods or of all goods. I admit that, at a macro-level, the latter is a somewhat meaningless question, as in the last resort and over a sufficiently long period of time the balance of payments must balance. But this is not the case with the stocks and flows of international investment; hence the concept of the investment development path does have some meaning.

Moreover, investment owned and controlled by multinationals is a different phenomenon from portfolio investment. So indeed is trade conducted within multinationals different from trade between independent parties. In other words, organizational issues do inject the need for a set of analytical tools different from those offered by traditional trade theory.

This is where I think Kojima's criticism of the eclectic paradigm (and of internalization theory) falls down. He will insist upon applying a strictly neoclassical framework of thought to the explanation of a phenomenon which is outside that framework of thought. Moreover, like neoclassical theory, his approach to international direct investment is more normative than ours. However, in various of my writings (see especially Dunning, 1988a: chapter 10) I have attempted to give some normative content to the eclectic paradigm in suggesting the conditions for optimizing the level and pattern of multinational activity into and out of the UK.

Buying an ownership advantage and conglomerate investment

One final criticism of the eclectic paradigm is that it fails to explain two particularly fast-growing forms of international investment. The first is that by companies, in both developed and developing countries, which engage in foreign investment in order to acquire assets in which they are deficient. The second is the growth of all forms of conglomerate investment.

As regards the first criticism, to which I have already alluded earlier, I would accept that, unless the firm has some kind of advantage in exploiting these assets which its competitors have not; or there is some degree of synergy between the assets already owned by the investing company and those acquired; or by acquiring the assets a firm controls the supply of the output generated by them, one cannot! However, the reason one cannot is that, in that case, as with many types of conglomerate investment, the investment is not really a direct investment at all, but rather the purchase of a set of assets which the firm is not intending to organize, manage or integrate in any way. The question of why a firm seeks to acquire such assets then comes down to its expectation that the assets it acquires will appreciate in value with time, or enable it to earn a better rate of return than it could get from any alternative use of resources. But, I repeat, in that case it is not a direct investment at all but a portfolio investment. And, as an aside to the main thrust of my thoughts, I would suggest that, because of the growing role of acquisitions and mergers as an entry or expansion route for international production, while at the same time there is some evidence of a hiving-off (i.e. disinternalization) of non-core assets by companies, it follows that any particular foreign investment, part of which may be sold off after acquisition, may indeed have the features of a portfolio rather than a direct investment.

Thus I would argue that the two apparent exceptions are not really exceptions to the eclectic explanation of international production. In the first, one has to judge the effect of investment on the competitive advantage of the company's existing investment, and the presumption is that the new investment will give the company an additional advantage (net of its cost) greater than it would otherwise have had (including, incidentally, a strengthening of its monopolistic position).[14] In the second, the investment, although classified as a direct investment, has all the attributes of a portfolio investment.

CONCLUSIONS

Let me conclude by re-emphasizing six points. The first is that, although I have sometimes illustrated the eclectic paradigm by reference to the individual firm, my main focus of interest is in explaining the international production of all firms from a particular country or group of countries. Because of this, I contend that it is not correct to compare the merits and demerits of the eclectic paradigm directly with those of internalization theory.

Second, I accept that some ownership-specific advantages are the direct result of firms internalizing the market for their intermediate products across national borders. However, since this very act of internalization puts the internalizing firms at an advantage relative to non-internalizing firms, I think it appropriate to refer to the benefit as an ownership-specific advantage and internalization as the modality by which this advantage is realized.

Third, I acknowledge that the eclectic paradigm, as originally conceived, is uncomfortable in dealing with the dynamics of international production. However, I would argue that it can help to explain why an industry or country's international investment profile may be different at two points in time. To link the two periods one needs to introduce changes in the exogenous or endogenous variables, including strategy, and how these in turn affect the OLI configuration.[15] I have illustrated from the investment development cycle how this may be done at a macro-level (which essentially evens out differences in strategic behaviour). At an industry or micro-level, only a detailed examination of the profile of individual firms can resolve the problem. The reclassification of firms into strategic groups (McGee and Thomas, 1986) is helping to show us that types of strategic behaviour are not an idiosyncratic variable but can be related to certain characteristics of firms (or groups of firms).

Fourth, I have endeavoured to explain differences between my approach and that of Kiyoshi Kojima, and I hope I have made it clear that the main difference between us is in emphasis and perspective rather than reasoning.

Fifth, I have suggested that there are certain types of investment classified as foreign direct investment which the eclectic paradigm apparently cannot explain. It may, however, be that at least some of these investments do not have the character or intent of a direct investment, and should be more appropriately thought of as portfolio investments.

Finally, I wish to stress that the eclectic paradigm is not an explanation of international production on the same level as (for example) the product cycle or appropriability theories. Its main advantage is that it offers a general framework for theorizing about all kinds of international economic involvement, including trade in goods and intermediate products. It main drawback, which applies no less to any generalized theory of trade, is that, because the motives in foreign production are so different, no one model can hope to explain equally well each and every kind of multinational activity.

This is why in the mid-1980s we began to refer to the eclectic *paradigm* rather than eclectic *theory* of international production. At the same time each of the specific theories is consistent with the tenets of the paradigm, and to this extent both the paradigms and the theories are necessary for a complete and operational explanation of all forms of foreign production by firms and countries.

NOTES

1 As explored by Caves (1980) by use of the 'separability' theory explaining why firms should wish to control separate, but related, value-added activities.
2 But see chapter 7 by E. Graham in this volume. Also, in a recent paper

(Dunning, 1990b), I have criticized both the internalization theory and the eclectic paradigm for failing to take on board the dynamics of international production.

3   It is these latter which are solely the result of the internalization of markets, which the internalization economists assert may be the only advantages which a foreign investor may have over a local firm. I agree, but, *de facto*, advantages of the first kind are likely to be no less important in explaining the initial act of foreign investment.

4   Which indeed is exactly what has transpired. For an examination of the impact of European economic integration on transatlantic production see Dunning (1990a).

5   See especially Dunning (1988b: chapter 4).

6   The only English source of Lundgren's thoughts on this matter is his comment on my paper for the 1976 Nobel Symposium in Ohlin *et al*. Birgitta Swedenborg took up and extended the theme in her excellent study on Swedish MNEs (1979).

7   For an explanation of the difference between a paradigm and a theory see, e.g. Dunning 1988a, chapters 1 and 2.

8   If there is no synergy between a firm's existing assets and those it acquires it is difficult to see how this can be thought of as a direct investment, although we readily admit there are such investments, which are classified in this way. See also pp. 131–2 above.

9   A net outward direct investment is one where the value of the stock of outward direct investment (or the flow of outward investment over a given period of time) exceeds the value of the stock of inward direct investment (or the flow of inward investment over a given period of time).

10 For a fuller exposition see Dunning (1988a).

11 It is worth noting that such advantages may stem from the forces of monopoly or of (dynamic) competition. Most references to the competitive advantages of firms embrace both types of advantage, and it is in this sense we use ownership advantages as well.

12 For example, by their competitors capturing markets which might otherwise be theirs.

13 But see Buckley and Casson (1985: chapter 5). Also, as early as 1975 Peter Buckley and I introduced the notion of the investment development cycle at a conference of the UK chapter of the Academy of International Business, in Manchester.

14 The fact that the company is prepared to pay a higher price for a set of assets than another firm presumably indicates that it perceives itself as better able to make use of the acquisition (an ownership advantage in its own right) than its competitors.

15 In this respect see some interesting work by John Cantwell (1989) and Paz Tolentino (1990) on the interaction between the technological capacity of a country and the OLI configuration affecting both its own and foreign-based firms. See also John Cantwell's contribution to this volume, chapter 2.

REFERENCES

Aliber, R.Z. (1970) 'A theory of foreign direct investment', in C.P. Kindleberger (ed.) *The International Corporation: a Symposium*, Cambridge, Mass: MIT Press.
—— (1971) 'The multinational enterprise in a multiple currency world', in J.H.

Dunning (ed.) *The Multinational Enterprise*, London: Allen & Unwin.

Bain, J. (1956) *Barriers to new Competition*, Cambridge, Mass.: Harvard University Press.

Baumann, H. (1975) 'Merger theory, property rights and the pattern of US direct investment in Canada', *Weltwirtschaftliches Archiv* III, 4: 676–98.

Buckley, P.J., and Casson, M.C. (1976) *The Future of the Multinational Enterprise*, London: Macmillan.

—— (1985) *The Economic Theory of the Multinational Enterprise: Selected Papers*, London: Macmillan.

Bye, M. (1958) 'Self-financed multi-territorial units and their time horizon', *International Economic Papers* 8: 147–78.

Cantwell, J. (1989) *Technological Innovation and Multinational Corporations*, Oxford: Blackwell.

Casson, M.C., ed. (1990) *The Multinational Enterprise*, London: Edward Arnold.

Caves, R.E. (1971) 'International corporations: the industrial economics of foreign investment', *Economica* 38: 1–27.

—— (1974a) 'Causes of direct foreign investment: foreign firms' share in Canadian and United Kingdom manufacturing industries', *Review of Economics and Statistics* 56: 272–93.

—— (1974b) 'Multinational firms, competition and productivity in host country markets', *Economica* 41: 176–93.

—— (1980) 'Investment and location policies of multinational companies', *Schweiz Zeitschrift für Volkswirtschaft und Statisik* 116: 321–7.

Clegg, L.J. (1987) *Multinational Enterprises and World Competition*, London: Macmillan.

Coase, R.H. (1937) 'The nature of the firm', *Economica* (New Series) 4: 386–405.

Dunning, J.H. (1958) *American Investment in British Manufacturing Industry*, London: Allen & Unwin (reprinted by Arno Press, New York, 1976).

—— (1972) 'The Location of International Firms in an Enlarged EEC: an Exploratory Paper', Manchester: Manchester Statistical Society.

—— (1973) 'The determinants of international production', *Oxford Economic Papers* 25: 289–336.

—— (1981) *International Production and the Multinational Enterprise*, London: Allen & Unwin.

—— (1988a) *Explaining International Production*, London: Unwin Hyman.

—— (1988b) *Multinationals, Technology and Competitiveness*, London: Unwin Hyman.

—— (1988c) 'The eclectic paradigm of international production: a restatement and some possible extensions', *Journal of International Business Studies* 19: 1–31.

—— (1989) 'Gloablization of Firms and the Competitiveness of Countries: Some Implications for the Theory of International Production', paper presented to Crafoord Symposium, Lund, Sweden, November.

—— (1990a) *The European Economic Community and Transatlantic Production: the Record Assessed*, University of Reading Discussion Papers in International Investment and Business Studies, Series B, No. 136.

—— (1990b) 'The Dynamics of International Production: Country and Firm-specific Characteristics', *Scandinavian Journal of Management* (forthcoming).

Frankel, M. (1955) 'Anglo-American productivity differences – their magnitude and some causes', *American Economic Review* 45: 94–112.

Hirsch, S. (1967) *The Location of Industry and International Competitiveness*,

Oxford: Oxford University Press.

Horst, T. (1972a) 'Firm and industry determinants of the decision to invest abroad: an empirical study', *Review of Economics and Statistics* 54: 258–66.

—— (1972b) 'The industrial composition of US exports and subsidiary sales to the Canadian market', *American Economic Review* 62: 37–45.

Hufbauer, G.C. (1965) *Synthetic Materials and the Theory of International Trade*, London: Duckworth.

Hymer, S. (1960) 'The International Operations of National Firms: a Study of Direct Investment', Ph.D. thesis, Massachusetts Institute of Technology, published by MIT Press in 1976.

—— (1968) 'La grande firme multinationale', *Revue Economique* 19: 949–73.

Kindleberger, C.P. (1969) *American Business Abroad*, New Haven, Conn.: Yale University Press.

Knickerbocker, F.T. (1973) *Oligopolistic Reaction and the Multinational Enterprise*, Cambridge, Mass.: Harvard University Press.

Kogut, B. (1983) 'Foreign direct investment as a sequential process', in C.P. Kindleberger and D. Audretsch (eds.) *The Multinational Corporation in the 1980s*, Cambridge, Mass.: MIT Press.

—— (1985) 'Designing global strategies: profiting from operational flexibility', *Sloan Management Review*, fall, 27–37.

Kojima, K. (1978) *Direct Foreign Investment: a Japanese Model of Multinational Business Operations*, London: Croom Helm.

—— (1982) 'Macroeconomic versus international business approaches to foreign direct investment', *Hitotsubashi Journal of Economics* 23: 1–19.

McGee, J., and Thomas, H. (1986) 'Strategic groups: theory, research and taxonomy', *Strategic Management Journal* 7: 141–60.

McManus, J.C. (1972) 'The theory of the multinational firm', in G. Paquet (ed.) *The Multinational Firm and the Nation State*, Don Mills, Ont.: Collier-Macmillan.

Ozawa, T. (1989) 'Japan's Strategic Investment Policy towards Developing Countries: from the *ad hoc* to a new Comprehensive Approach', mimeo.

Rostas, L. (1948) *Comparative Productivity in British and American Industry*, Cambridge: Cambridge University Press.

Rugman, A.M. (1980) 'Internalization theory and corporate international finance', *California Management Review* XIII: 73–9.

—— (1986) 'New theories of multinational enterprises: an assessment of internationalization theory', *Bulletin of Economic Research* 38: 101–18.

Swedenborg, B. (1979) *The Multinational Operations of Swedish Firms: an Analysis of Determinants and Effects*, Stockholm: Almquist & Wiksell.

Tolentino, P.E. (1990) *The Internationalization of Philippine Firms*, London: Routledge.

Vernon, R. (1966) 'International investment and international trade in the product cycle', *Quarterly Journal of Economics* 80: 90–207.

—— (1974) 'The location of economic activity', in J.H. Dunning (ed.) *Economic Analysis and the Multinational Enterprise*, London: Allen & Unwin.

—— (1979) 'The product cycle hypothesis in a new international environment', *Oxford Bulletin of Economics and Statistics* 41: 255–67.

—— (1983) 'Organizational and institutional responses to international risk', in R.J. Herring (ed.) *Managing International Risk*, Cambridge: Cambridge University Press.

6 Multinational enterprise as strategic choice: some transaction cost perspectives

Neil M. Kay

The role of transaction costs in the analysis of multinational enterprise has now become a major focus of economic analysis and research; see, for instance, the previous two chapters. Its development as a major explanatory device in this area has been rapid and its influence is now such that it represents the dominant theme in many accounts of multinational behaviour.

However, transaction cost economics is subject to many interpretations, and there is no single route in this area. This is frequently obscured; for example, Oliver Williamson (1986: 174–91) identifies 'the' transaction cost approach with his specific variant, the 'markets and hierarchies' approach. Such territorial imperatives are not legitimate and it is important to recognize that transaction cost theorizing encompasses all perspectives that involve the costs of co-ordinating the economic system that Coase talked of in his seminal 1937 article.

In this chapter we shall develop a simple resource-based or supply-side analysis to set the context for some transaction cost explanations of corporate strategies, including foreign direct investment in multinational enterprise and joint venture activity. Multinational enterprise is analysed in terms of the opportunity cost of other strategies not pursued, and a lexical ordering of strategies is a natural implication of this resource-based analysis.

The four major strategies analysed are specialization, diversification, multinational enterprise and joint venture. Joint venture is taken here to mean co-operative agreement in which a separate unit is set up by two or more parents and a degree of independence in decision-making is awarded to the child (though with continuing parental involvement which may include the provision of assets such as managerial resources). The selection and restriction of strategic analysis to these types may appear strange at first sight, especially in choosing only joint venture as a collaborative strategy. After all, why not also include licensing, subcontracting and know-how agreements as examples of co-operative strategies? There are two main reasons for selecting joint ventures only. First, joint venture involves internalization and co-operation over decision-making resources, not just physical or informational exchanges. For example, in licensing or sub-contracting, information or components to be exchanged may be specified in advance; joint ventures typically leave such decisions to be made in the future, so co-operating over strategy formulation itself as well as outcomes. Second, each of these strategies has implications for internal organization and corporate strategy/structure relationships. By way of contrast, licensing and subcontracting may leave these issues relatively unaffected.

In the first section we shall utilize a stylized case of corporate growth to develop our resource-based transactional approach. In the next two sections we shall consider the relevance of Williamson's 'markets and hierarchies' approach to the analysis of corporate strategy and structure in general, and, second, to analysis of multinational enterprise in particular. The role of transaction costs in influencing the incidence and form of joint venture activity is discussed with particular reference to the work of Buckley and Casson. The concluding section argues that transaction cost is useful for the analysis of multinational enterprise and joint venture activity, but that there are problems with certain interpretations, in particular the 'markets and hierarchies' approach.

A STYLIZED CASE OF CORPORATE GROWTH

Suppose we have a small, specialized manufacturing firm, Manfac. Manfac's managers have a growth objective and have to choose between specialization and diversification strategies to achieve this objective. Diversification, by definition, has fewer common resources in the form of common marketing, distribution, technology and/or production than does a specialized strategy. Specialization offers scale economies, diversification more limited synergies or scope economies. Supply-side and opportunity cost considerations favour specialization over diversification, in Manfac's view, because of the richer set of shared resources and potential economies specialization offers, *ceteris paribus*.

So what would encourage Manfac's managers to diversify? It would require the existence of blocks or barriers inhibiting the ability of Manfac to exploit specialization economies. For example, product obsolescence, market saturation, anti-trust action (real or potential) may all make the firm itself more vulnerable to failure by tying the firm into a limited set of market and technological links.[1] Thus the supply-side 'tug' towards specialization may have to be tempered by demand-side 'shove' factors towards diversification;[2] if demand is limited, declining or inelastic, diversification may be encouraged. Nevertheless, the typically significant opportunity costs of specialization associated with diversification should ensure that the supply-side 'tug' will encourage the firm to concentrate and specialize on core skills so far as possible, subject to satisfying the demand-side 'shove' factors.[3]

Manfac has therefore been 'shoved' into diversification in pursuit of its growth objective. Suppose now that, in pursuing further growth, Manfac has to choose between domestic expansion or going multinational and so servicing overseas markets by adding significant value through operations in host-country subsidiaries. Although Manfac has been forced to diversify because of demand-side limitations, the supply-side 'tug' has meant that it has diversified around core skills, as far as possible. Multinationalism offers only limited shared resources between home and host-country operations; marketing and distribution resources have to be replicated in the host country, separate production facilities have been set up and there are a whole set of country-specific skills and resources relating to the economy, law, social and cultural relations, and even language that may have to be duplicated. By way of contrast, domestic diversification around core skills could exploit a variety of marketing, distribution, technology and production-level economies, as well as benefiting from country-specific economies such as a common language as well as the shared social and economic context. The only significant economies multinationalism can offer are typically informational in character, such as technological or marketing knowledge. This helps to explain why so many multinationals are R&D or marketing-intensive (e.g. IBM and Unilever respectively). However, domestic diversification could exploit many of these economies as well as additional human and physical economies due to shared resources in marketing, production and country level of operations. Thus supply-side and opportunity cost considerations would tend to favour diversification over multinationalism in Manfac's view because of the richer set of shared resources and potential economies specialization offers, *ceteris paribus*.[4] (For similar reasons, if Manfac is going to service overseas markets, it would prefer to do so by exporting rather than going multinational. At least exporting allows the consolidation of technological and production activities that multinationalism duplicates. However, the host trading bloc has brought to bear a variety of anti-dumping laws, local content requirements and rules of origin to frustrate that strategy.)

So what would encourage Manfac's managers to go multinational? Again, it would imply the existence of blocks or barriers inhibiting the ability of Manfac to exploit economies of scale and scope from domestic growth. On the supply side, the thinness of resource links across multinational operations means that it would not be difficult for Manfac to contrive a domestic diversification strategy that would beat multinationalism on the basis of potential economies alone. As was the case with the specialization/diversification choice, the answer lies again in terms of problems or inhibitors on the demand side. For example, Manfac's managers have observed an aluminium ski manufacturer diversifying into aluminium tennis rackets, exploiting market and technological synergies in the process. They have observed the same manufacturer further diversifying into aluminium cricket bats, and baseball bats, failing miserably in the process to make an impact on those traditional markets. There was no problem on the supply side as far as the second diversification move was concerned, since it provided similar market and technological economies to the first. The problems lay in the demand-side limitations of diversification. For Manfac, as for the aluminium sports goods manufacturer, demand-side limitations on domestic diversification means that growth through the more costly multinational option may be forced on to the corporate agenda.[5]

Manfac is now diversified and multinational. Further growth opportunities related to core skills can be expected through full-scale internalization (diversification or multinational expansion), or through joint venture. Considered at the level of individual ventures, supply-side considerations unambiguously favour full-scale internalization. First, joint ventures typically involve significant bargaining costs in negotiating and policing agreements. Second, they involve a dual system of parental control of the child, with duplication of monitoring effect and potential for confusion and conflict in directing the venture. Third, intellectual property and other intangible assets may be appropriated by partners taking advantage of the degree of intimacy such collaboration involves. This latter type of loss may be regarded as a redistribution of gains rather than a straightforward deadweight loss, as in the first two cases. However, incorporating allowances for 'leaky' intangible assets is notoriously difficult to achieve in contracts, and so all three sources of costs may discourage joint ventures.

So what would encourage Manfac to pursue joint ventures? More specifically, for a given venture opportunity, why should Manfac choose the typically more expensive joint venture solution rather than one of the simpler single-ownership alternatives that could be pursued through internal growth or acquisition? At first sight this is puzzling, even paradoxical. If we are comparing alternative modes of organizing a given venture opportunity, then we have identical demand-side characteristics, irrespective of organizational mode (unless we wish to invoke quality effects on performance contingent on choice of organizational mode),[6] while joint venture is a most costly organization form. In those circumstances, why should anyone ever joint-venture? Obviously demand-side considerations cannot drive the choice of strategy, as in diversification or multinationalization, if we are considering a *given* venture opportunity. However, at a deeper level, similar considerations still apply to the choice of strategy. Supply-side influences (which in this case relate to the cost of organizing the venture) generally favour full internalization of venture opportunities through diversification or multinational expansion rather than in the form of joint ventures. Joint ventures will be chosen only when blocks or barriers to single-ownership solutions impede the adoption of diversification or multinational strategies.

What kind of blocks or barriers are likely to impede adoption of the multinational option? One obvious impediment is governmental restrictions on multinational expansion, such as some Third World requirements to the effect that a local partner is a prerequisite of market access. Alternatively small privately owned entrepreneurial firms may not be prepared to sacrifice sovereignty, in which case joint venture may be the only realistic option; if the firm is not for sale, joint venture may be the only strategic alternative on offer. Further, even though joint venture may be the most expensive form of organization at local divisional level, it may be the only practical internalization solution because of externality effects beyond divisional level. We illustrate this in Fig. 6.1. Manfac and Otfac are two large diversified firms both operating five divisions. The respective firms exploit a choice of marketing and distribution (*M*) and technological (*T*) links between divisions. A venture possibility (*V*) could exploit the marketing resources of Manfac's A division and the technological skills of Otfac's B division. Why not merge the two divisions A and B to exploit V?

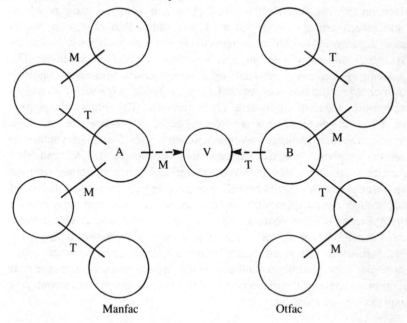

Manfac   Otfac

Figure 6.1

If Manfac and Otfac merged to exploit V, we would have a considerably enlarged and complex bureaucracy for the sake of a limited and localized venture; a sledgehammer to crack a nut (Kay *et al.*, 1988).[7] If A was sold to Otfac or B sold to Manfac, there would be the potential opportunity costs of marketing or technological economies that could have been exploited with other divisions if they had stayed in their original homes. Therefore although joint venture may be *locally* the most expensive option for participating divisions, it may be adopted if the alternative method of single-ownership internalization involves costly system-wide effects such as the above. Consequently, joint venture may evolve naturally as the last-resort internalization strategy where resources have to be integrated between large diversified firms. Processes of growth by diversification may 'shove' the firm towards joint venture as a major strategic option.

Focusing on the supply side therefore suggests a natural lexical ordering of strategies in the direction: specialization → diversification → multinationalism → joint ventures (or specialization → diversification → joint venture if international operations are excluded). The stylized case described above is sympathetic to growth processes and strategic choices described by Penrose (1959) and Marris (1964),[8] and emphasizes the role of exploitable core skills in determining the form and content of strategy. The decision process described is itself consistent with the early problemistic search process developed by Cyert and March (1963), in which satisficing agents search for progressively more distant (costly) solutions as nearer and more familiar solutions fail to satisfy aspirations. The ordering incorporates implicit opportunity costs; strategies 'shoved' further down the line are pursued at the potential expense of strategies with more focused supply-side characteristics. This point may appear in retrospect obvious but it is often neglected in practice; for example, it is common to compare co-operative strategies like joint venture to non-cooperative competitive strategies that would duplicate R&D and other activities. In such cases it is easy to rationalize the existence of joint ventures as strategies that internalize control, impede free-riders and avoid duplication. Such explanations are misleading and do not properly explain the existence of joint ventures – indeed, they force such awkward questions as why they have not appeared in greater proliferation if they have such attractive efficiency characteristics. Lexical ordering helps place strategies in proper context and avoid such failures of analysis. In the next section we consider the implications of this perspective for transaction cost explanations of the firm.

TRANSACTION COSTS, MARKETS AND HIERARCHIES, AND THE THEORY OF THE FIRM

It is essential to distinguish between transaction costs in general and specific theoretical developments utilizing transaction cost reasoning such as Williamson's 'markets and hierarchies' approach. It is misleading to talk of 'the' transaction cost approach when there are in fact a number of variants of transaction cost reasoning in this area. Nevertheless, Williamson's approach is often taken as delineating the basic paradigm of transaction cost economics and so we shall concentrate on the applicability of this approach to corporate strategies.

Before we do so, however, it should be noted that the lexical ordering of strategies described in the previous section depends on implicit transaction costs for its existence. If two similar firms could co-ordinate economies in marketing, R&D and production through a system of market contracts at zero cost, there would be no supply-side 'tug' towards incorporation of shared core skills within one firm. Similar considerations apply to the diversification/multinational and multinational/joint venture decisions. If there are no cost problems of search, negotiation, policing and appropriability, then a nexus of firms linked by networks of market contracts could co-ordinate the exploitation of economies through resource sharing at zero cost. In fact it is the pervasiveness of transaction costs that provides the glue binding the firm to its specialized core skills. Remove transaction costs and there is no reason why the components of the firm should stick together.

These issues are discussed at greater length in Kay (1982, 1984). For our purposes it is sufficient to acknowledge the transactional underpinnings of the resource-based lexical ordering above. Consequently, it would seem natural to draw upon Williamson's 'markets and hierarchies' approach to deepen our analysis of the evolution of the corporation and build on the supply-side picture developed above.

Unfortunately there are major problems in doing so. In this connection it is useful to consider Williamson's most recent synthesis and clarification of his version of transaction cost economics (1985). In his view, bounded rationality (cognitive and language limits on 'individuals'' ability to process and act on information) asset specificity (specialization of assets with respect to use or user) and opportunism (self-interest seeking with guile) are central issues influencing transaction costs.

Williamson argues that if any of these three conditions are not met in a given transactional situation, then the market mechanism can relocate resources effectively. If *bounded rationality* is not a problem and all relevant information can be processed and acted on, all further contingencies may be anticipated and incorporated in market contracts. If *asset specificity* does not exist, and substitutes are easily found, mistakes can be swiftly rectified and opportunism does not pose irrevocable problems. If *opportunism* does not exist, unexpected developments and problems can be easily resolved if parties operate on the basis of equity and fairness (1985: 30–2). Williamson applies his framework to the evolution of both strategies (such as vertical integration, conglomerateness and multinational enterprise) and structures (notably the evolution of the multidivision or M-form corporation).

Multinational enterprise may be characterized as involving a strategic decision to adopt a hierarchical structure rather than a market solution, and indeed this is how Williamson regards it. Consequently, analysis of his treatment of multinational enterprise should properly consider first of all his views on how strategies and structures evolve, the role of decision-making, and the nature of transaction in influencing choice of form of economic organization. Discussion of these issues should help illuminate Williamson's analysis of the multinational. Accordingly we shall first of all consider Williamson's explanation for the evolution of the conglomerate strategy.

Strategies, structures and conglomerates

According to Williamson, the conglomerate exists because of failures in the external capital market. First, internalization of the capital market may improve the quality and quantity of information available to decision-makers and facilitate direct monitoring and control. Second, divisionalization may facilitate the operation of profit centres organized around decision units. These characteristics help generate the efficiency gains that the M-form provides in Williamson's analysis.

The curious thing about this explanation is that, while it may help to explain why markets are internalized, it in no way helps to explain why a conglomerate strategy should be adopted over a more specialized strategy. In principle, there is nothing to stop the firm exploiting internalization, using a specialized strategy built around similar product markets, whether through internal growth or acquisition. Indeed, our earlier analysis suggests that such a strategy could exploit additional efficiency gains closed off to the conglomerate, in so far as the existence of internal corporate umpires may facilitate internal resource-sharing and exploitation of economies of scale and scope. The true opportunity cost of conglomerateness is represented by specialization, not the external capital market as in Williamson's analysis.[9]

So what about a theory of *related* diversification in Williamson's framework, if the explanation for unrelated diversification turns out to be faulty? There is no consideration of such strategies in Williamson (1975,

1985, 1986), which appears curious at first sight. After all, the conglomerate is a very rare strategy, as Rumelt (1974) confirms; most diversification exploits some marketing , technology or production core skills and associated economies of scope.

In fact Williamson cannot develop a theory of related diversification. By definition, related diversification internalizes economies resulting from *shared* assets. Williamson's explanation of internalization totally depends on asset specificity, i.e. assets *specialized* in use or user. Williamson's own restrictions on reasons for the choice of hierarchy over market means his theory cannot be extended to related diversification – by definition. If the theory is applicable at all, it can be applicable only to the limit case of the single-product firm and its intermediate product markets.

However, there are further difficulties with Williamson's approach. Not only is the explanation of corporate diversification unsatisfactory, so also is his explanation of how the internal organization evolved to deal with the resulting problem of scale and diversity. According to Williamson, the adoption of an M-form structure and associated decision-making apparatus mitigates control loss problems, since most decisions can be taken at a lower level. Top management are freed to concentrate on strategy, while divisional profit centres facilitate the creation of an internal capital market.

These arguments are reasonable – indeed, widely accepted. The problem is Williamson's explanation of how the M-form structure evolved. The M form organizes activities by quasi-autonomous operating divisions and by major strategic decisions organized and co-ordinated at headquarters. According to Williamson, in the functionally specialized or U-form structure:

> the ability of the management to handle the volume and complexity of the demands placed upon it became strained and even collapsed . . . the U-form structure laboured under a communication overload while the pursuit of subgoals by the functional parts (sales, engineering, production) was partly a manifestation of opportunism.
>
> (1985: 280–1)

> Faced with the need to retrench or to develop a new set of internal contracting relationships, organisational innovators devised the M-form structure.
>
> (1985: 295)

> Eventually the U-form structure defeats itself and results in the M-form structure to solve these problems.
>
> (1971: 350)

On the surface such a theory and description of structural evolution appears plausible. In fact it is highly problematic. Williamson sees this process of M-form development as an evolutionary one, operating according to natural selection criteria (1985: 296), consistent with the role of the competitive process in weeding out inferior forms over the long run through natural selection (1985: 22–3, including footnote).

In fact Williamson's description of the evolutionary process has the effects the wrong way round if he wishes to invoke natural selection. In natural selection it is the appearance of the superior form which causes problems in the inferior form, not problems in the inferior form stimulating the adoption of a superior form. Natural selection selects from *available* forms not the set of all existing and potential forms. In natural selection, the form does not 'defeat itself', as Williamson suggests above – it is competition from other forms that defeats it. In natural selection the relatively efficient win; if the U form has over-extended itself and run into problems of diseconomies of scale, a natural selection interpretation would identify limits to the size of firm, with smaller, more specialized firms competing success-fully against the larger ones, not organizational innovation.

If Williamson's interpretation of competitive processes is unsatisfactory, so also is the role of decision-making in his theory. Williamson's transaction cost framework is virtually alone in the modern theory of the firm in having no explicit decision-making criteria. As Elster (1983) points out, theories of intentional explanation tend to be based on either optimizing or satis-ficing criteria, as is typically observed with other theories of firms, old and new. Williamson does not utilize any explicit criteria, and indeed it is difficult to see which he could use. Satisficing is hardly consistent with his claims that the most efficient form of organization will win in the end, while optimizing is not consistent with the assumption of bounded rationality.[10]

It is also worth noting that the concept of 'transaction' itself is not defined in Williamson (1975, 1985), and when it is defined in Williamson (1986) it is in two parts that are not necessarily mutually consistent:

> Each feasible mode of conducting relations between technologically separate entities can be examined with respect to the . . . costs . . . [of] the [explicit or implicit] contract that joins them. A transaction may thus be said to occur when a good or service is transferred across a technologically-separable interface.
>
> (1986: 139)

Transaction is thus both the process of exchange and physical transfer across separable interfaces. Pick up a pen and stick it behind your ear. Is that a transaction? Yes, in the physical transfer sense, no in the exchange sense. The problem is that non-exchange-based transactions grossly outnumber exchange-based transactions. Exchange, whether explicit or implicit, is a very rare form of transaction, as any casual census of types of decisions involved in specific economic activities reveals. This distortion is reflected in the general treatment of markets and hierarchies, which is not actually about markets v. hierarchies in general, but rather about internal markets versus external markets. For example, Williamson (1975) contrasts internal intermediate products, internal labour markets and internal capital markets with their external counterparts. However, where hierarchy is analysed it is essentially in terms of hierarchy v. hierarchy (U form v. M form), not hierarchy v. market. Consistent with the limited exchange-based definition of transaction, Williamson's approach is essentially a comparative analysis of market exchange, both internal and external. Broader considerations of transaction and hierarchy are neglected, or sealed off from the exchange-based analysis, as in the self-contained analysis of U-form and M-form structures.

Thus the 'markets and hierarchies' approach has to be limited to the single-product case by definition, and is extremely problematic in its treatment of decision, transaction and hierarchy. In the next section we shall consider the implications for Williamson's explanation of the existence of multinational enterprise.

MARKETS, HIERARCHIES AND MULTINATIONAL ENTERPRISE

Williamson (1985) argues that his version of transaction cost economics helps account for the existence of the multinational; in his brief explanation (pp. 290–4) for the existence of the multinational Williamson again relies on asset specificity as the critical determinant.

> A more harmonious and efficient exchange relation . . . predictably results from the substitution of an internal government relation for bilateral trading under those recurrent trading circumstances where assets, of which complex technology transfer is an example, have a highly specific character.
>
> (1985: 294)

Thus asset specificity again leads to the internalization decision, in this case to go multinational and put corporate boundaries around trading relations. Unfortunately Williamson's explanation obscures the fact that it is *non*-specificity of assets that is typically cited as a major transactional issue in cross-frontier economic activity. As Casson (1987: 29) points out, because knowledge has the characteristics of a public good the firm with privileged knowledge tends to become multinational.

Public goods are an extreme form of asset non-specificity in which not only is the good not specialized by use or user, there are major property right problems in trying to ensure that such specialized use or user actually obtains in practice. Appropriability and free-rider problems attend the lack of asset specificity associated with intangible goods such as technology transfer, the reverse of the transactional problems of dependence and specialized use identified by Williamson as encouraging the adoption of multinational enterprise.[11]

As Casson points out (1987: 41), Williamson appears unaware of earlier transaction cost reasoning in this area. However, it could be argued strongly that recognition of this literature leads to a rejection of the 'markets and hierarchies' interpretation of the multinational enterprise as a consequence of asset specificity. In addition, it leads to the same limited interpretation of hierarchy discussed in the previous section. For example, Rugman (1981) explicitly builds on Williamson's 'markets and hierarchies' approach as a framework for analysing the existence of multinationals. Rugman defines internalization as the process of making a market within a firm in which:

> internal prices (or transfer prices) of the firm lubricate the organisation and permit the internal market to function as efficiently as a potential (but unrealised) regular market.

> (1981: 28)

> Resource allocation processes that are internalised are those carried out in a centralised manner. Williamson's book highlights the complexities that result when internal decisions of the firm are centralised. Thus the theory of internalisation is also a theory of centralisation in decision making.

> (1981: 29-30

The problem with Rugman's interpretation of internalized markets as an explanation of multinational enterprise is that it is inconsistent in much the same way that Williamson's definition of transaction is inconsistent. Internalization is defined as both the creation of an internal market and centralized decision-making in Rugman's analysis. However, just as transaction need not involve exchange processes, so internalization need not involve transfer prices.[12] Centralized decision-making may involve non-exchange decision processes, whether they are autonomous (the corporate equivalent of sticking your pen behind your ear) or *fiat* (telling someone else to stick a pen behind your ear). As Coase pointed out in his early statement of transaction costs and the nature of the firm, 'if a workman moves from department Y to department X, he does not go because of a change in relative prices but because he is ordered to do so' (1937: 387). *Fiat* is more general than exchange. Transfer pricing (the corporate equivalent of paying someone to stick a pen in your ear) is a very rare event in the spectrum of internalized decision processes, and indeed may not necessarily be involved in the internalization at all. By definition transfer pricing is associated with vertical multinational strategy, and so is not applicable to the more common strategy of horizontal multinational expansion.[13] As Dunning and Norman (1985) point out, the gains from such horizontal strategies are typically those of protection of proprietary rights and the monitoring of quality control. Rugman's analysis is therefore limited to single-product vertical relations, just as is Williamson's, and also involves a very limited perspective on the internalized decision processes even in that context.

In the next section we shall take the analysis a step further, and consider transaction cost perspectives on the last stage of corporate evolution described earlier, joint ventures, with specific reference to international joint ventures.

TRANSACTION COSTS AND JOINT VENTURES

The evolution of collaborative strategies like joint ventures has focused attention on why co-operative activity may take place between firms. Williamson is quite clear on the pervasive nature of the concept of opportunism, even in the case of Japan:

> The hazards of trading are less severe in Japan than in the United States because of cultural and institutional checks on opportunism . . . the same principles that inform make or buy decisions in the United States and in other Western countries also apply in Japan.
>
> (1985: 122)

In fact Williamson is forced to argue that individuals are intrinsically opportunistic, in Japan as in the US. Since he has already assumed that the absence of opportunism would ensure there were no serious transactional problems, it is essential in his perspective to retain the individualistic, self-interested, opportunistic model of human behaviour, even for a society which has been widely described as valuing group loyalty, co-operation and con-ciliation as central norms. Such values operate only as constraints, in Williamson's view, not as objectives and targets in their own right.

Interestingly, other writers on joint ventures have argued that a central role may be played by trust and goodwill even in Western joint ventures. Casson (1987: 1134) suggests joint ventures may operate under a co-operative 'mystique'. In such circumstances, intelligent parents encourage loyalty to the joint venture itself, and the avoidance of conflict may not pose severe problems. Buckley (1988) also argues that forbearance (from cheating) can help build up trust and effective co-operation in joint ventures.

We therefore have the interesting contrast between Williamson's argu-ment that Japanese transactions are characterized by the 'Western' characteristics of opportunism and self-interest (albeit heavily constrained by society and constitution) and Casson and Buckley's argument that joint venture agreements in general may be infused with 'Japanese' characteristics of loyalty, co-operation, self-denial and goodwill. They may all be right, but if they are it is a curious reversal of the conventional wisdom.

My own feeling is the conventional wisdom gets it more nearly right in the cases implied above than do the respective authors. There is a whole variety of Japanese phenomena that are easier to understand and explain if it is perceived that there is a Japanese emphasis on 'group rather than individual, on co-operation and conciliation aimed at harmony, on national rather than personal welfare' (Patrick and Rosovsky, 1976: 53). Overlapping systems of ownership and control, lifetime employment, 'just in time' and heavy reliance on subcontracting are all examples of Japanese industry characteristics that make sense if Patrick and Rosovsky's perspective is adopted rather than Williamson's picture of the potentially self-interested opportunistic trader limited by social and institutional constraints.[14]

At the same time, it may be a mistake to connect the existence of collaborative arrangements between Western firms and between Western and Japanese firms with the existence of overriding tendencies towards trust, loyalty and honesty between partners. The apparent suspension of the competitive ethic in Western economies and societies in these cases is something that should be viewed with suspicion, and an individualistic explanation would generally seem to be both simpler and more reasonable as a first approximation in these cases.

Is it possible to develop explanations of joint venture behaviour without having recourse to 'Japanese' qualities as a prop? In general, yes, as we have done in the earlier sections. If two escaped prisoners are sitting in a bus handcuffed together they may co-operate to hide their manacles – not because of instinctive or even learnt qualities of loyalty and trust, but because there is no reasonable alternative. Similarly joint venture may be pursued as a strategy even in cases where partners are opportunistic, self-interested, deceitful and downright untrustworthy – if there is no reasonable alternative. Examples of circumstances leading to the adoption of joint venture as a device of last resort owing to high levels of transaction costs were discussed earlier. These include government forcing partnership for local access, the independence of the smaller partner being non-negotiable, and co-operation at divisional level between large, diversified firms.

In Kay, *et al.* (1987) the implications of this interpretation for multinational enterprise and joint ventures are explored further. The article helps explain the comparatively recent proliferation of joint ventures, and their relative scarcity in earlier years. Merger was the obvious means by which economies and complementarities could be internalized in areas with small, specialized firms and atomistic industry structures, while joint venture may be forced on firms as a last-resort strategy following processes of growth and diversification. To the extent that scale and diversity are precursors of the pursuit of joint venture as last-resort strategy their recent evolution becomes comprehensible, even inevitable. Other implications for analysis of joint ventures also follow from this perspective. In Kay (1989) it is argued that the Cecchini report's[15] predictions of the likely effects of 1992 on cross-frontier joint ventures are likely to be misplaced. Cecchini *et al.* (1988: 88) argue that the harmonization of company law and the elimination of other barriers to co-operation that 1992 will achieve will increase as a direct consequence of 1992: 'international co-operative link-ups between EC partner firms have up to now proved less frequent than those with a non-EC participant. The scope for correcting this balance is considerable once the barriers came down'.

In fact the direct effect of 1992 on multinational joint ventures is likely to be the opposite. The European Commission's own research found that a great deal of the motivation for existing collaborative activity derives from non-tariff barriers to trade and the need to involve a local partner for market access. It is consistent with other studies that found that, the more 'difficult' the market, the greater the propensity to adopt joint ventures.[16] Barriers to trade were *associated* with joint ventures; they were not impediments to their formation, as the Cecchini report suggested.

A direct effect of 1992 will be to give firms unilateral access to other EC markets as processes of harmonization and mutual recognition remove impediments to trade. The 'last resort' of multinational joint venture may not be necessary. Indeed, the effects of completing the internal market may be to erect further stategic barriers to joint venture activity; if appropriability problems are severe in certain sectors, such as the high-technology industries, low or non-existent trade fences between partners may make them more vulnerable to subsequent threats from former partners. Even if such threats are more imaginary than real, they may be sufficient to further deter collaboration. There are obvious implications here for EC policies, such as ESPRIT, designed to encourage multinational collaborative activity. All other things being equal, we would expect 1992 to diminish joint venture activity relative to alternative strategies of merger or direct access, and/or put up the price of inducing collaboration in the form of subsidies required to effect cross-frontier co-operation.

Kay (1989) examined a number of studies and databases in the area and generally found the effect of completing markets to be consistent with these predictions. For example, joint venture increased in frequency relative to mergers in line with the general level of barriers to trade. Thus joint ventures were infrequent within national markets relative to merger activity, increased in frequency relative to mergers when cross-frontier EC economic activity was considered, and become even more frequent relative to mergers for

EC/non-EC economic activity. The evidence supports the contention that the direct effect of 1992 will be to inhibit rather than encourage cross-frontier joint venture activity within the EC.

The extension of the earlier supply 'tug' analysis to joint ventures helps in our analysis of the evolution of this strategy. The reasons for its being a device of last resort in our earlier lexical ordering have their origins in transaction and organization costs, and indeed the ordering of strategies depends on these costs for its existence. However, the interpretation of the role and form of transaction costs is rather different from that postulated by Buckley and Casson, and leads to different predictions and policy conclusions.

Therefore transaction cost economics is not a single theoretical framework, but an area in which a variety of approaches have been developed. Williamson's approach has particular problems, and it is difficult to see how it could be usefully applied to the areas we have been discussing. Casson and Buckley's analysis of transaction costs appears to be more appropriate, especially in its explicit recognition of the public good nature of many technological issues and associated appropriability problems.[17] The transaction cost perspective developed in this chapter differs from Casson and Buckley in terms of the interpretation of the likely roles of co-operation and trust in joint venture activity, but these may be reduced to differences in emphasis and can in any case be resolved through empirical testing of derived hypotheses.

CONCLUSION

It is helpful to analyse the strategic choices facing the firm in terms of a natural ordering running in the direction: specialization → diversification → multinationalism → joint ventures. In doing so, the supply-side 'tug' encouraging the consolidation and exploitation of core skills is made explicit. It is also a useful base for the development of transaction cost theorizing, as we found in the later sectors. However, Williamson's 'markets and hier-archies' approach in transaction cost economics is not seen as being applicable to problems identified here, despite the author's claim to generality. The framework is flawed in significant respects, both in terms of its internal logic and in terms of its empirical relevance. The transaction cost perspective developed by Buckley and Casson is more obviously applicable to the issues discussed, especially in the explicit recognition of property rights as a transactional problem. Differences in transaction cost reasoning between that approach and the resource-based transaction cost perspective developed here may be resolved by empirical testing.

Transaction cost economics is a paradigm, not a theory, despite the tendency of some authors of to talk of 'the' transaction cost approach. It is neither useful nor enlightening to claim that the multinational enterprise exists because of transaction costs. What counts is what form these transaction costs take and the internal integrity and coherence of the frameworks within which the explanations are developed.

NOTES

1   These points are developed at length in Kay (1982).
2   The 'tug' and 'shove' metaphors should not be confused with supply 'push' and demand 'pull' metaphors.
3   A specialization constraint on the supply side may be limited possibilities for highly related diversification as, for example, the petroleum companies have discovered.
4   See Galbraith and Kay (1986) for further discussion of this argument.
5   Again, a further constraint in practice may be that the supply side affords few opportunities for diversification into related fields.
6   Michael Dietrich, Newcastle-upon-Tyne Polytechnic, has argued in an unpublished paper that such effects may operate in some circumstances.
7   This paper looks at determinants of joint venture activity, especially in high-technology industry.
8   It also represents a continuation of themes discussed in Kay (1982, 1984).
9   There are therefore two parallel sets of internalization issues, one set concerning whether or not to internalize, the second concerning which strategy (specialization, diversification) is appropriate for internalization. It is this latter set that is neglected by Williamson.
10   Conditions under which it is possible to utilize maximizing rules when uncertainty exists at lower levels were a concern of Kay (1979, 1982).
11   See Galbraith and Kay (1986) for further discussion along these lines.
12   See Kay (1983) for earlier discussion of this point.
13   Payments from divisions for shared overheads or central services should not be construed as transfer pricing in the sense in which the term is usually used.
14   At an Industrial Economics Study Group meeting in London Business School (November 1989) Robin Marris pointed out that the Japanese system of industrial organization could be a recipe for disaster if operated by another culture.
15   The Cecchini report represents the official analysis of the likely effects of 1992, sponsored by the Commission.
16   See Commission of the European Communities (1988) for further discussion and elaboration of this research.
17   Buckley and Casson (1976) provide an analysis of multinational enterprise based on transaction cost reasoning that incorporates appropriate recognition of appropriability problems, especially those associated with technological innovation. It is property rights issues such as these that are neglected by Williamson, to the detriment of his theory.

REFERENCES

Buckley, P.J. (1988) 'Organisational forms and multinational companies', in S. Thompson and M. Wright (eds.) *Internal Organisation, Efficiency and Profit*, Oxford: Philip Allen.

Buckley, P.J. and Casson, M. (1976) *The Future of the Multinational Enterprise*, London: Macmillan.

Casson, M. (1987) *The Firm and the Market*, Oxford: Blackwell.

Cecchini, P., Catinat, M. and Jacquemin, A. (1988) *The European Challenge: 1992*, Reading: Wildwood House.

Coase, R.M. (1937) 'The nature of the firm', *Economica* 4: 386–405.

Commission of the European Communities (1988) *The Cost of Non-Europe* 7, Brussels: CEC.

Cyert, R.M. and March, J.G. (1963) *A Behavioural Theory of the Firm*, Englewood Cliffs, New Jersey: Prentice-Hall.

Dunning, J.H. and Norman, G. (1985) 'Intra-industry production as a form of international economic involvement: an exploratory analysis', in A. Erdilek (ed.) *Multinationals as Mutual Invaders*, London: Croom Helm.

Elster, J. (1983) *Explaining Technical Change*, Cambridge: Cambridge University Press.

Galbraith, C. and Kay, N.M. (1986) 'A theory of multinational enterprise', *Journal of Economic Behaviour & Organisation* 7: 3–19.

Kay, N.M. (1979) *The Innovating Firm: the Allocation of Resources to Research and Development in the Firm*, London: Macmillan.

—— (1982) *The Evolving Firm: Strategy and Structure in Industrial Organisation*, London: Macmillan.

—— (1983) 'Multinational Enterprise: a review article', *Scottish Journal of Political Economy* 30: 304–12.

—— (1984) *The Emergent Firm: Knowledge, Ignorance and Surprise in Economic Organisation*, London: Macmillan.

—— (1989) 'Corporate Strategies, Technological Change and 1992', Standing Commission on the Scottish Economy, working paper, Glasgow.

Kay, N.M., Robe, J.A. Zagnoli, P. (1987) 'An Approach to the Analysis of High Technology Joint Ventures', European University Institute, working paper, Florence.

Marris, R. (1964) *The Economic Theory of Managerial Capitalism*, London: Macmillan.

Patrick, H. and Rosovsky, H. (1976) *Asia's new Game: how the Japanese Economy Works*, Washington, D.C.: Brookings Institution,

Penrose, E.T. (1959) *The Theory of the Growth of the Firm*, Oxford: Blackwell.

Rugman, A.M. (1981) *Inside the Multinational: the Economics of Internal Markets*, London: Croom Helm.

Rumelt, R.P. (1974) *Strategy, Structure and Economic Performance*, Boston, Mass.: Harvard University Press.

Williamson, O.E. (1971) 'Managerial discretion, organisation form and the multi-division hypothesis', in A. Marris and A. Wood (eds.) *The Corporate Economy: Growth, Competition and Innovative Potential*, London: Macmillan, 343–86.

—— (1975) *Markets and Hierarchies: Analysis and Antitrust Implications*, New York: Free Press.

—— (1985) *The Economic Institutions of Capitalism: Firms, Markets, Relational Contracting*, New York: Free Press.

—— (1986) *Economic Organisatison: Firms, Markets and Policy Control*, New York: Free Press.

7 Strategic management and transnational firm behaviour: a formal approach

Edward M. Graham

It is largely accepted among economists that analysis of the multinational enterprise (MNE) is an extension of the study of large firms (e.g. see Caves, 1982). Thus this analysis properly belongs in the domain of industrial organization, a field that has witnessed considerable development over the past two decades or so, giving rise to what is often termed the 'new' industrial organization. The 'new' industrial organization is treated comprehensively by Tirole (1988).

A major distinction between industrial organization and traditional microeconomics is the context in which the decisions of the firm are made. Large firms operating in concentrated industries, when formulating decisions with respect to the setting of price or output and how much to invest in new product development, must take into account the likely reactions of their competitors to these decisions, whereas firms operating in competitive industries do not. The distinction can be summarized by saying that the former firms must make decisions 'strategically', whereas the latter do not.

In spite of this distinction, much of the modern literature specific to the multinational enterprise largely ignores the effects of rivalry on MNE decision-making. Thus, for example, the 'internalization' theories of Buckley and Casson (1976) and Rugman (1986) and the 'eclectic' theory of Dunning 1988 focus largely on factors internal to the firm in analysing why MNEs make the decisions they do. (See also chapters 4 and 5 of this volume.) There have indeed been some efforts to account for inter-firm rivalry in this literature (e.g. Knickerbocker, 1973; Flowers, 1976; Graham, 1978; Casson, 1987; Yu and Ito, 1988). But on the whole the literature has concentrated on explanations other than rivalry.

The intent of this chapter is to bring some concepts from the 'new' industrial organization to bear upon the multinational enterprise. Much of the 'new' industrial organization is derived from modern game theory, and the aim in this chapter is to apply certain concepts from non-cooperative game theory to the understanding of MNE rivalry.

The chapter is divided into three sections. The first presents some basic concepts. Two firms, each a monopolist in a national market, are considering entering each other's home market. Given certain simplifying assumptions, under what circumstances will entry take place, and what then will be the reaction of the other firm? The second section extends this analysis to the case where one firm is subject to economies of learning and each firm possesses incomplete or imperfect information. The third section attempts to draw some conclusions relevant to the real world from the results of the first two.

SOME BASIC CONSIDERATIONS

In this section, rivalry between two multinational firms operating in two markets is examined. In order to keep the formal analysis tractable, a number of simplifying assumptions are made. These assumptions are relaxed in the following sections, where more realistic considerations are discussed.

Let us consider a world consisting of just two firms operating in two national markets. Each firm enjoys a monopoly in its home market. The firms are named A and B, with home markets market A and market B respectively. There are insurmountable barriers to trade between the two markets, and hence, if either firm wishes to participate in the market of the other, it must do so by means of investment. The firms produce a single undifferentiated good. Each firm knows both its own and the other firm's cost structure, and each firm can observe the other firm's past strategy. We will further assume that each firm's strategy is based on a Cournot conjecture, that is, each firm sets its quantity of output in the current period on the assumption that rival firms will not change their output. Thus, regarding the other firm's strategy, what is important is that each knows the quantity of output produced in any market period by the other. These assumptions can be summarized by saying that each firm works with complete and perfect information.

In order to prevent confusion, let us introduce the following conventions. Variables having a single subscript pertain to a market. For example, the variable P_A is the price of the good in market A. Variables with double subscript pertain to a firm in a market. The first subscript identifies the market, and the second the firm. For example, Q_{AB} indicates the quantity produced by firm B in market A.

Suppose that the total demand in market A (for the product produced by both firm A and firm B) is given by the following inverted demand function: $P_A = D_A - m_A Q_A$. (The underlying demand function $Q_A = 1/m_A (D_A - P_A)$ clearly can be inverted because it is continuous, strictly decreasing and everywhere differentiable.) Here m_A and D_A are constants and Q_A is the total amount of the product demanded. Likewise, suppose demand in market B can be written as $P_B = D_B - m_B Q_B$. Each firm will of course price monopolistically in its home market as long as the other firm remains outside that market, but if either market is entered by the outside firm, the two firms will initially compete with one another, following Cournot conjectures, so that the outcome will be a Cournot equilibrium. We further assume that the equilibrium is reached instantaneously after entry, and that there are no costs associated with entry. We first ask, given these assumptions, under what conditions will the lower-cost firm – we will arbitrarily designate it firm A – choose to enter market B? (For reasons that follow, the higher-cost firm B does not consider entry of market A unless its home market has already been entered by firm A.)

To keep things interesting but manageable, let us assume further that firm A produces at constant marginal cost C_A and that firm B produces at constant marginal cost C_B, where, as noted, $C_A \leq C_B$. If firm A stays at home, it will retain a monopoly there and can garner a monopoly profit per period π_A^m equal to $(D_A^2 - C_A^2)/4m_A$, assuming of course that the firm chooses to produce at all (which happens if $D_A > C_A$). One further assumption will be made in the name of tractability: neither firm discounts future profits. The profit earned by firm A in market B will then be:

$$\pi_{BA} = (D_B^2 - 4C_AD_B + 2C_BD_B + 4C_A^2 + C_B^2 - 4C_AC_B)/9m_B \quad (1)$$

subject to the constraint that the quantity produced by firm A in market B is positive. This quantity is given by:

$$Q_{BA} = (D_B - 2C_A + C_B)/3m_A$$

It will be positive if firm B produces in market B prior to the entry of firm A, because for firm B to do so it is necessary that $C_B < D_B$, and by assumption $C_A < C_B$. The reader can easily verify if $C_A = C_B = C$ then the expression for π_{BA} reduces to the more familiar result for the Cournot duopoly equilibrium

$$\pi_{BA} = (D_B - C)^2/9m_A$$

The reader can also easily verify that π_{BA} is always positive if firm B produces in market B (again because $C_A < C_B$). Finally, the reader can verify that if C_B is sufficiently high and C_A sufficiently low, after the entry of firm A into market B firm B would operate at a loss at the Cournot equilibrium and hence would choose to withdraw from the market. In what follows we shall assume that this lattermost does not in fact happen.

Even so, we would be near the end of our story if it were not for the reaction of firm B to firm A's entry into market B. If there were no counter-entry, then under our assumption that firm A's entry into market B is costless, firm A would surely enter in order to garner $\pi_{BA} > 0$. Obviously, if there were some cost of entry K_{BA}, then the entry would occur only if the expected present value of profits from the entry exceeded this cost. (Under our assumption of no discounting, this would always be met if $\pi_{BA} > 0$. But of course the story would be different if firm A discounted future profits.) The following proposition then is straightforward: firm B's best response to firm A's entry into market B is to enter market A if it can achieve positive profit from doing so.

We remind ourselves that a best response is a strategic move by a firm that maximizes its pay-off in the current period on the condition that its rival(s) continue to play the same strategic move in the current period as they played in the period immediately preceding. Because the Cournot duopoly equilibrium is a Nash equilibrium in market B, firm B maximizes its profits in that market by continuing to hold to this equilibrium in market B (on the assumption, of course, that firm A will continue to hold to the same strategy). But if firm B can achieve positive profits by entering market A, it will increase its total profits by doing so. By assumption, the outcome there will also be a Cournot duopoly equilibrium, and by the Nash property no strategy of firm A can reduce firm B's profits in market A. Hence if $\pi_{AB} > 0$, entry of firm B into market A is a best response to the entry of firm A into market B.

Again, this proposition depends upon the assumption that there is no entry cost to firm B in entering market A. If there were to be such a cost, entry would be a best response only if the expected present value of the entry exceeded that cost. These considerations again figure, of course, only if firm B discounts future profits, which by assumption it does not.

Firm B will not necessarily be able to garner a profit by entering market A. The profit to firm B from doing so is equal to:

$$\pi_{AB} = (D_A^2 - 4C_B D_A + 2C_A D_A + 4C_B^2 + C_A^2 - 4C_A C_B)/9m_A$$

subject to the constraint that Q_{AB} is positive. There is a C_B sufficiently high and a C_A sufficiently low that firm B would operate at a loss were it to enter market A at any (positive) level of output by firm A there.

But if this does not happen, then, by entering market B, firm A faces the loss of profit in its home market as a result of the subsequent entry of firm B. Continuing with the assumption that firm A does not discount its future profits, and firm B does respond by entering market A when firm A enter market B, firm A's criterion for entry of market B is thus that:

$$\pi_{BA} + \pi_{AA} > \pi_A^m \tag{2}$$

where π_{BA} and π_{AA} are respectively the Cournot duopoly profits to firm A in markets B and A respectively and π_A^m is the monopoly profit to firm A in market A.

Under what conditions will this last inequality hold? If one writes out the inequality in its entirety, the only thing that is immediately clear is that the expressions are not easy to evaluate. Let us assume for the moment that the slopes of the demand curves in the two markets are equal. Then the following can be said, defining $\pi_A^C = \pi_{BA} + \pi_{AA}$:

$$\delta \pi_A^C / \delta D_B > 0 \tag{3a}$$

In other words, the lower C_A relative to C_B, the more likely firm A will choose to enter market B. It should be noted that this result is completely consistent with the early theory of the MNE, dating to Hymer (1959), wherein it has been held that a firm must hold a cost advantage relative to its overseas rivals before it makes sense for that firm to extend its operations multinationally.

Let us now drop the assumption that $C_A < C_B$. We then find that:

$$\delta \pi_A^C / \delta D_B > 0 \tag{3b}$$

In other words, the larger market B is relative to market A, the more likely it is that firm A will enter market B, irrespective of the relative costs of firms A and B. Indeed, for any D_A, C_A and C_B there is a D_B sufficiently large that $\pi_A^C > \pi_A^m$, so that it would pay firm A to enter market B.

This result is consistent with the observation that multinational firms from smaller countries do exist. However, it is fair to note that these firms are typically very efficient producers (i.e. something like our assumption $C_A \leq C_B$ also holds true).

It intuitively makes sense that if $dD_B/dt > dD_A/dt$ (that is, if market B were growing faster than market A), *ceteris paribus*, this would lead to a higher likelihood that firm A would enter market B than if $dD_B/dt \leq dD_A/dt$. This is consistent with inequality 3b above.

Following entry of each firm into the other's home market, there are circumstances under which it would pay for both firms to collude in both markets to appropriate and share full monopoly rent (e.g. this would be the case if $C_A = C_B$ and the sharing rule were to be that each firm received half the rent in each market). Under these circumstances the Friedman version of the 'folk theorem' for infinitely repeated non-cooperative games holds: the strategy of appropriation and splitting of monopoly rents, under the assumptions that both firms intend to participate in the markets in perpetuity and that the rate at which the firms discount future profits is below some threshold level, is a sub-game perfect Nash equilibrium. This 'repeated game' Nash equilibrium will Pareto-dominate the Cournot equilibrium, and hence the new equilibrium will be preferred by both firms to the Cournot equilibrium. (See Friedman, 1971; Graham, 1990.)

It should be noted, however, that this holds only so long as the underlying circumstances continue to hold. If the costs of the two firms are too disparate, no repeated game Nash equilibrium will exist. Thus, if collusion is initiated at a time when $C_A = C_B$ and the sharing rule is that rents in both markets are divided equally, but in some subsequent time interval one firm succeeds in lowering its costs faster than the other, it is possible that the lower-cost firm could eventually prefer to revert to the Cournot duopoly equilibrium in the two markets rather than continue to appropriate and split monopoly rents equally. This possibility could give both firms an incentive to continue to reduce costs even while they were colluding to appropriate monopoly rents.

Even so, if one firm did succeed in reducing its costs relative to the other, both firms would always prefer to collude to maximize total rents under some unequal sharing rule (for example, a rule to split profits according to market share under the Cournot equilibrium) than to revert to the Cournot equilibrium.

A variant on this theme can come about if we drop our initial assumption that upon the entry of one firm into the other's home market, the outcome (without collusion) is an immediate Cournot equilibrium. Suppose instead that for some reason (customer loyalty?) it takes time for the new entrant to build market share. Suppose further that $C_A = C_B = C$. Then there is a share of market below which the new entrant (again, assume it is firm A in market B) would prefer the Cournot equilibrium to collusion to maximize total profits and to split them on the basis of market share. The condition is that:

$$[(S_{BA}/4)\ (D_B^2 - C^2) < (D_B - C)^2/9]$$

where S_{BA} is the share of firm A in market B, $0 < S_{BA} < 1$. Thus it is possible that a new entrant into the market will choose to compete rather than collude until it achieves a certain threshold share of the market, whereupon it will be willing to consider a more co-operative approach to things than it had previously been willing to.

Before closing this section, one should note that significant policy and welfare implications follow from the preceding discussion. Many are self-evident. But to give a synopsis none the less, let us begin by summarizing our main result: (1) under reasonable assumptions, entry by a firm from one country into the market of another country already served by a local firm can, under plausible circumstances, trigger entry of the second firm into the home market of the first but (2) the cross-entry will not necessarily lead to price competition by the two firms in the two markets. The dynamics of the entry and cross-entry as described (in the admittedly very simplified and stylized analysis of this section) might help explain such phenomena as the increasing propensity of major industrial countries to be both home and host to foreign direct investment to and from other such countries (see, for example, Graham and Krugman, 1989). Even though cross-entry could result in collusion of the cross-entrants to appropriate jointly monopoly rents, other forms of rivalry could prevail; we have discussed the possibility of continuing cost-reducing efforts. Were the discussion to be extended to allow for product differentiation, the rivalry could be manifested in product improvement and new product innovation.

Does this help us to explain firm behaviour in the real world? This issue is taken up in the third section of this chapter, but here let us rule simply that price collusion among oligopolists combined with rivalry with respect to cost reduction and new product development can be demonstrated in fact to occur in real life. The best example with which the author is familiar is that of the semiconductor producers in Japan, who, according to many accounts, enjoy a closed home market for their products.

These producers seem to collude to hold domestic prices high, but to price competitively in external markets. Also, they compete vigorously in both the development of new products and the reduction of cost of existing products. The latter behaviour is possibly motivated by competition from strong non-Japanese rivals in markets external to Japan. Thus it can be claimed that these producers act jointly as a monopoly at home but as oligopolists in external markets, along the lines postulated by our model. But a fuller accounting of the behaviour of these firms must also take into account economies of learning, introduced in the next section.

TWO-MARKET DUOPOLY WHERE FIRMS ARE SUBJECT TO LEARNING AND WHERE INFORMATION MAY BE INCOMPLETE OR IMPERFECT

Two restrictive and unrealistic assumptions in the previous section's analysis were that firms operated with constant marginal costs and complete and perfect information. In this section we attempt to extend the analysis by relaxing these assumptions (but retaining the equally unrealistic and restrictive assumptions of a two-firm, two-market world, a completely homogeneous product and costless entry which leads immediately to a new equilibrium). Even so, a full analysis of the two-market, two-firm situation where returns to scale are not constant and information is incomplete and imperfect would be a considerable task, beyond the scope of this section. Here the analysis is limited to a first pass.

To begin, let us consider the case where firms, rather than having constant marginal costs, instead are subject to economies of learning (dynamic scale economies). That is, the marginal cost is a declining function of the total accumulated production volume of the firm. A special case of economy of learning has been extensively analysed by Spence (1981). The marginal cost at time t of a firm (call it $C(t)$) decomposes into a constant M and a component which declines exponentially with respect to total accumulated production $Q(t)$:

$$C(t) = M + A_0\exp(-bQ(t))$$

$$Q(t) = \int_0^t q(\tau)d\tau$$

and $q(\tau)$ is the instantaneous rate of production of the product.

Spence uses the calculus of variations to show that the firm will maximize profits (under an assumption of no discounting of future profits) not by setting current marginal revenue equal to current marginal costs but by setting current marginal revenue equal to marginal costs as they will be at the end of the life cycle of the product. This result is difficult to operationalize, because, in general, firms do not know what their marginal costs will be at the end of the life cycle of the product. (Spence gets around this by assuming that the firm faces a known stationary demand curve and a tractable exponential learning curve given by the equations above, and knows exactly the life span of the product; but the first and the last of these assumptions are clearly unrealistic.) The practical result of the Spence analysis is that a firm subject to economies of learning will set price lower than will a monopolist or a colluding oligopolist in order to maximize profits by 'sliding down' the learning curve faster than would be possible at a higher price and lower per period volume of output.

What effects will this have on the decision of firm A with respect to entry to market B? If firm A recognizes that it is subject to economies of learning, so that its marginal costs at future time t will behave according to some relation of the form $C(t) = C(0)\exp - rQ(t)$, it will want to increase its total per period volume of output over the optimal volume, given constant marginal costs $C(0)$. This will imply that it will price in its home market at a level below the static monopoly price, offering a higher volume of output to the market.

This will lead to a different situation from that considered in the previous section, but the mechanics of the analysis will none the less remain largely the same. What changes is the algorithm by which the firm maximizes its profits.

A full-blown analysis of the dynamics of duopoly with complete and perfect information where each firm is subject to economies of learning is beyond the scope of this chapter and is not attempted here. We focus instead on the situation where information is incomplete and imperfect. Imperfect information implies that each firm is missing information with respect to exactly what are some of the fundamental characteristics of its competitor (e.g. is it subject to economies of learning?). Incomplete information means that some aspect of the information needed by a firm to determine an optimal strategy is missing and that the firm knows that the information is not available (e.g. what is the value of the parameter m_A or m_B?). We content ourselves here with some relatively qualitative observations pertaining to this situation.

We noted in the previous section that the propensity of firm A to enter market B depends in part upon the relative costs of firms A and B. But suppose that firm A does not really know for sure the costs of firm B, but can observe that market A is growing faster than market B and hence believes that it is moving down a learning curve faster than firm B. The decision of firm A to enter market B would clearly be influenced by whether or not the learning garnered in market A was transferable by firm A to market B, and vice versa. If the learning were to be transferable, firm A might bet that it would eventually produce in both markets at lower cost than firm B. And if participation in market B enabled firm A to accelerate its own learning, it would then reduce the (profit-maximizing) price it charged in its home market. This reduction in price would serve to deter the counter-entry of firm B into market A.

So would firm A enter market B? The answer also depends in part upon firm A's estimates of the cost structure of firm B. Again, this information is imperfect and incomplete. Information that firm A does have is the price being charged and the level and rate of growth of equilibrium demand in market B. Firm A must infer the costs of firm B from these price and quantity data. Entry will occur only if firm A calculates that at the post-entry equilibrium it will achieve marginal revenue equal to or greater than marginal cost. But marginal cost here is long-run marginal cost after all learning has taken place. If this cost is low relative to current marginal cost, it is possible that firm A would enter even if it were to incur a current operating loss.

It is worth asking, under circumstances as above but where firm A has not entered market B, would firm B be likely to enter market A? Market B, we recall, is the relatively slow-growth economy. It is thus likely that firm B is moving much more slowly down a learning curve than is firm A. Firm B can also observe the rate of growth of realized demand in market A and from it infer that firm A is likely on a faster learning curve. But failure of firm A to enter market B might be taken by firm B as an indication that firm A was currently a high-cost producer; further information would be given by the current price in market A. Also, firm B must consider whether it could accelerate its own learning by entering market A. Obviously, if it believed that it could, it would be more likely to enter than if it felt otherwise.

Of course, each firm is uncertain with respect to how much information is in the hands of the other. Hence, from the perspective of either firm, failure of the other to enter could simply be the product of uncertainty.

So exactly what can be said about entry and counter-entry under these circumstances? The following proposition seems safe enough. If the first firm to enter the other's market has as its home the faster growing market, so that the entering firm is on a faster learning curve in its new market than is the firm already established there, it is less likely that the established firm will counter the move by entry into the first firm's home market than if both firms were to have constant marginal cost. It is tempting to say also that the faster-learning firm will be more likely to enter in the first place. But, absent further information, it is truly difficult to say under what circumstances an initial entry would take place and by whom.

It is quite clear that there is considerable room for more research into the dynamics of firm rivalry when firms are subject to economies of learning and when information is incomplete or imperfect. Indeed, little research has been attempted in this area. Thus this section does little more than raise some issues without really resolving them.

CAN ANY OF THIS BE APPLIED TO THE REAL WORLD?

The real world, of course, consists of more than two countries, and in each country there are typically to be found more than one industry and more than one firm in each industry. Do any of the observations offered in this chapter, other than ones of the order of 'the world is complex and it is hard to know', have any bearing upon actual corporate strategy?

The main theme of this chapter is, of course, that the conduct of multinational firms depends in part upon inter-firm rivalry, and that such rivalry has been largely ignored in the literature on these firms. One point worth making is that just as two firms operating in a rarified two-market duopoly, as posited in the first two sections of this chapter, must take into account the likely reactions of the other in making strategic moves, so must firms operating in multiple markets with multiple rivals be conscious of the consequences of their strategic moves upon rivals' behaviour. In the real world, multinational firms do indeed tend to watch their rivals' moves closely and to react to them.

This truism aside, there are points from the earlier sections of this chapter that do generalize to multinational corporate strategy in the world as we know it. A best response to the new entry into a national market by a firm already established in some other market can indeed be counter-entry into that firm's established market by its rival. It has already been suggested that this counter-action may account for the very marked propensity for large firms from most of the industrialized countries to cross-penetrate each others' home markets.(See, for example, Graham, 1978; Yu and Ito, 1988.)

Such cross-entry is indeed observable, with one notable exception: Japan. Japan is an outlier with respect to the proportion of its economic output that is accounted for by local subsidiaries of foreign-controlled firms (see Julius and Thomsen, 1988; Graham and Krugman, 1989). For many reasons, Japan is a mystery in this regard. In recent years Japanese multinationals have been particularly aggressive with respect to entry to other industrial countries' markets. In particular, both the EC countries and the United States have witnessed massive rates of new entry by Japanese-based firms.

Japan's outlier status may be accounted for by reasons hinted at in the previous section: Japan's firms tend to be subject to rapid economies of learning, and their resulting cost advantages presumably both are transferable to other economies and serve as entry barriers to Japan itself. But other factors doubtless contribute to Japan's outlier status. These would almost surely include the virtual prohibition of foreign direct investment in Japan that was in effect from the end of the Allied occupation in the early 1950s until the late 1970s (but why has there been so little entry by multinationals into Japan following termination of official barriers to entry?). Cultural factors, including the noted propensity of Japanese firms within Keiretsu groups to buy only from other Keiretsu members, doubtless also have played a role.

Certain other aspects of the conduct of new Japanese entrants, if the accounts of this conduct that have appeared in the business press are accurate, may be explainable via arguments put forward in the previous sections of this article. The business press has noted that Japanese new entrants into non-Japanese markets often underprice the established firms in order to build market share. It is claimed that the underpricing is often such that the Japanese firms sustain current operating losses. A possible explanation centres on the argument in the first section of this chapter that a firm which is a new entrant to a market is likely to behave rivalistically as long as its market share is low; it will prefer a Cournot equilibrium to joint appropriation of monopoly rent and sharing of that rent according to market share. But at some threshold level of market share its preferences will change. The joint appropriation and sharing will at this threshold be preferred to the Cournot equilibrium, and the firm will then be willing to enter into co-operative strategies with rival firms. According to this argument, Japanese firms would then cease underpricing once a threshold market share had been attained. In some industries this seems in fact to have happened, e.g. in the US automobile industry.

It may be noted (and the reader can easily verify) that under the assumptions of the first section above a firm will prefer a co-operative strategy at a much lower threshold market share in a new market if its home market is counter-entered than if it is not. (That is, if the rival firms enter the home market of the new entrant, and then offer to co-operate there in exchange for the new entrant's entering into a co-operative arrangement in their home markets, the new entrant is more likely to do so at a low market share than if no counter-entry takes place.) Thus one reason for the reported continued aggressive pricing of Japanese firms in markets outside Japan even after substantial market share has been gained could very well be the failure of non-Japanese firms to penetrate the Japanese home market.

An alternative explanation of the same phenomenon (aggressive price competition by Japanese firms that are new entrants into a market outside Japan) rests on arguments offered in the second section, notably that a firm subject to economies of learning may sustain current operating losses upon entry into a new market if the additional volume of output attained in that market enables the firm to accelerate its overall rate of learning. And, as noted previously, this acceleration of learning will in fact serve as a barrier to entry to the Japanese market itself.

The issue of Japan as an outlier aside, arguments presented in previous sections suggest that multinational firms that have cross-penetrated each others' home markets may collude to hold prices high (i.e. at monopoly levels) but may none the less engage in rivalistic behaviour along other dimensions (e.g. cost reduction, product improvement, new product innovation, marketing, etc.). The major reason for this behaviour is actually defensive, e.g. if one firm were to lower its costs relative to all others, it might pay that firm to initiate price competition, whereas if all firms were to lower their costs in tandem the conditions for a repeated game, sub-game perfect Nash equilibrium (which Pareto-dominates a one-period Nash equilibrium) would be maintained. Thus the dynamics of rivalry can help to explain why multinational firms often seem to compete more on a non-price than on a price basis.

The author hopes that the main point of this chapter, that inter-firm rivalry must be part of any explanation of multinational firm behaviour, is adequately demonstrated, even if some of the details are missing. Indeed, the missing details suggest that there is much work yet to be done on the dynamics of rivalry of these large firms. Until this work is carried further it must be said that the theory of the strategic behaviour of the multinational firm is incomplete.

REFERENCES

Buckley, Peter J., and Casson, Mark C. (1976) *The Future of the Multinational Enterprise*, London: Macmillan.

Casson, Mark C. (1987) *The Firm and the Market*, Cambridge, Mass.: MIT Press.

Caves, Richard E. (1982) *Multinational Enterprise and Economic Analysis*, Cambridge: Cambridge University Press.

Dunning, John H. (1988) 'The eclectic paradigm of international production: a restatement and some possible extensions', *Journal of International Business Studies* 9, 1: 1–31.

Flowers, Ed B. (1976) 'Oligopolistic reactions in European and Canadian direct investment in the United States', *Journal of International Business Studies* 7, 3: 43–55.

Friedman, James W. (1971) 'A noncooperative equilibrium for supergames', *Review of Economic Studies* 38, 1: 1–12.

Graham, Edward M. (1978) 'Transatlantic investment by multinational firms: a rivalistic phenomenon?', *Journal of post-Keynesian Economics* 1, 1: 82–99.

—— (1990) ' "Exchange of threat" between multinational firms as an infinitely repeated noncooperative game', *International Trade Journal*, 4, 3: 259–77.

Graham, Edward M., and Krugman, Paul R. (1989) *Foreign Direct Investment in the United States*, Washington, D.C.: Institute for International Economics.

Hymer, Stephen H. (1960) 'The International Operations of National Firms', Ph.D. dissertation, Massachusetts Institute of Technology, published by MIT Press in 1976.

Julius, DeAnne, and Thomsen, Stephen (1988) *Foreign-owned Firms, Trade, and Economic Integration*, Tokyo Club Papers, No. 2, London: Royal Institute of International Affairs.

Knickerbocker, Frederick T. (1973) *Oligopolistic Reaction and the Multinational Enterprise*, Cambridge, Mass.: Harvard University Press.

Rugman, Alan M. (1986) 'New theories of multinational enterprise: an assessment of internalisation theory', *Bulletin of Economic Research* 38, 2: 101–18.

Spence, A. Michael (1981) 'The learning curve and competition', *Bell Journal of Economics* 12, 1: 49–70.

Tirole, Jean (1988) *The Theory of Industrial Organization*, Cambridge, Mass: MIT Press.

Yu, Chwo-Ming J., and Kiyohiko Ito (1988) 'Oligopolistic reaction and foreign direct investment: the case of the US tire and textile industries, *Journal of International Business Studies* 19, 3: 449–60.

8 The importance of distributional considerations

Roger Sugden

Why are there transnational corporations? That is, supposing firm A initially produces in country X, why should it acquire production facilities in country Y, either where in initially produces in X or where it initially produces in X and Y? In answering this question analysis has traditionally followed the general rule of economics, to be obsessed with (Pareto) efficient outcomes. However, this chapter is different: it pursues an analysis emphasizing distribution.

Briefly, the plan of the chapter is as follows. Accepting that transnational corporations are merely some form of firm[1], the first section begins to answer 'Why transnationals?' by contrasting two approaches to the question 'Why firms?', namely: internalization analysis, emphasizing efficiency, and Marglin's study of the rise of the factory, emphasizing distribution. It is argued that Marglin's work provides real insights. Consequently – and in contrast to existing work on transnationals – subsequent sections pursue a Marglinian analysis. The second section develops a general theoretical framework based upon product market domination and the third takes up one aspect of this – labour market domination – in theoretical and empirical detail. Finally, section four concludes with a short summary. Throughout liberal use is made of notes to compare the analysis with others.[2]

'WHY FIRMS?' AS A FOUNDATION FOR 'WHY TRANSNATIONALS?'

Because it begins at the beginning, a reasonable starting point is to consider 'Why firms?'. This question has been dominated by so-called internalization analysis, associated originally with Coase (1937) and more recently the likes of Williamson (1975). As regards transnationals, this approach is associated very much with Buckley and Casson (1976). Accordingly it is worth outlining their argument.

Firms are seen as a means of co-ordinating 'interdependent activities

linked by flows of intermediate products' (p. 36). The issue 'Why firms?'
really asks: why should interdependent activities be co-ordinated 'internally'
by a firm rather than by *the* alternative, namely 'externally' by market
forces? The answer is that internal co-ordination is used because of the
incentives to bypass imperfect external markets, i.e.:

> It is well known to economists that under certain conditions . . . the
> co-ordination of interdependent activities by a complete set of perfectly
> competitive markets cannot be improved upon. An important corollary
> of this is that there is no advantage in replacing a *perfect* system of markets
> by a centrally administered control system. Thus the incentive for internal
> co-ordination of activities by a firm does not rest on the advantages of
> centralisation *per se* . . . . In fact, it is a consequence of the result above
> that a necessary condition for an internal market to be more efficient
> than an external one is that the external market is imperfect.
>
> The benefits of internalisation stem from the avoidance of
> imperfections in the external market, but there are also certain costs of
> internalisation which may affect the potential benefits. The optimal scale
> of the firm is set at the margin where costs and benefits of further inter-
> nalisation are equalised.
>
> (pp. 36–7)

Why, then, are there transnationals? A transnational 'is created whenever
markets are internalised across national boundaries' (p. 45).[3] Exactly when
this is likely is explored in more detail by Buckley and Casson but such details
need not detain us here; our concern is the concept of internalization and the
contrast with an alternative, preferable foundation for answering our question.

In so far as it goes, it is not wrong to view a firm as a means of co-ordinating
interdependent activities linked by flows of intermediate products. Similarly,
it is not wrong to argue that the *raison d'être* of a firm is the net benefits
arising from its existence. But such general statements do not go very far,
and when we delve more deeply genuine dispute arises. More specifically,
mention of benefits suggests the need to consider *who* benefits. Exploring
this reveals real problems with internalization. Its concern is efficiency but
an understanding of this concept merely gives *one* approach to whose benefits
matter, and moreover an approach which is seriously lacking.

A situation in which no one can be made better-off without making
someone else worse-off is said to be 'efficient'. It is in this sense that a
complete set of perfectly competitive markets cannot be improved upon.
A situation is said to be 'more efficient' than an alternative if no individual
is worse-off and at least one is better-off than in the alternative. Thus the
consequence that an internal market is more efficient than an external one
only if the latter is imperfect is undoubtedly correct. But why is this

important? The implication is that an internal market is in fact more efficient than an external market, otherwise it would not exist.

This is a crucial implication of internalization analysis. The underlying reasoning can be shown by a simple example. Suppose individuals A and B are engaged in interdependent activities within a firm. The argument typically runs: the fact that a firm exists implies that A and B are better off – or, at least, neither is worse-off – using a firm organization rather than an external market, otherwise they would have chosen to use the external market. That is, all participants in a firm receive non-negative benefits from internalization.[4]

However, this argument assumes that the option of using the external market is available, and it says nothing about any other options. The importance of this is shown by Marglin's (1974) discussion of the rise of the factory in the English textile industry, 1750–1850.[5]

Prior to the factory, production was organized on the 'putting-out' system: a capitalist divided production into separate tasks, each being carried out by workers in their own homes at the pace they dictated. Under the factory system the division of labour remained, but workers were brought under one roof and the capitalist dictated when and how much work was done. This control of the work process was the critical reason for the introduction of factories: as a result, capitalists could increase their profits by decreasing workers' utility. Efficiency was not in issue. By working in a factory a worker revealed no preference for the factory system:

> The question is not so much whether or not factory employment was better for workers than starving – let us grant that it was – but whether or not it was better than alternative forces of productive organisation that would have allowed the worker a measure of control of product and process, even at the cost of a lower level of output and earnings. But to grow and develop in nineteenth century Britain . . . such alternatives would have had to have been profitable for the organiser of production. Since worker control of product and process ultimately leaves no place for the capitalist, it is hardly surprising that the development of capitalism . . . did not create a long list of employment opportunities in which workers displaced from the traditional occupation of their parents could control product and process.

> (p. 37)

That is, Marglin sees control of the firm as exercised in the interests of capitalists – who benefited from the factory – rather than workers – whose utility fell within the introduction of the factory. Moreover whereas the worker's option was whether or not to work at all, the capitalist's was which method of organizing production – be it use of the price mechanism (i.e.

external organization) or one of the many possibilities for internal organization – would benefit *him* the most.

The concern of this chapter is not the English textile industry, 1750–1850.
However, Marglin's work has interesting implications for analysing transnationals. Particularly important is the need to focus in detail on the
characteristics of a firm's activities. Put another way, real insight is obtained
by focusing in detail on the characteristics of a transaction (involving an
intermediate product) executed within a firm. For example, why *this* transaction rather than *another*, internal or external? Moreover, as a result of
this focus, Marglin (1974) emphasizes *distributional* considerations, in direct
contrast with the efficiency emphasis of internalization; in short, the factory
arose because it allowed capitalists to gain at workers' expense. This contrast is vital from a welfare standpoint.

The remainder of this chapter examines 'Why transnationals?' within
this Marglinian framework, focusing in detail on the characteristics of a
firm's activities, and emphasizing distributional considerations,

A GENERAL THEORETICAL FRAMEWORK

The key to understanding fruitfully the characteristics of a firm's activities
is to conceptualize its environment. Using this, we can draw upon a
considerable body of existing literature to give two sets of reasons to explain
the existence of transnationals.

If a firm operates in a perfectly competitive product market, it receives
normal profits. Thus, assuming a firm seeks maximum profits, it will attempt
to get away from a perfectly competitive environment and obtain above-
normal profits; it will try to dominate its product market and, in the limit,
obtain monopoly returns. The crucial issue is: can it? In fact it can. Above-
normal returns are obtainable.

Particularly vital in this respect is the possibility of firms colluding,[6]
a concept discussed as regards pricing by Baran and Sweezy (1966):

> The typical giant corporation . . . is one of several corporations
> producing commodities which are more or less adequate substitutes for
> each other. When one of them varies its price, the effect will be felt
> by others. If firm A lowers its price, some new demand will be tapped,
> but the main effect will be to attract customers away from firms B, C
> and D. The latter, not willing to give up their business to A, will retaliate
> by lowering their prices, perhaps even undercutting A. While A's original
> move was made in the expectation of increasing its profit, the net result
> may be to leave all the firms in a worse position . . .
> Unstable market situations of this sort . . . are anathema to the big

corporations . . . . To avoid such situations therefore becomes the first concern of corporate policy . . .

(p. 67)

Thus collusion derives from recognition of rival producers' 'retaliatory power': a firm accomodates its rivals' presence because it cannot drive them from the industry. If circumstances arise in which rivals can be driven out, a firm will not hesitate to become a pure monopolist. Likewise, a firm will appreciate that rivals tolerate its presence because they believe they cannot drive it from the industry.

Bearing in mind this conceptualization of a firm's environment – namely, collusive behaviour existing alongside and deriving from a ready willingness by each firm to drive rivals from the market; the coexistence of rivalry and collusion, as Cowling (1982) puts it – the literature on oligopolistic reaction and transnationals is of interest. Consider, for instance, one of the most prominent earlier works on this: Knickerbocker (1973).[7]

Suppose, for example, that rivals A and B initially supply country X from production facilities outside X, but that A then produces in X.[8] B could see A's move as posing important risks. For example, production in X may expose A to new technologies, giving it an advantage over B. With such risks, Knickerbocker suggests:

> prudence argued for the adoption of a risk-minimising strategy of industry rivals matching each other's moves. To illustrate, if firm B matched, move for move, the acts of its rival . . . B's gains, either in terms of earnings or in terms of new capabilities, would parallel those of A. And if some of firm A's moves turned out to be failures, B's losses would be in the range of those of A.

(pp. 24–5)

The qualification Knickerbocker attaches to this is that when collusion is 'very strong' firms may divide markets among themselves, e.g. A and B agree to be monopolists in X and Y respectively. There is then no possibility of matching.

Buckley and Casson (1976) criticize Knickerbocker (1973) on the fundamental grounds that the objectives of firms are never clearly stated. This is correct. It is not certain from Knickerbocker (1973) why firms pursue a risk-minimizing strategy. Moreover, whilst firms will not undertake unnecessary risks, the risk-minimization hypothesis goes too far. It implies that if a risk can be avoided it will not be taken, no matter what the potential rewards. In reality even though a firm may be risk averse it seems likely that it will take some risks.

Nevertheless the analysis in Knickerbocker (1973) has relevance. In a world characterized by the coexistence of rivalry and collusion – and accepting Knickerbocker's qualification regarding the division of markets when collusion is very strong – the risks taken by B in not matching firm A ultimately reduce to one thing, namely: firm A may be able to drive B out of the market, or at least force a new situation in which B obtains reduced profits. Even if B is risk-neutral this threat may induce it to acquire production facilities in X.

A more specific example may clarify the argument. Assume that the initial position, in which both firms supply X from elsewhere, leaves B with profit π_b^* from that market. Suppose now that firm A acquires production facilities in country X. B has two choices. It either (1) matches A or (2) continues to supply X from elsewhere. For simplicity, assume that if (1) is chosen B obtains profits of π_b^+ and if (2) it will get zero profits with probability p and π_b^* with probability $(1-p)$, where p = the probability B attaches to being driven from market X if it does not acquire production facilities in X_s. If (1) is chosen, B's profits are π_b^+. If (2), B's expected profits are $(1 - p)\pi_b^*$. Then, even if B is a risk-neutral profit maximizer, it will acquire production facilities in X if $(1 - p)\pi_b^* < \pi_b^+$. The higher is p the more likely is B to acquire facilities abroad. If, for example, B is convinced that A will gain no advantage from producing in X, $p \to 0$ and B is unlikely to follow suit. Similarly, the higher is π_b^+/π_b^* the more likely is B to match A's move.

Thus firm B may acquire production facilities in various countries because of the risk in not matching A – in short, because B *defends* its position. Its risk refers to any factor influencing A's ability to drive B from the market, or to force a new situation where B obtains reduced profits. Any determinant of production cost[9] is therefore vital, because lower costs may enable A to undercut rivals. Significant costs are emphasized in the existing literature – albeit *not* within the general framework being presented here. For instance, production in various countries may reduce the costs of raw materials, transporting goods from and between factories, and taxes, e.g. import tariffs, investment subsidies and profits tax (bearing in mind the possibilitiy of avoiding these by transfer pricing); see, for example, Hilferding (1981) and Frank (1970). In addition the determinants of demand are vital, and again the existing literature provides some interesting insights – see, for example, the seminal contribution on product differentiation in Caves (1971).[10]

More generally, matching is only one aspect of defensive behaviourT leading to transnationals. This can be seen by considering three further points. First, an issue associated in particular with Graham (1978). Suppose firms A and B produce and sell all their outputs in country X and, with no other rivals, collude to maximize joint profits. However, firm C, producing a similar good in country Y, begins to produce and sell in X. Graham hypothesizes that C's entry 'is likely to disrupt established patterns of conduct within that market, since the foreign subsidiary engages in pricing and product strategies designed to capture some of the market share from local firms' (p. 88). To pre-empt C becoming too disruptive, A and B could acquire production facilities in Y. This would be 'a purely retaliatory defensive move' – if A and B can threaten C in Y, C may be less disruptive in X. This clearly fits neatly alongside the matching analysis.

Second, firms require entry barriers in their industries to prevent new arrivals undermining their position – existing firms in an industry cannot obtain above-normal profits if there are potential entrants ready and willing to drive profits down. Thus they will defend their market dominance against potential rivals by seeking entry barriers. This can explain the existence of transnationals. Two possibilities are:

1. Developing a differentiated product. As the Caves (1971) analysis suggests, this is facilitated by producing where the good is marketed.
2. Securing access to raw materials, thereby preventing potential rivals from obtaining vital ingredients of the production process.

A third additional point about defensive action concerns Knickerbocker's (1973) view that matching does not explain why a firm makes the initial move in producing in various countries; it explains only the activity of firms that follow. Whilst this is correct, Yamin (1980) notes that the initial move may be a defence against rivals' threatened moves. As such it is closely related to matching behaviour and again fits neatly alongside the matching analysis.

In short, then, we have identified a whole set of reasons explaining the existence of transnationals: they may arise because a firm defends itself against rivals, fearing the latter will undermine its market position.

Moreover, and following on from this, Yamin, (1980) also recognizes the crucial point that the initial move by a firm to produce in various countries may be an *attack* on rivals,[11] that is, an attempt to obtain advantages enabling gain at rivals' expense. The source of these advantages is once more cost and demand factors. In other words, the coexistence of rivalry and collusion implies that firms look to maintain *and* improve their market dominance; and the factors underlying defensive moves also underlie attacks. But remember: firms will not attack if they believe rivals' response will leave them worse-off – they will collude to avoid such an outcome.[12]

Accordingly we now have a second set of reasons explaining the existence of transnationals; they may arise because a firm attacks rivals, i.e. seeks its own cost or demand advantages that will undermine rivals' market positions.[13]

They key to this entire argument is the coexistence of rivaly and collusion, which gives our general theoretical framework its focus on the characteristics of a firm's activities. Rather than examining internal co-ordination of activities versus the alternative, external co-ordination by market forces, our analysis takes a wider perspective. For instance, in discussing Graham's (1978) analysis of defensive behaviour, it was supposd that firms A and B initially supply country X from production inside X, that C then produces inside X, and that A and B therefore must decide whether or not to acquire production facilities in Y, where C also produces; i.e. A and B must decide whether to produce in one or two countries. These options are *both* means of internally co-ordinating activities, simply being a choice of where to locate production facilities, given the rivalry and collusion environment. Neither contemplates the possibility of external co-ordination by market forces.

Furthermore the focus on the characteristics of a firm's activities has distributional implications, in *direct contrast* to internalization analysis. Suppose, for instance, that firms A and B initially supply country X from production in Y, where B employs individual I. When A begins production in X, B's choice is to match or not match. If it matches, suppose B reduces its operation in Y and no longer employs I. The vital point is that I's welfare may *decline* as a result of B's relocation; then the transnational is not an efficient outcome in the sense implied by internalization analysis. Why? As argued by others, in a world characterized by the coexistence of rivalry and collusion there is a tendency towards unemployment – see, for example, Kalecki (1939), Baran and Sweezy (1966), Cowling (1982) and Cowling and Sugden (1987). Moreover whilst B's decision may condemn I to unemployment, evidence suggests that workers would rather be employed than unemployed. Consider, for example, Payne *et al.*'s (1983) UK survey of approximately 400 unemployed males, over 90 per cent of whom agreed with the statements 'Having a job is very important to me' and 'I hate being on the dole'. Also suggestive is Field (1979), reporting that in 1977 there were 640,000 individuals in the UK living in households receiving income below supplementary benefit level, despite the household having a wage from full-time work.

The crucial fact is that a firm matching rivals is concerned with its profits and not with the possibility that its dismissed workers are unemployed.[14] At most, workers can attempt to dissuade matching by, for example, accepting such low wages – and thereby cutting employers' costs – that not matching is found to be the most profitable choice. But it may simply be that no wage sufficient to live off is low enough to have an influence. Very importantly, it could also be that when negotiating a wage to prevent matching, workers do not believe a firm's threat to produce elsewhere unless lower wages are accepted. Yet, if workers are wrong, firms will produce elsewhere. These arguments, concerning bargaining, involve issues taken up in the next section.

There are also other vital distributional implications resulting from the focus on the characteristics of a firm's activities. Consider, for instance, consumers' utility. A hornets' nest of controversy surrounds, for example, the consequences for consumer utility of product differentiation. Space constraints alone prevent these issues being explored here. However, one example illustrates the view that transnationals may arise to the detriment of consumer utility. Consider the case of a firm acquiring production facilities in various countries to prevent potential rivals from entering its industry – e.g. the firm secures vital raw material supplies. The entry barriers (at least could) imply a higher product price than would otherwise be the case. Assuming their money incomes are unchanged, consumers of the firm's product are therefore worse-off.[15]

LABOUR MARKET DOMINATION

In the previous section we outlined a general theoretical framework, which obviously leaves room for exploring specific reasons in more detail. The purpose now is to move on to this next stage by examining an issue that is new *vis-à-vis* the 'Why transnationals?' question.

The section has two parts. The first considers a theoretical analysis and the second some empirical evidence. The focus is lower labour costs, a potentially important determinant of defensive and attacking behaviour.[16] More particularly, we will concentrate on the endogeneity of bargaining power between labour and its employers, a point discussed quite extensively in literature looking at the domestic sphere; see, for example, Marglin (1974), Edwards (1979) on workplace hierarchy, and the reviews of McPherson (1983) and Marginson (1986). The theory is implicit in such existing works as Frobel *et al.* (1980) but our analysis is more detailed and in a different context. The empirics draw heavily on existing reports.

As a final introductory comment, note that the aim is to establish labour market domination as an at least contributory reason for the existence of some transnationals; it is not to establish labour market domination as *the* reason for *all* transnationals. Underlying this is the view that in any one case there are likely to be a number of reasons contributing to a firm's decision.

Theoretical analysis

In general, utility-maximizing workers and profit-maximizing firms are in conflict over wages (per unit of work effort); *ceteris paribus* (and bearing in mind the discussion of costs in considering rivalry and collusion in the previous section), a firm will try to push wages down – it looks to dominate its labour market, in the limit paying subsistence wages – whereas workers look to increase their wages. The outcome of this conflict is determined by the bargaining power of workers and employers. Moreover, following Burkitt and Bowers (1979), for example, workers generally have a weaker bargaining position when they do not act[17] collectively because, for instance:

1 The loss of potential utility to workers from failure to settle the conflict is more severe than for employers. A worker's sole means of livelihood is the sale of his or her labour, a quick sale generally being essential because accumulated savings are small relative to expenditure commitments; see also Preiser (1971). In contrast employers can often replace specific workers and/or rearrange the activities of remaining workers to offset the loss of profits.
2 There is usually greater competition for jobs than for workers, and greater competition implies a weaker bargaining position.
3 Individual workers are often ignorant of their value to particular employers and are less skillful at wage negotiation.

In contrast, collective worker action – e.g. via trade unions – does not suffer these disadvantages to the same extent.[18]

Of course this entire discussion of bargaining power assumes imperfect labour markets. One important aspect of this is that in a perfect labour market any attempt by employers to depress wages and thereby obtain above-normal profits would be met by other firms entering the market, paying higher wages and obtaining normal profits. In such a case bargaining power is not a useful concept. However, it is reasonable to rule out this situation as unrealistic. In practice, industry entry barriers limit the set of potential employers,[19] who can also be expected to avoid competition for workers that pushes wages to the point where only normal profits are obtained. That is, employers can be expected to collude over wages.[20] Furthermore if there is an excess supply of workers collusion is unnecessary because there will be plenty of workers for all – and, as noted earlier, in a world characterized by attempts to dominate product markets there is a tendency towards unemployment.

Against this background of worker/employer conflict, what is the importance of transnationals? Suppose individual I is a typical worker in country X, employed by firm A. Consider the case where A can choose between two methods of production: it can either produce only in country X or it can produce in countries X and Y. Define I's wages in these two situations as w^n and w^t, respectively. Because the choice affects the ability of workers to act collectively, in general there is a tendency towards $w^t < w^n$.

That is, by choosing to be a transnational corporation firm A may *increase its profits* by decreasing I's wages and hence *decreasing I's utility.*

Lane (1982), for example, discusses problems faced by British trade unionists in a multi-plant firm producing in one country, let alone a transnational. Whereas workers could theoretically elect representatives to plan collective action across plants – i.e. they could form 'combine committees' – Lane notes practical difficulties arising from inter-plant differences in union development, and the historical organization of unions:

> From the trade unionist's point of view the multi-plant firm raises a host of not readily resolvable problems. The wide dispersion of plants over considerable distances, with location in areas differing in their labour movement traditions, means that within the divisional structure of any one firm uneven development of trade union practice as between plants is the norm. Attempts at forming combine committees always fall foul of this problem – and doubly so where combine committees organise on an inter-divisional or inter-company basis. If there are difficulties in involving activists in such schemes, imagine the problems of interesting rank and file.
>
> (p. 11)

He continues:

> These circumstances are compounded by internal union organisation. Full-time officers in most unions have, so to speak, a portfolio of companies within a given geographic area for which they are responsible. It follows that the employees of a multi-plant company operating in a number of regions must have contact with a number of full-time officers. Constraints of time, resources and variation in outlook as between these officers ensures that they neither meet nor exchange information on a regular and systematic basis. The only point of convergence is through the national officer responsible for the company concerned – who suffers from precisely the same constraints.
>
> (p. 11)

And when a number of plants are spread across various countries these difficulties increase considerably. For instance,[21] Counter-Information Services (1978) points out with regard to Ford workers across Europe:

> It's difficult enough for Ford workers in one country, sharing a common language and separated by comparatively small distances, to organise effectively against the company on anything more than a local plant or shop level. Even here, major problems of communication, sectionalism, and cumbersome national union machinery arise. On a European

scale the problems are multiplied many times. Workers in France, Germany, Belgium, Spain and the U.K. use six different languages plus those of the immigrants. It means much greater distances – over a thousand miles from Halewood to Valencia, with disproportionately large travel and telephone costs as a result. There are that many more unions – and another layer, the international union organisation, on top.

(p. 30)

Furthermore, this analysis suggests a second, closely related explanation for the existence of transnationals. Suppose, for instance, firm A decides to erect production facilities to manufacture a particular good. *Ceteris paribus*, it will employ those workers accepting the lowest wages. This is again determined by bargaining. If all potential workers act collectively, employers will simply have to settle for the best they can negotiate with, for example, the trade union. However, if workers do not act collectively, employers can play off one group against another – bearing in mind the factors weakening the workers' position when they are divided – and thereby secure lower wages. For instance, having asked workers in country X their price, A can tell workers in Y that if they accept lower wages, they get the jobs. When workers in Y concede, firm A can return to workers in X and seek still more gains. On some occasions A will produce in just one country because workers in that country always accept the lowest wages. But this will not always be so, in which case transnationals arise.

Thus we have two specific reasons for the existence of transnationals. An appropriate description covering either of these bargaining situations is 'divide and rule' (see Marglin, 1974): by dividing workers into country-specific groups employers improve their bargaining position, thereby gaining *at the expense* of workers.

A possible criticism of this is as follows: 'if workers are better off when a firm produces in one country, why do they not offer their services more cheaply to the firm if it continues to produce solely in one country, and thereby avoid its acquiring production facilities elsewhere?'[22] This criticism can be countered.

Consider first the case of bargaining when a firm erects new production facilities. The argument here recognized that a firm may in fact locate in one country. But with a work force divided into groups that can be played off against each other, a game involving bluff and counter-bluff, threat and counter-threat is played; perhaps, for example, workers in country X simply do not believe that their failure to accept lower wages will lead to a firm producing elsewhere. As a result, transnationals may arise. The criticism is therefore not valid.

Whereas this aspect of 'divide and rule' concerns bargaining over new investments in, say, period t, the first case outlined earlier examines the wage conflict in periods $t + 1$, $t + 2$ and so on, albeit still referring to a decision to become a transnational in period t. Compare now two situations. In the first, firm A produces solely in country X, where it faces workers' acting collectively. In the second, A is a transnational producing in X and Y, and facing two groups of workers. Considering again the three aforementioned factors illustrating the importance of collective action, if A chooses the first situation rather than the second it might face a work force that could in fact: (1) inflict greater loss of profits on the firm if the wage conflict is not settled; (2) compete less – indeed, not at all – within itself for jobs; (3) obtain greater information on the value of particular workers to A. So will A choose to produce in one country because the work force will restrain itself by not attempting to use factors like these? Yes, if workers: (a) can accurately assess employers' beliefs regarding workers' increased bargaining power when production is in just one country; (b) choose not to use that power; and (c) convince employers that this is the case. But (a) and (c) again involve a game of bluff, etc., and accordingly transnationals will sometimes arise. The criticism is not valid.

Even more to the point, why should workers choose to restrain themselves in periods $t + 1$, $t + 2$, ... simply because the firm could have chosen to produce elsewhere in period t? If workers ignore future investments they will make full use of factors like (1)–(3), simply because what happened in the past is in the past. If they do not ignore future investments, fear that the firm will subsequently become a transnational may temper their behaviour. But as this is again a game of bluff, etc., there will be times when employers believe that if they do not produce in various countries workers may use their full collective strength, at least on some occasions. For example, workers may seek as much as possible immediately because they are unsure whether A will make more new investments. Thus, whether or not workers ignore future investments, transnationals arise. The crucial point is that any improvements in a firm's bargaining power as a result of its ability to become a transnational are *guaranteed* only by its actually being a transnational. Again, the criticism is not valid.

This can be simply illustrated. Define π_a^T = firm A's profits if it produces in countries X and Y; π_a^{N1} = A's profits if it produces only in X, and workers use their full collective strength; π_a^{N2} = A's profits if it produces only in X and workers do not use their full collective strength; p = the probability employers attach to workers using their full collective strength when A produces only in X. (If workers ignore future investments, $p = 1$; if they may use their full collective strength, $0 < p < 1$.) Then, if A is a risk-neutral profit maximizer, it will become a transnational if: $\pi_a^T >$ $p\,\pi_a^{N1} + (1 - p)\,\pi_a^{N2}$. If the only effect on A's profits from becoming a transnational is this wage affect, $\pi_a^T = \pi_a^{N2} > \pi_a^{N1}$ and $p < 0$ means A will become a transnational.[23]

Accordingly we have presented a theoretical analysis showing that firms' attempts to dominate labour markets lead to production in various countries. Apart from the fact that this analysis sits within our general theoretical framework, with its distributional emphasis, the concern with labour market domination is clearly fundamentally about distributional considerations: our theory clearly and explicitly suggests that transnationals may be formed to increase profits *at the expense* of workers' utility[24]. Efficiency is not the concern.[25]

This is a vital implication. However, and *not* to undermine any of the theoretical analysis developed in this chapter, the value of further theoretical discussion is limited; no matter how detailed theoretical arguments become, without supporting empirical evidence they tend to be accepted at best with scepticism. The concern of the remainder of this chapter is therefore to examine empirical evidence related to the 'divide and rule' concept.

Empirical evidence

Is there evidence concerning the following 'divide and rule' hypothesis? An at least contributory reason for the existence of some transnationals is the division of workers into country-specific groups, enabling a firm to pay less wages when it is a transnational than when it produces in just one country.

It is interesting to examine analyses of wage levels in different types of firm. In particular, consider the typical analysis[26] contained in Buckley and Enderwick (1983) and Blanchflower (1984).[27] This examines senior management's estimates of employees' average weekly gross pay. The data are from the 1980 Workplace Industrial Relations Survey and cover British manufacturing plants. Each plant is identified as UK or non-UK-owned. The conclusion drawn is as follows: the data support the view that, in general, non-UK-owned plants offer wages comparable to or higher than their indigenous rivals. Is this result fatal to the divide-and-rule hypothesis?[29] No, for several reasons.

First, the result does not distinguish transnationals and other firms. Clearly a UK-owned plant could be part of a transnational. Then, if a UK-owned transnational pays sufficiently low wages, non-UK plants can pay more than UK plants whilst transnationals pay less than firms producing in just one country. Second, the data ignore effort. This is a crucial omission, because our hypothesis refers to wages *per unit of work effort*;[29] see again

p. 176. Third, a finding that transnationals tend to pay more than firms producing in only one country does not undermine the possibility of *some* transnationals paying less. This is important because the hypothesis refers to an at least contributory reason for the existence of some transnationals. Fourth, even if all transnationals pay higher wages than all firms producing in just one country, the existence of a transnational paying higher wages may nevertheless be explained by the 'divide and rule' concept. Suppose firm A is a wage leader in country Y and that, dividing workers into country-specific groups to thereby pay less wages, it acquires production facilities in country X. In X, A can be a high-payer – for example, because it feels this brings forth better workers, or because it faces workers well organized within X. Yet it can still pay less than if it produced entirely in Y, facing a work force acting collectively. For instance, A may use its X production to undermine a strike by workers in Y and thereby secure lower wages in Y; and/or, in making its initial investment in X, A may play off two separated yet individually well organized work forces to obtain lower wages. In addition, even though A uses its production base in X to undermine workers in Y, it can remain a wage leader in Y – for example, because it continues to face the best organized workers in Y, or because of historical inertia. In short, firm A can be a high-payer in X *and* Y, even though 'divide and rule' is a reason for its producing in both countries. The critical factor in our hypothesis is simply that a firm's wages are less when *it* divides workers across countries than when *it* produces in only one country; whether the firm is a high-payer *or a low payer* relative to rivals is irrelevant.

Accordingly studies analysing wage levels in various types of firm have not reached the heart of our hypothesis and will *never* do so. In contrast, the heart of the matter is reached when examining the views of participants in the firm, and actual cases of firms dividing workers into country-specific groups.

As regards the former, ILO (1976a) is useful as it summarizes some trade union views. It notes:

> union concerns that some multinational enterprises are adopting the policy of 'dual' sourcing. Under such a policy a multinational enterprise would *deliberately* seek to have alternative sources of production for given products or components, and thereby reduce the impact of a strike in any one country.
>
> (p. 20; emphasis added)

This indicates a belief that firms become transnationals at least partly to divide their workers into country-specific groups, enabling them to pay less wages. More generally, ILO (1976a) also comments:

One of the most serious charges that unions make, from time to time, vis-à-vis multinational companies is that the latter use their internationally-spread facilities as a threat to counter union demands and power. If the union will not yield, the company can or will threaten to transfer its production to another country, or the company may utilise already existing facilities in another country to penalise the 'demanding' union, or the company may threaten to curtail its future investments in the country in which the union is making 'unreasonable' (in the company's judgement) demands. All of these tactics are subsumed by the unions under the general head of threats to shift production as part of the labour tactics of multinational enterprises.

(p. 19)

This is supported by 'typical' views from various European unions, for example:

In many companies the existence of alternative sources of supply gives management scope to threaten to switch products to other locations. This can be a very effective bargaining counter.[30]

(p. 19)

the numerous transfers to countries in which wage costs are lower weigh heavily on general wage levels and undermine the many social benefits which have often been acquired after many years' struggle by the workers.[31]

(p. 19)

Multinational companies have wide opportunities of moving their capital from one country to another. This . . . makes it more difficult for trade union organisations to pursue their demands for higher wages, employment and workers' influence in the firm.[32]

(pp. 19–20)

In so far as these views are representative, they imply that firms divide workers into country-specific groups that are played off against each other. They do not say firms consequently become transnationals but they are strongly suggestive.

Also interesting is Greer and Shearer (1981), reporting a survey of US unions, fifty in all, thirteen having experience with non US-owned companies. Table 8.1 reproduces some results. These again raise the dual sourcing issue, and the use of threats to shift production elsewhere. Moreover, that these are *not* entirely empty threats is revealed by the *actual* 'use of foreign production to undercut U.S. union's bargaining position' and 'to undercut U.S. union's position during a strike'. This still does not establish conclusively that a reason for 'foreign production' is to undercut

Table 8.1 Number of unions reporting on the use of multinational bargaining tactics by foreign-owned US firms

Company tactic	Firms frequently use	Firms seldom use	Firms never use
Use of foreign production to undercut US union's bargaining position:			
Threatened	0	1	7
Actual	0	2	4
Use of foreign production to undercut US union's position during a strike:			
Threatened	1	1	5
Actual	1	1	4
Movement of US production facilities abroad or new investments abroad to strengthen US bargaining position:			
Threatened to move/ invest abroad	0	2	6
Actually moved/ invested abroad	0	2	5

Source: Greer and Shearer (1981).

US unions, but it does add to the suggestion. Even more persuasive is the claim from two unions (out of seven) that firms *do actually* move their US production facilities elsewhere or *do actually* make new investments abroad *to strengthen their US bargaining position*. These results are clear evidence favouring our hypothesis.

In addition Greer and Schearer (1981) report a survey of twenty-nine US companies, each non-US-owned. Seven out of twenty-six firms agreed they would consider using production in various countries to discourage US strikes, whilst one out of twenty-eight agreed they had actually done so. Again, whilst this does not say firms become transnationals to improve their bargaining power, it is suggestive; if firms recognize a means by which they can benefit from being transnationals, this means is likely to be a contributory factor explaining their becoming transnationals. These results are also supported by ILO's (1976a) reference to the Chrysler Corporation chairman extolling the benefits of dual sourcing *vis-à-vis* bargaining power. Thus it would seem that trade unionists are not paranoid in their views of firms' activities – at least, not paranoid all the time.

This is important. In general, a problem when examining any views – firms' or unions' – is the interference of political considerations. For example, the division of workers into country-specific groups to reduce their bargaining power is not something firms are likely to advertise.[33] Yet the evidence of firms' own views is that at least some of them *do* divide workers. Thus from both parties to the wage conflict there is evidence favouring our hypothesis. Precisely because it comes from *both* parties, despite the political considerations problem, the evidence is strong. The fact that ILO (1976a), for instance, also refers to firms denying that they divide workers does not undermine this conclusion. The vital point is: it is not denied by all firms.

Nevertheless the political considerations problem is acute. Always the issue is: does this union/firm really mean what it is saying, or are its comments merely political rhetoric? Because of this there are narrow limits to the value of accumulating view after view. Accordingly, consider now actual cases of firms dividing workers. In particular, consider evidence from the car industry – a comparatively well documented example. This supports the evidence of participants in the firm.

Steuer and Gennard (1971) report that in February 1970 Henry Ford was questioned by Halewood shop stewards about rumours of new investment going to Germany rather than the UK, it being known that Detroit was unhappy with UK industrial relations. This is taken up by ILO (1976a). Referring, for example, to 1971 and the Ford strike in Britain:

> While this dispute was under way . . . Henry Ford . . . was reported to have declared that parts of the Ford Escort and Cortina models . . . would in the future no longer be made in the United Kingdom but would be manufactured in Asia . . . .
>
> Mr. Ford came to London shortly thereafter, and in a meeting with [then] British Prime Minister Heath, he is reported to have let it be known, with regard to the company's labour difficulties, that if improvements were not forthcoming, the company would take its business elsewhere.
>
> (pp. 21–2)

Moreover, the threats are seemingly not empty:

> In 1973 when the company decided to locate the bulk of its small car engine production in the United States (for the Pinto model, sold largely in the United States), the *Financial Times* (22 June) reported: 'It is no secret that industrial disputes in Britain priced the United Kingdom out of the market. . . . ' The same paper added, 'There was, of course, no guarantee that Britain would ever have been selected for such a major development but the comments of Henry Ford . . . [in] the early part

of the year made it clear that the United Kingdom had dropped out of the running. . . . ' The same report added, 'the fear of similar labour unrest in Germany in the future may have entered into the company decision to locate the plant in the United States'.

(p. 22)

Nor is Ford the only company concerned:

Difficult labour disputes at the Chrysler plants in the United Kingdom in 1973, provoked somewhat similar overtones or visions of production transfers out of the country, or future reductions of company investment in the country.

(p. 22)

And ILO (1976a) continues:

More seriously, the *Financial Times* . . . observed the labour disputes at Chrysler were currently leading company planners to consider switching substantial production to its French (Simca) plants, and/or to a partner operation in Japan.

(p. 23)

The catalogue of Ford threats against workers in one country by comparison with workers elsewhere is also documented in Counter-Information Services (1978). Even more interestingly this reports Ford's decision deliberately to dual-source Fiesta components to reduce worker bargaining power. For instance, engines:

in the event of a shutdown of the Dagenham Fiesta engine line, the company's aim would be to boost output of the Valencia engine line to supply extra units to the Dagenham and Saarlouis assembly lines. With a higher output of the Valencia-engined cars from these two plants, stocks of the Dagenham engines could be stretched out to minimise interruptions in supply of any model. Similarly, if the Valencia engine plant were shut down. . . .

(p. 30)

Finally, and coming more up to date, reports from the *Financial Times* reveal that the threats at Ford continue:

Mr. Paul Roots, Ford employee relations director, told the [UK] unions that the company was suffering from high labour costs because of overmanning, inefficient working practices and failure to achieve production targets.

'This year, to date, we have achieved only 62 to 64 per cent of capacity at Halewood and Dagenham against 100 per cent at Saarlouis in West

Germany and 96 per cent at Valencia, Spain,' he said. 'If we do not get our costs down we cannot compete and if we cannot compete we will not survive in Britain as a manufacturing company.'[34]

Also, referring to the vice-president for manufacturing at Ford of Europe, during a dispute with UK workers over investment plans:

> Although Mr Hayden denied that Ford was running down its British plants, he gave a stiff warning that the consequences for future investment would be serious if the productivity gap with European plants was not closed.[35]

Thus, whereas claims of dual sourcing and so on were examined earlier as evidence favouring the 'divide and rule' hypothesis, the car industry gives actual examples which are likewise powerful evidence. All in all, there is strong empirical justification for accepting our hypothesis. It is reasonable to claim that an at least contributory reason for the existence of some transnationals is the division of workers into country-specific groups, enabling a firm to pay less wages when it is a transnational than when it produces in just one country.

CONCLUSION

In analysing the 'Why transnationals?' question this chapter has rejected the traditional obsession with (Pareto) efficient outcomes and instead emphasized distributional considerations.

The chapter's contrast between the internalization approach and Marglin's explanation of the rise of factories led to the conclusion that Marglin's work is particularly important because it shows the need to focus in detail on the characteristics of a firm's activities and, as a result of this, the significance of distributional considerations. Accordingly the chapter went on to pursue a Marglinian analysis of 'Why transnationals?'. A general theoretical framework was developed. The existence of rivalry and collusion gave this framework its focus on the characteristics of a firm's activities. Two sets of reasons for the existence of transnationals were provided: defending against rivals and attacking rivals. The concern with distribution rather than efficiency was illustrated in different ways. For example, matching behaviour leading to unemployment and hence decreased utility was discussed. Attention then turned to a more specific explanation for transnationals' existence: labour market domination. A theoretical analysis was developed and empirical evidence examined. Apart from the fact that the analysis sat within our general theoretical framework, with its distributional emphasis, the concern with labour market domination clearly and explicitly suggested that transnationals may be formed to increase profits at the expense of workers' utility. It was argued that by dividing workers into country-specific groups employers improve their bargaining position and thereby gain at the expense of workers. Efficiency was not a concern.

NOTES

1   See, for example, Buckley and Casson (1976) and the discussion in Cowling and Sugden (1987).

2   The paper is *not* a literature survey, for which see Hood and Young (1979), Buckley (1981), Caves (1982), Dicken (1986) and chapter 2. See also chapter 3.

3   Dunning (1977, 1979, 1980, 1981) has proposed an 'eclectic theory' which requires (among other things) that internalization of activities is preferable to external co-ordination and that a firm has a 'monopolistic advantage' over rivals. This contrasts with our interpretation of the literature: internalization on its own explains the existence of firms, including transnationals. There is a discussion of this point in Dunning (1988), which also contains other interesting references. See also chapters 2 and 5.

4   It is unclear whether internalization in Dunning's eclectic theory has efficiency implications. If it does not, the point is not pursued.

5   See also Marglin (1984).

6   See Cowling and Sugden (1987) for a more detailed discussion of the importance of price collusion, and its determinants. Note that in this chapter collusion does not mean joint profit maximization. Compare chapter 7.

7   The comments in Magdoff and Sweezy (1969) and Brewer (1980) are also interesting, for instance. See also chapter 7.

8   As Vernon (1972) notes, the analysis merely requires that firms are rivals, not that they both supply X initially. For example, they may both serve Y, and A's move into X may cause B to fear that A will supply Y more cheaply from X.

9   Adjusting for input quality, of course.

10   See also MacEwan (1972).

11   See also Hymer (1975).

12   Although Yamin (1980) presents a general framework based upon rivalry, collusion is ignored. A further fundamental difference from this paper is Yamin's acceptance of the view – based upon Kindleberger's (1969) interpretation of Hymer (1960) – that a 'monopolistic advantage' is necessary for a firm to become a transnational. This is *not* required in our general framework. Clearly this is not to claim that imperfect markets are unimportant. Indeed, the analysis favoured in this chapter is similar to the Hymer–Kindleberger approach: it emphasizes imperfect markets, and draws upon literature in the Hymer–Kindleberger tradition. However, it is different in so far as we do not begin with 'costs of operating at a distance' and conclude that markets must be imperfect for there to be transnationals; our analysis begins with imperfect markets and concludes with implications for 'Why transnationals?'. The latter cannot be criticized on the grounds that established transnationals do not incur costs of operating at a distance, a point raised in Buckley (1981), because such costs are not a critical issue in our analysis.

13 Cowling and Sugden (1987) identify a theoretical possibility for a third set of reasons explaining the existence of transnationals. This focuses on attempts to increase profits with no regard for attack or defence but it is dismissed as irrelevant in practice.

14 As argued by Cowling and Sugden (1987), this situation arises owing to the absence of democratic control of firms.

15 As another example of distributional implications, it could be that, if vital raw material supplies were not secured by becoming a transnational and entry did occur, the entrant would have an identical cost function to existing firms and joint profits would continue to be maximized. But in that case the implication of the firm becoming a transnational (and here preventing entry) would be redistributon of profit, i.e. the existing firm would not lose profit to the entrant. Again, this is not an efficient outcome.

16 Points in this paragraph are taken from Cowling and Sugden (1987).

17 It is not simply collective bargaining that is at issue. For instance, contacts between workers to foster information-sharing are important. See, for example, Enderwick (1983).

18 For example: (i) acting together increases the loss of utility to employers from failure to settle the conflict; (ii) collective action prevents many sellers competing amongst themselves; (iii) at relatively very little cost to each worker, trade unions, for instance, can acquire information about a firm's activities, and negotiating skill.

19 ·For a general discussion of entry barriers see, for instance, Encaoua *et al.* (1983).

20 See the evidence of collusion over wages in Forsyth's (1972) survey of Scottish firms.

21 See also Gennard (1972), Craypo (1975), Ullman (1975), ILO (1976a), Northrup (1978), Kujawa (1979a, b) and Helfgott (1983). Dunning (1980) suggests that a transnational's monopolistic advantage may be its ability 'to reduce the impact of strikes or industrial unrest in one country by operating parallel production capacity in another . . . ' (p. 10). Nevertheless Dunning's theory is very different from the approach in this chapter, as earlier notes indicate.

22 This would not necessarily increase workers' utility, but would mean that divide-and-rule does not answer the question 'Why transnationals?'.

23 Observe how this analysis of bargaining in periods $t + 1, t + 2, \ldots$ is closely linked with bargaining over new investments. When employers bargain with workers over new investment in period t, they will bear in mind how those workers have behaved in the past.

24 See also the much wider discussion of distribution in Cowling and Sugden (1987).

25 Cantwell (1984) criticizes the concern with distribution in (an earlier version of and therefore) this chapter, arguing that efficiency is likely to be the central issue in a dynamic framework, albeit recognizing that distribution plays some role. This is based on the view that changes in period t, even if they involve distributional rather than efficiency considerations at t, are likely to inspire more efficient outcomes in the longer run, e.g. because of the technical innovations that follow. To return to Marglin's (1974) analysis, for example: even if the factory implied short-run distributional rather than efficiency changes, in the long run it leads to the development of machinery, etc., that implies all are better-off than in earlier periods. But this does *not* analyse the fact that efficiency versus distribution in a dynamic framework requires comparison

of *alternative growth paths*, e.g. whilst factory production leads to certain machines being developed, so too would *other* forms of production, technological innovation being tailored to the demands of the innovator. See Cowling (1982).

26   Typical in the sense of the conclusion drawn and of the criticism that can be made of it as a test of our hypothesis.

27   See also Steuer and Gennard (1971), Gennard (1972), Dunning (1976), ILO (1976b) – giving a useful general survey – and Dunning and Morgan (1980).

28   This point has been raised in numerous discussions of earlier versions of this chapter.

29 ˇ Steuer and Gennard (1971), referring to the UK, note: 'the foreign subsidiary, particularly the American-owned firm, is alleged to utilise labour more effectively, which could be a nice way of saying people work harder' (p. 119).

30   Comments from a British Trades Union Congress Conference report.

31   The view of the French CGT.

32   A statement from a Swedish Metalworkers' Union Congress.

33   See ILO (1976a), where this point is recognized.

34   29 October 1983, p. 3.

35   23 February 1984, p. 1.

REFERENCES

Baran, Paul A., and Sweezy, Paul M. (1966) *Monopoly Capital*, Harmondsworth: Penguin

Blanchflower, David (1984) 'Comparative pay levels in domestically-owned and foreign-owned manufacturing plants: a comment', *British Journal of Industrial Relations*.

Brewer, Anthony (1980) *Marxist Theories of Imperialism*, London: Routledge.

Buckley, Peter J. (1981) 'A critical review of theories of the multinational enterprise', *Aussenwirtschaft*.

Buckley, Peter J. and Casson, Mark C. (1976) *The Future of the Multinational Enterprise*, London: Macmillan.

Buckley, Peter J., and Enderwick, Peter (1983) 'Comparative pay levels in domestically-owned and foreign-owned plants in UK manufacturing – evidence from the 1980 Workplace Industrial Relations Survey', *British Journal of Industrial Relations*.

Burkitt, Brian, and Bowers, David (1979) *Trade Unions and the Economy*, London: Macmillan.

Cantwell, John A. (1984) 'The Relevance of the Classical Economists to the Theory of International Production', paper presented at the annual conference of the Academy of International Business, Bradford, April.

Caves, Richard E. (1971) 'International corporations: the industrial economics of foreign investment', *Economica*.

—— (1982) *Multinational Enterprise and Economic Analysis*, Cambridge: Cambridge University Press.

Coase, Ronald H. (1937) 'The nature of the firm', *Economica*.

Counter-Information Services (1978) *Anti-report: the Ford Motor Company*, Anti-report No. 20, London: CIS.

Cowling, Keith (1982) *Monopoly Capitalism*, London: Macmillan.

Cowling, Keith, and Sugden, Roger (1987) *Transnational Monopoly Capitalism*, Brighton: Wheatsheaf.

Craypo, Charles (1975) 'Collective bargaining in the conglomerate multinational firm: Litton's shutdown of Royal Typewriter', *Industrial and Labour Relations Review*.

Dicken, Peter (1986) *Global Shift*, London: Harper & Row.

Dunning, John H. (1976) *United States Industry in Britain*, Chichester: Wilton House Publications.

—— (1977) 'Trade, location of economic activity and the multinational enterprise: a search for an eclectic approach', in Bertil Ohlin, Per-Ove Hesselborn and Per Magnus Wikjkman (eds.) *The International Allocation of Economic Activity*, New York: Holmes & Meier.

—— (1979) 'Explaining changing patterns of international production: in defence of the eclectic theory', *Oxford Bulletin of Economics and Statistics*.

—— (1980) 'Toward an eclectic theory of international production: some empirical tests', *Journal of International Business Studies*.

—— (1981) 'Explaining the international direct investment position of countries: towards a dynamic or developmental approach', *Weltwirtschaftliches Archiv*.

—— (1988) *Explaining International Production*, London: Unwin Hyman.

Dunning, John H., and Morgan, Eleanor J. (1980) 'Employee compensation in US multinationals and indigenous firms: an exploratory micro/macro analysis', *British Journal of Industrial Relations*.

Edwards, Richard (1979) *Contested Terrain*, London: Heinemann.

Encaoua, David, Geroski, Paul, and Jacquemin, Alexis (1983) 'Strategic competition and the persistence of dominant firms: a survey', in F. Matthewson and J. Stiglitz (eds.) *New Developments in the Analysis of Market Structure*, Cambridge, Mass.: MIT Press.

Enderwick, Peter (1983) 'Multinational Collective Bargaining: an Increasingly less likely Prospect?', mimeo, Queen's University of Belfast.

Field, Frank (1979) *One in Eight: a Report on Britain's Poor*, Low Pay Papers No. 28, London: Low Pay Unit.

Forsyth, David J.C. (1972) *US Investment in Scotland*, New York: Praeger.

Frank, Andre Gunder (1970) 'On the mechanism of imperialism: the case of Brazil', in Robert I.Rhodes (ed.) *Imperialism and Underdevelopment: a Reader*, New York: Monthly Review Press.

Frobel, Folker, Heinrichs, Jurgen and Kreye, Otto (1980) *The New International Divison of Labour*, Cambridge: Cambridge University Press.

Gennard, John (1972) *Multinational Corporations and British Labour: a Review of Attitudes and Responses*, British-North American Committee.

Graham, E.M. (1978) 'Transatlantic investment by multinational firms: a rivalistic phenomenon?', *Journal of Post-Keynesian Economics*.

Greer, Charles R., and Shearer, John C. (1981) 'Do foreign-owned US firms practice unconventional labour relations?', *Monthly Labour Review*.

Helfgott, Roy B. (1983) 'American unions and multinational companies: a case of misplaced emphasis', *Columbia Journal of World Business*.

Hilferding, Rudolf (1981) *Finance Capital*, London: Routledge.

Hood, Neil, and Young,Stephen (1979) *The Economics of Multinational Enterprise*, London: Longman.

Hymer, Stephen (1960) 'The International Operations of National Firms', Ph.D. thesis, Massachusetts Institute of Technology, published by MIT Press in 1976.

—— (1975) 'The multinational corporation and the law of uneven development', in Hugo Radice (ed.) *International Firms and Modern Imperialism*, Harmondsworth: Penguin.

International Labour Office (1976a) *Multinationals in Western Europe: the Industrial Relations Experience*, Geneva: ILO.

—— (1976b) *Wages and Working Conditions in Multinational Enterprises*: Geneva: ILO.

Kalecki, Michal (1939) *Essays in the Theory of Economic Fluctuations*, London: Allen & Unwin.

Kindleberger, Charles P. (1969) *American Business Abroad*, New Haven, Conn.: Yale University Press.

Knickerbocker, Frederick T. (1973) *Oligopolistic Reaction and the Multinational Enterprise*, Cambridge, Mass.: Harvard University Press.

Kujawa, Duane (1979a) 'Collective bargaining and labour relations in multinational enterprise: a US public policy perspective', in Robert G. Hawkins (ed.) *Research in International Business and Finance* 1, Greenwich: Jai Press.

—— (1979b) 'The labour relations of United States multinationals abroad: comparative and prospective views', *Labour and Society*.

Lane, Tony (1982) 'The unions: caught on an ebb tide', *Marxism Today*.

MacEwan, Arthur (1972) 'Capitalist expansion, ideology, and intervention', in Richard C. Edwards, Michael Reich and Thomas E. Weisskopf (eds.) *The Capitalist System*, Englewood Cliffs, N.J.: Prentice Hall.

Magdoff, Harry, and Sweezy, Paul M. (1969) 'Notes on the multinational corporation, Part Two', *Monthly Review*.

Marginson, Paul (1986) *Labour and the Modern Corporation: Mutual Interest or Control?*', Warwick Papers in Industrial Relations, No. 9.

Marglin, Stephen A. (1974) 'What do bosses do? Part I', *Review of Radical Political Economics*, page numbers refer to the reprint in Andre Gorz (ed.) *The Division of Labour*, Brighton: Harvester, 1976.

—— (1984) 'Knowledge and power', in Frank Stephen (ed.) *Firms, Organization and Labour: Approaches to the Economics of Work Organization*, London: Macmillan.

McPherson, Michael (1983) 'Efficiency and liberty in the productive enterprise: recent work in the economics of work organization', *Philosophy and Public Affairs*.

Northrup, Herbert R. (1978) 'Why multinational bargaining neither exists nor is desirable', *Labour Law Journal*.

Payne, R., Hartley, J., and Warr, P. (1983) 'Social Class and the Experience of Unemployment', mimeo, MRC/SSRC Social and Applied Psychology Unit, University of Sheffield.

Preiser, E. (1971) 'Property, power and the distribution of income', in K.W. Rothschild (ed.) *Power in Economics*, Harmondsworth: Penguin.

Steuer, Max, and Gennard, John (1971) 'Industrial relations, labour disputes and labour utilisation in foreign-owned firms in the United Kingdom', in John H. Dunning (ed.) *The Multinational Enterprise*, London: Allen & Unwin.

Sugden, Roger (1983) *Why Transnational Corporations?* Warwick Economic Research Papers, No. 222, Coventry: University of Warwick.

Ullman, Lloyd (1975) 'Multinational unionism: incentives, barriers, and alternatives', *Industrial Relations*.

Vernon, Raymond (1972) *The Economic and Political Consequences of Multinational*

Enterprise: an Anthology, Cambridge, Mass.: Harvard University Press.

Williamson, Oliver E. (1975) *Markets and Hierarchies: Analysis and Antitrust Implications*, New York: Free Press.

Yamin, M. (1980) *Direct Foreign Investment as an Instrument of Corporate Rivalry: Theory and Evidence from the LDC's*, University of Manchester Department of Economics Working Paper, No. 13.

ACKNOWLEDGEMENTS

Earlier versions of this chapter were entitled 'Why Transnational Corporations?'; it first appeared as Sugden (1983). I would like to thank several people for very helpful comments and assistance in writing these earlier versions, in particular Keith Cowling and Norman Ireland but also David Blanchflower, Peter Buckley, Mark Casson, Peter Enderwick, Paul Geroski, Charles Jones, Charles Kindleberger, Paul Marginson, Manfred Neumann, Christos Pitelis, Geoff. Stewart and Raymond Vernon. I would also like to thank Keith Cowling in another respect. Some of the points raised in earlier versions (and related arguments) have been pursued in Cowling and Sugden (1987). This has also significantly influenced the contents of this chapter.

9 The transnational corporation: demand-side issues and a synthesis

Christos N. Pitelis

A conspicuous aspect of the theory of the transnational corporation (TNC), as for example exemplified in the preceding pages of the present volume, is the focus on the supply side alone of firms' decisions to transcend their national borders. The underlying assumption appears to be one where, given the prevailing demand-side conditions (effective demand, aggregate profitability, liquidity, etc.) firms decide to become TNCs or not on the basis of supply-side considerations, usually the exploitation of firm-specific ownership advantages (see chapter 2) or the internalization of market transaction costs (see chapter 4).

Keeping the demand side constant for methodological purposes can be perfectly legitimate if the aim of the analysis is then to proceed to relax the assumption. This, however, is almost never done, implicitly relegating the demand-side issues to unimportance or secondary importance. We consider this unsatisfactory. The possible influence of aggregate demand factors in firms' decisions to become TNCs needs to be discussed, so that a reasoned decision be made as to their relative influence and importance. My aim in this chapter is to take a step in that direction.

The introduction of demand-side considerations in the analysis raises a question: can the two sides be synthesized so that an integrated demand/supply-side theory obtains? Attempts at a synthetic theory of the TNC have indeed been made, most notably Dunning's – see, for example, chapter 5 in this volume – also Calvet (1981). Such attempts, however, tend to focus on the supply-side factors. They also draw eclectically on these supply-side factors, often at the expense of such non-mainstream supply-side factors as, for example, those discussed by Sugden in this volume, chapter 6. Another aim of this chapter is to redress this imbalance.

My attempt at a synthesis intends to account for these limitations by providing a more comprehensive integration of the existing supply-side factors and then by examining their potential link with demand-side factors. One claim of this chapter is that there are *ex ante* and *ex post* factors explaining the TNC. The former include factors such as the exploitation of monopolistic advantages, the internalization of market transaction costs and the control of foreign (and domestic) labour. The latter are mainly the result of oligopolistic rivalry and/or the international competition between national states.

The central thesis of this chapter is as follows. Competition on the supply side between firms (capitals) and capital and labour tends to result in increasing monopolization of markets. The latter creates demand-side de-eficiencies associated with increased liquidity, both of which provide an incentive for firms to undertake overseas activities. The choice of the institutional form of the TNC (as opposed to alternatives such as exporting and/or licensing) is made on the basis of the cumulative supply-side advantages that this form conveys to their owner-controllers.

In the next section I provide a brief historical account and proposed synthesis of the supply-side theories (both mainstream and radical). This is followed by a section introducing some demand-side considerations. A brief synthesis of the two provides our *ex ante* theory of the TNC in the following section. *Ex post* factors and theories are discussed in the following section. A discussion of policy implications and concluding remarks are given in the final section.

SUPPLY-SIDE THEORIES OF THE TNC: A SYNTHESIS

Hymer's doctoral thesis, completed in 1960 but first published in 1976 (after having become the established reference on the TNC) is widely acknowledged to be the first serious attempt to analyze the TNC phenomenon, within the broad mainstream tradition. There is an on-going debate as to exactly what Hymer regarded as the main reason for TNC activity, as reflected in chapter 2 of this volume. It seems undisputable now that Hymer recognized three main factors pertaining to a firm's decision to become a TNC. First, the possession of an oligopolistic (often called ownership or monopolistic) advantage,[1] the removal of conflict and the internalization of market imperfections. Regarding the latter, and despite a reference to Coase's classic 1937 article on the nature of the firm (see Yamin's chapter 3 in this volume), Hymer emphasized structural market imperfections rather than transactional ones (see Dunning and Rugman, 1985). As I have pointed out elsewhere (Pitelis 1987b) this *choice* cannot constitute an argument against Hymer's claim to the parenthood of what is now called the internalization theory of the TNC.

The three main traditions subsequently developed within the mainstream research programme all build upon Hymer's original insights. Kindleberger (1969, 1984) and Caves (1971, 1982) are the best-known to have expanded the 'monopolistic advantage' aspect of Hymer's theory. The main idea here is that there exist natural disadvantages for a foreign firm operating outside its country of origin: language, cultural and other related problems. Accordingly, for a firm to still be able to undertake overseas activities through direct foreign investment (DFI), it must be the case that the firm possesses an advantage which indigenous firms do not. Technology, know-how, management and liquidity-related advantages could thus be exploited in order to overcome the inherent disadvantages of DFI and make contemplated overseas operations more attractive.

An implication of this Hymer–Kindleberger–Caves (HKC) tradition is that TNCs need not be Pareto-efficient. Their monopolistic advantages may facilitate a process of monopolization abroad, thus potentially reducing the welfare of the host countries.[2] Although proponents of the theory, for example Kindleberger (1969), express the belief that the long-run benefits of TNCs will offset any short-run costs, the fact remains that the HKC tradition recognizes the possibility of the existence of both efficiency and inefficiency aspects of TNCs' operations. The possibility that TNCs will consciously try to monopolize global markets so as to obtain monopoly profits and that in so doing they will tend to behave collusively (eliminate conflict) has been developed by the 'global reach' variant of Hymer's theory (see Jenkins, 1987). Vaitsos (1974) and Newfarmer (1985) are important contributions along this line of thought, as also is a good part of Cowling and Sugden's (1987) more recent contribution.[3] Unlike Kindleberger, this line of thought emphasizes the (Pareto) inefficiency aspects of TNCs' operations.

The case with the internalization school is different. Affiliates of this school emphasize the internalization of market imperfections aspect of Hymer's theory. Unlike Hymer's own emphasis on structural imperfections, however, such as bilateral monopoly problems, they suggest that TNCs internalize 'cognitive' or 'natural' market imperfections, defined as those arising out of excessive market transaction costs, (see Dunning and Rugman, 1985). The basic notion that the firm exists in order to reduce the costs associated with the operation of the price mechanism dates back to Coase (1937). The forceful reintroduction and extension of Coase's insight is due principally to Williamson (1975, 1981). For Williamson three main factors – bounded rationality, opportunism and asset specificity – give rise to high market transaction costs, such as the costs of searching, contracting, negotiating and policing agreements. These costs can often be reduced if the market is superseded by a hierarchical structure, such as the firm. The existence of firms can thus result in decreased transaction costs.[4]

The transaction costs/internalization theory has been developed independently by McManus (1972) and Buckley and Casson (1976), who also focused specifically on the TNC. Hennart (1982), Teece (1981, 1982) and Rugman (1986) are also major contributors to this theory. The main claim is that the use of market alternatives to DFI, such as licensing, can result in excessive transaction costs due to the 'public goods' nature of a number of intangible assets, such as knowledge, managerial skills and technology, and the associated appropriability problems. The supersession of the market by TNCs (the choice of the institutional form of the TNC) resolves these problems, thus economizing in transaction costs. The why and how of this outcome are discussed in some detail by Hennart in chapter 4 of this volume. Suffice it to note here that this economizing attribute of the TNC and the associated private efficiency gains are claimed by internalization theorists to render the TNC a more efficient – and thus desirable – alternative to the market.[5]

An early synthesis of the HKC and the internalization/transaction costs tradition has been offered by Dunning's (1981, 1988) 'eclectic theory', (see also this volume). In Dunning's theory ownership advantages and internalization of market transactions are the reasons for TNCs as well as 'locational factors', namely factors specific to the 'host' country. Indeed, Dunning's early work on the TNC (1958) explained US TNCs' activities in Europe in terms of such locational factors (see also Fieldhouse, 1986). The role of such factors has received little attention from other authors, partly owing to the belief that locational differences between developed countries are of no importance (see Gray, 1985). Rugman (1986) moreover has suggested that Dunning's ownership advantages need to be internalized before TNCs can result. Accordingly the eclectic theory can be seen as internalization–cum–locational factors, which is internalization only if the latter factors are not important![6]

The HKC and internalization/transaction cost theories focus on the final product markets and intermediate goods market respectively. Marglin (1974) focused attention on the labour market. Starting from the classical dichotomy between capital and labour, Marglin suggested that the emergence of the factory system from the putting-out system was more likely to have been due to the desire of capitalists to increase their control over the work force than to any alleged technological superiority of the factory system. Accordingly the emergence of the more hierarchical structure from the more decentralized 'market'-based one need not necessarily be associated with exclusively (Pareto) efficiency attributes. Labour, for example, may not perceive the change of institutional form as an improvement (see Sugden, 1983).

The last-mentioned author has extended Marglin's analysis to the TNC (see also chapter 8 of this volume). According to Sugden, the TNC allows firms to increase their control over global labour, which thus allows them to pursue 'divide and rule' policies in order to reduce further the power of trade unions, by playing off country-specific worker groups against each other. The potential mobility of TNC operations, as compared to the inherent immobility of country-specific labour groups, increases TNCs' bargaining power, allowing them to derive distributional gains from labour. This redistributional aspect of TNCs definitionally implies Pareto-inefficiency.

It can be suggested that the 'divide and rule' hypothesis fits very well into the internalization tradition. Consider, for example, a firm, X, contemplating the choice between a licensing agreement with an overseas firm, Z, or undertaking DFI. If X chooses to proceed with licensing Z, it faces the problem of inadequate (or absent) control over Z's work force. One way out is for X to take over Z, thus internalizing the market (firm Z) and also what from the point of view of X represents a potential labour market inefficiency, i.e. Z's work force. A problem with this extended-internalization theory is that by extending the concept of internalization to labour market 'inefficiencies' it sacrifices the short-run Pareto-efficiency aspect of the simple internalization view; firm Z's work force, for example, may not 'prefer' to face having to bargain with a powerful, potentially mobile TNC. What is more, the very possibility of a take-over emphasizes, in a different context, a point raised by Malcolmson (1984), namely that the very internalization of transaction (here labour-related) costs may facilitate the acquisition of monopoly power by firms; in this case firm X, which takes over firm Z.

To summarize, supply-side theories of the TNC, mainly emanating from Hymer's original insights, tend to emphasize the exploitation of monopolistic advantages by firms (the HKC tradition and 'global reach' theories), the internalization of market transaction costs, an eclectic synthesis of the two (an eclectic theory), or the increased power over labour markets ('divide and rule' theory). In principle (subject to the qualifications expressed in note 5), all these theories can be integrated within the general concept of internalization. TNCs can be argued to arise in order to reduce 'natural' and structural market costs (as suggested by Rugman, 1986), as well as what they view as labour market imperfections (the extended internalization view). The problem for the internalization of transaction costs theory, resulting from this integration, is that the efficiency-only property of this theory fades away. The internalization of monopolistic advantages may result in the restriction of competition, which need not be Pareto-efficient or socially beneficial despite its private gains to the TNC itself.[7]

Moreover, this is more blatantly clear in the case of the internalization of subjectively perceived labour market inefficiencies, which can give rise to TNCs with increased power over markets and global labour. Again, however beneficial this may be for the TNC itself, the outcome is neither

Pareto-efficient (the welfare of the owners and/or labour of the firm taken over in our example may be reduced), nor necessarily socially beneficial.

However disturbing the above implications are to the arguably dominant internalization of transaction costs research programme, a synthesis along the above lines is not only possible but also powerfully suggested by one of the less disputed tenets of economic theory, that of profit maximization. Once this is accepted as an aim it becomes very difficult to justify to external observers, often our own students, why a firm should stop short of redeploying its whole arsenal to achieve it. The arsenal can include the reduction of market transaction costs, as well as the reduction of labour costs, or the increase of prices through the monopolization of markets.[8] The very ability of a TNC to achieve all the above may in fact be viewed as a supply-side reason *per se* why firms choose to become TNCs. It is instructive to note that, unlike economists, TNCs themselves have few qualms admitting following 'divide and rule' policies (see Cowling and Sugden, 1987). Further, that some TNCs try their best to restrict competition so as to increase their profits is eloquently admitted by such 'insiders' as Stanley Adams (1985) in the case of the Swiss drug TNC Hoffman La Roche. We economists must often feel very lonely in refusing to see what everybody else does.

THE IMPORTANCE OF THE DEMAND SIDE

The supply-side approaches of the previous section help us to establish the reasons for the choice between institutional forms, given the internationalization of production. The latter is explained only to the extent that the choice of any institutional form represents a decision to undertake international production. But why international production to start with? In particular, could other reasons, besides the static 'choice between alternatives' framework of the previous section, help to explain the internalization of production? I believe the answer to these questions should be in the affirmative. In particular I suggest here (see also Pitelis, 1987b, 1990) that demand-side, effective demand-type reasons have a useful role to play in providing the general framework within which firms' decisions concerning the choice between existing alternatives are taken.

There is nothing new under the sun, and my claim is no exception. In fact, a long tradition of Marxist theories of imperialism, dating back to Luxemburg (1963), Hilferding (1981, first published in 1910) and Lenin (1917), among others, regarded imperialism as the result of the inherent tendency of capitalist economies to crisis – usually of the effective demand type (underconsumption and realization crises) and/or the increasing organic composition of capital/declining rate of profit type. Extensive surveys of these theories can be found in, for example, Bleaney (1976), Brewer (1980) but also in mainstream texts such as Hood and Young (1979). In this framework, the suggestion is that the underlying crisis is a reason for firms to undertake overseas investment, so as to relieve their profitability pressures, be they due to supply-side problems, demand-side problems, or a combination of the two. In this framework the TNC is simply regarded as the institutional manifestation of the crisis-induced international production, that is, the 'agent of imperialism'.

The potential importance of effective demand on firms' decisions to seek 'external markets' has also been acknowledged by Kalecki (1971) in his critique of Rosa Luxemburg. Based on this and other contributions by Kalecki, Steindl (1952) and earlier work of their own, Baran and Sweezy (1966) generated a revival of interest in such ideas. Their main point is that most domestic industries of advanced industrial countries today are dominated by giant firms, which jointly attempt to charge the joint profit-maximizing (monopoly) price. This pricing policy generates the tendency of the 'surplus' (gross profits, rent, interest and 'wasteful' expenditure by firms and the state as on advertising and armaments) to increase. For reasons related to the stability of the dividend pay-out ratio as well as firms' reluctance to introduce new inventions before the end of the useful life of existing fixed capital, consumers' expenditure and investment expenditure are claimed to be insufficient to 'absorb' (realize) the 'surplus', leaving wasteful expenditures, such as on armaments and, partly as a result of that, overseas markets, as the only available way of surplus absorption.

Baran and Sweezy's theory attracted both interest and substantial criticism regarding both the generation of the 'surplus' and its absorption (see, for example, Pitelis, 1987a for more). Their main point, however, that oligopolistic pricing can lead to an increasing share of gross profits to income, has been proved formally by Cowling (1982), under the assumption of successful strategic entry deterrence (of the excess capacity investment type) by incumbents. Pitelis (1985, 1987a), moreover, has argued that perhaps the main route through which monopolization of markets is achieved, the emergence of the joint stock company, provides another independent source of demand-side deficiencies in market economies.

According to this argument, a major way of firm growth is through the socialization of ownership by joint stock companies, through direct or indirect (often compulsory) shareholding, in particular through occupational pension funds. This socialization process increases the internal finances of joint stock firms but simultaneously reduces the income available for consumption. Given the evidence on the less than perfect substitutability between different types of saving, the result is a tendency towards declining consumer expenditure. *Ceteris paribus*, this leads to effective demand pressures, combined with the availabilty of 'excess' liquidity, in terms of corporate retentions and pension fund surpluses in the hands of the corporate sector. The two, combined, generate a need for overseas markets, that is, the internationalization of production.

The most serious attack on the Baran–Sweezy 'stagnationist' theory of international production has come from the Marxist tradition, mainly from the proponents of the 'internationalization of capital' school; see, for example, the collection in Radice (1975) and more recently Jenkins's (1987) contribution. In summary, the main arguments of this school are as follows. First, Baran and Sweezy's focus on monopoly is based on a neoclassical-type 'quantity theory of competition' which regards competition and monopoly as polar opposite types of market structure. In actual fact competition should be viewed as a process which dialectically links competition and monopoly, as indeed Marx argued. Accordingly increasing concentration need not imply monopoly power, given actual and potential competition by rival firms.[9] Baran and Sweezy's theory, moreover, fails to explain the direction of DFI from capital exporting countries, such as the US, to other capital exporting countries, such as the European ones.

The 'internationalization of capital' theorists' alternative is to explain the emergence of the latter in terms of the inherent competition in capitalist economies between capital and labour for the generation of 'surplus value' (potential gross profit) on the one hand and inter-capitalist differences on the other (for the appropriation of such profit). This competitive process suffices to provide a supply-side incentive for the 'internationalization of capital'; where labour power exists, so does profit potential, and the first to exploit it will do better in the competitive struggle.

The 'monopoly versus competition' debate is still raging within both the Marxist and the mainstream traditions. The recent debates on 'contestable markets' and on 'strategic entry deterrence' by incumbents is living proof of this (see Pitelis 1989a for a discussion). In fact what the debate shows is that the epitaphs on the Baran and Sweezy insights may be premature. To the extent that incumbents behave strategically to prevent new entry, and/or global TNCs decide to collude rather than compete, the aggregate tendency to monopolization may well be on the increase. Accordingly demand-side problems may still help to provide a general incentive for the internationalization of production. This is particularly the case if such problems can arise even in the absence of monopolization tendencies, as suggested before (see Pitelis, 1987a). Further, the introduction of a Marxian-type competition motive in the Baran–Sweezy argument does not undermine their argument, as it provides an explanation of their assumption of profit maximization. Rather, it enhances the argument in that it makes it consistent with Marx's own prediction of increasing concentration and centralization of capital (see below).

It follows from the above that, on theoretical grounds at least, a case for a demand-side-induced tendency to internationalization of production can legitimately be made. According to it, existing effective demand deficiencies may provide an incentive to firms to seek profitable outlets for their products overseas. The idea has been emphasized by Cowling and Sugden (1987) too, who consider it as one factor in internationalization along with their discussion of product and labour market domination supply-side factors.

Despite the fact that demand-side issues such as the above are usually ignored or played down by mainstream theorists, questions such as liquidity in the form of retained earnings are acknowledged in, for example, the 'monopolistic advantage' theory (see Koutsoyiannis, 1982). Demand-side questions from the point of view of the firm also enter Vernon's (1966) 'product cycle' hypothesis. Further, high-growth regions or countries, can be seen by firms facing demand-side problems as locationally advantageous. In this sense the absence of demand-side deficiencies may be viewed by potential TNCs as a 'locational advantage', as in Dunning's 'eclectic theory'. Such advantages could provide an answer to the other critique of the Baran–Sweezy tradition, regarding the direction of DFI. To the extent that the United States, for example, faces demand-side problems before, for example, Europe, the latter could be seen as an attractive location to invest in by US firms. This issue is pursued further in the next section.[10]

To summarize, demand-side deficiencies are here claimed to be a reason (general incentive to firms) for the internationalization of production. Indeed, they can arise from a competition-induced tendency towards monopolization, an idea that marries two apparently contrasting schools of thought in the Marxist tradition. Although this demand-side argument helps to counterbalance the exclusive focus of the mainstream theories on the supply side, it is the case that the demand-side argument as it stands fails to address directly the issue of the choice between institutional forms. It provides a partial answer to the question 'Why internationalization?' but has little to say on 'Why TNCs?' as opposed to exporting, licensing and/or subcontracting. To answer this question, we believe, it is necessary to go back to the supply-side theories of the previous section.

A DEMAND AND SUPPLY-SIDE THEORY . . . AND EVIDENCE

Given our interest in explaining the *emergence* of international production and the TNC, it appears legitimate to start by focusing on pre-internationalization closed economies so as to reveal the factors that led to internationalization. In such a framework, we suggest that competition between capitals and between capital and labour can lead to a supply-side tendency towards monopolization, and hence a tendency towards a deficiency on the aggregate demand side. This deficiency can provide a general incentive for firms to undertake overseas activities. Granting its possibility, the question arises as to how individual firms will respond to its presence.

To the individual firm, aggregate demand-side deficiencies will tend to manifest themselves in terms of declining demand for its products, and hence declining rates of return to capital, often combined with 'excess' liquidity, i.e. corporate retentions and/or pension fund surpluses. Obviously different firms will be affected to different degrees, depending on their market conduct, the stage of the life cycle of their products, etc. Most, if not all, firms, however, will be faced with the 'option' of either cutting production, reducing prices or finding demand-liquidity outlets abroad.

In oligopolistic markets, cutting prices may not be an attractive alternative, as it can give rise to potentially destructive price wars. Non-price competition is more likely to arise here (see Koutsoyiannis, 1982). The cost of such competition to firms can itself be a reason for seeking new markets. Cutting production, is a realistic possibility in oligopolistic market structures, working at below full capacity levels (see, for example, Rowthorn, 1981). Firms particularly concerned with their short-run profitability may thus adopt this strategy. This in itself will tend to accentuate the demand-side deficiency (from the investment side this time), providing a further impulse towards overseas markets. For all the above reasons, this latter possibility will thus have to be contemplated by, in particular, firms interested in their longer-term profitability. The exploitation of economies of scale and scope associated with choosing to operate in global rather than domestic markets is the obvious way of doing so.

Going back to the firm's immediate concern relating to demand-side deficiencies, going abroad obviously relieves the pressures of demand and liquidity in terms of finding new markets. Vernon (1971), Caves (1971) and Agarwal (1980), among others, discuss this point further. From the point of view of production costs, moreover, TNCs can achieve a reduction in such costs, if they find cheaper labour and/or material costs overseas. In the longer term TNCs can also achieve higher profits by operating in concentrated/high barriers to entry industies and/or by themselves contributing to increased monopolization of 'host' countries' markets (see Hymer 1976). Further, the adoption of 'divide and rule' policies can lead to further reductions in labour costs by increasing the power of TNCs *vis-à-vis* labour, both overseas and domestic (given their relatively higher mobility).

Coming to the market transaction costs side, economizing in such costs – for example, choosing the TNC form rather than licensing – will help reduce total costs, and therefore relieve firms' profitability pressures. So will the internalization of labour market 'inefficiencies' (from the point of view of the firm) by, for example, taking over a foreign firm.

It should be clear that not all the above motives or reasons for internationalization are equally well placed to explain the choice of the institutional form of the TNC. Reduction in demand-side pressures, for example, can be achieved through exports. Cheap raw materials and even labour can be imported. Liquidity 'problems' can be resolved by investing in the shares of other firms, domestically and/or overseas. Internationalization of market transaction costs and/or labour market inefficiencies may be better able to explain 'why TNCs' rather than, for example, exports or licensing. The fact, however, is that it is the TNC which has all these potential benefits at its disposal. This should be viewed as a reason *per se* for the choice of this institutional form.

It is worth stressing that (the coexistence of) all the above supply-side reasons for TNCs fit perfectly within the general framework of obtaining maximum possible long-run profits. Accordingly it is plausible to suggest that firms will not exclude any of them from their possible strategies. In this sense the above synthesis of supply-side micro reasons (itself taken within a supply-side framework of competition leading to monopoly and hence demand-side deficiencies) represents a powerful *ex ante* reason for TNCs.

There is some evidence in support of the supply-side aspects of the synthesis proposed above. Such evidence is discussed and surveyed by the proponents of the various constituent parts of the above synthesis, for example Cowling and Sugden (1987), for 'divide and rule' aspects and Dunning (1989) for 'eclectic' (monopolistic, internalization and locational) factors. Accordingly they need not detain us further here. Suffice it to note that the very existence of evidence for such 'rival' theories points to the need for integrated non-unidimensional theories.

Regarding the demand side of our framework, some evidence has been put forward in Pitelis (1990) and is summarized here. It is concerned with the issue that a stylized fact of TNC operations in the 1950s and 1960s is that such firms were US-based and undertook operations in the main in other developed countries (see Casson, 1987). Why then should firms suffering from demand-side problems domestically choose to expand to other countries potentially suffering from similar problems?

There are a number of theoretical reasons answering the above and also some empirical evidence. I start with the former. First, a firm may have a different (sufficiently differentiated) product to offer. Given similarities in tastes or needs in other developed countries, they would be the obvious choice. Second, the proximity of other developed countries to sources of cheap labour and raw materials, in this case, for example, the proximity of northern European countries to southern Europe and North Africa. Given this, developed countries can be the base through which easier access to less developed countries can be achieved. The better infrastructure of developed countries makes them definitionally a good base, as does their greater politico-economic stability. Third, the acquisition of a stronghold within the emerging common European market and the associated avoidance of tariffs and other such barriers to firms' operations. Fourth, there are the advantages of being transnational *per se*, with the resultant reduction in labour and other costs and the increase in market power. Fifth, and more important in our framework, the timing and/or severity of demand-side problems may differ among developed countries.

Given this latter possibility, it is interesting to examine the demand/profit share/liquidity situation of the US economy in the period preceding the growth of TNCs and DFI. Starting, for example, from the post-1929 Depression period, consumer expenditure as a percentage of after-tax gross private (personal and corporate) income declined from 96.24 per cent in 1930–4 to 90.01 per cent in 1935–9 and 82.64 per cent in the 1945–9 period. Corporate retentions in the same periods increased from a mere 1.63 per cent to 5.85 per cent and 9.16 per cent respectively. The profit share also increased from 7.23 per cent to 11.24 per cent and 12.42 per cent respectively. All three measures became relatively stable up to the mid-1960s. It is exactly in the period during and following the above dramatic decline in consumer expenditure and increase in profit share and liquidity that US DFI took off – nearly tenfold between 1946 and 1969 (see Tugenhat, 1971).

Much of this investment was directed to the UK. This makes examination of the UK data for the period interesting. The share of consumer expenditure in fact was far more stable than in the USA. From 92.99 per cent in the 1930–4 period it declined to 89.24 per cent in the 1935–9 period and to 88.23 per cent in the 1945–9 period. Consumer demand, therefore, was more buoyant in the UK at the time, a point also supported by Cantwell (1988, and this volume). More interestingly, following US DFI to Europe the US consumer expenditure share effectively stabilized. The UK share declined dramatically, by nearly 10 per cent from the mid-1940s to the mid-1960s. This was followed by a dramatic increase in UK DFI (see Stopford and Dunning, 1983).

The above does not provide conclusive evidence of a demand-side framework. It does, however, provide an explanation of the direction of DFI which is consistent with it. There is little doubt that a host of other reasons were in operation; the post-war reconstruction boom, the 'specific' (technological) advantages of the US firms and more generally the US hegemony at the time. It seems, however, that demand-side pressures were also a contributory factor. Given this, it is logical, we believe, to suggest that demand-side considerations have a useful role in explaining DFI and the TNC.

To summarize this section, we have argued that competition tends to result in monopolization and (thus) demand-side problems for capitalist economies and in the internationalization of production. The TNC represents an institutional manifestation of this tendency. *Ex ante* it is chosen from the alternatives for a host of supply-side reasons such as internalization of transaction costs and increased power over product markets and labour.

EX POST FACTORS

So far I focused on *ex ante* factors leading to TNCs, namely factors providing a general incentive to international production and/or TNCs. Once the first TNC has appeared, however, oligopolistic rivalry and/or international competition between nation states can lead to a further increase in internationalization and the growth of TNCs. These last factors provide a primarily *ex-post* explanation of the growth of TNCs, although they can, and have been suggested to, provide *ex ante* reasons for TNC operations too.

Theories of the TNC based on oligopolistic rivalry are associated with Knickerbrocker (1973), Graham (1978) and Vernon (1981). The crucial insight of this tradition is that TNCs can and should be seen in terms of strategic interactions between oligopolistic firms. In this framework, whether a firm will become TNC is related to factors such as its relative costs, but also to whether rival firms have become TNCs. Rivalry can lead to a firm becoming transnational because its rival has done so, and accordingly its relative position is threatened. Such rivalry can explain the 'TNC fad' or 'bandwagon' phenomenon. It is primarily an *ex post* explanation, as the starting point (see, for example, Graham in chapter 7 of this volume) is rivalry between existing TNCs. However, it can be suggested that rivalry is also an *ex ante* reason for TNCs, to the extent that the uncertainty associated with the possibility or threat that a domestic rival will become transnational and thus reduce its costs so as to potentially undercut a rival may induce the latter to move first.[11]

Another, primarily *ex post* factor leading to TNCs is international competition between states. Once the assumption of a closed economy is relaxed, the reality of many nation states provides a new dimension to the analysis. The possibility of a number of TNC home states benefiting from the operations of 'their' firms abroad (through, for example, repatriated profits) poses a distinct threat to the international competitiveness, and thus the economic autonomy, of states with weaker capitals.[12] It is likely that threatened countries will try to increase their international competitiveness by promoting and/or creating 'national champions', often TNCs.

Instructive here is the debate on the 'American challenge' (see Jenkins, 1987, for a survey), that is, the idea that in the 1960s and 1970s Europe was technologically dependent on the US (the 'Servan-Schreiber, 1968, condition'). This led European states favouring substantial merger activity in the 1970s to counteract the challenge (see also Pitelis, 1989b). Similarly instructive is the recent debate on industrial and competition policy, where again 'national champions' are seen as the means of facing increasing international competition. Pitelis (1989b) discusses the point further. It should not be surprising if, in an internationalized world, conscious 'developmental policies' by national states were to provide another reason for TNCs. International competition can be the *raison d'être* of, in particular, TNCs of less developed countries (LDCs) and those of the centrally planned economies.

It should be noted that here again the role of international competition need not be operating only *ex post*. Underlying the Marxist theories of dependence, for example, is the very idea that dominant nations attempt to 'exploit' the natural resources and/or labour of the 'periphery' (see Brewer, 1980; Jenkins, 1987, for surveys). The obvious problem in these theories is the failure to explain why most post-Second World War DFI is within developed countries, that is, countries of the 'centre'. Given this, it appears more plausible to consider international competition between nation states as a primarily *ex post* factor leading to TNCs.

The scenario we have developed so far is one of capitalist competition giving rise to monopolization/socialization of capital, and leading to stagnation, internationalization of capital and TNCs. In concluding it should be noted that in its turn internationalization of capital may tend to result in the globalization of the monopolization and the socialization of capital ownership tendencies and thus eventual global capitalist stagnation. See Cowling (1985), Pitelis (1985, 1987a) and Cowling and Sugden (1987) for more on this issue.

CONCLUSIONS AND POLICY ISSUES

We have suggested here that existing theories of the TNC are limited in that they primarily focus only on the supply-side factors, affecting a firm's decision to go abroad. Our proposed synthesis starts from capitalist competition leading to a tendency to monopolization and the socialization of capital in industrialized market economies. This leads to a demand-side framework of stagnation, a contributory factor to the process of internationalization of capital and the TNC. Within this framework a host of supply-side factors were suggested to explain why the TNC is preferred to the alternatives; in particular market power, internalization-transaction costs and increased power over labour (and states), Following the first firm's decision to become a TNC, moreover, oligopolistic interdependence and international competition between nation states are additional factors. Overall, there appears to be no persuasive reason to focus on unidimensional theories.

From the point of view of policy, the above seem to point to the conclusion that in the short run TNCs have both efficiency and inefficiency implications. On the one hand, they tend to remove market inefficiencies, by internalizing the market on a global scale. They can create new markets in 'host' countries, export technology and exploit previously unexploited markets. At the same time, however, the actions of TNCs can close markets, reduce consumer welfare, reduce the bargaining power of labour and (home and 'host') states. In the longer term, moreover, our analysis points to the possibility of a tendency towards global stagnation.

The above considerations raise some doubt over the optimistic attitude of internalization-transaction costs theorists. Their position appears to be the simple result of their exclusive focus on short-run supply-side internal aspects of a firm's decision to become transnational. Our analysis would point to the conclusion that it is in the interest of labour at least to try to restrain the (excesses of) TNCs. Alliances with non-transnational capital also potentially threatened by the TNCs are possible here. Similarly, possible conflicts between TNCs and nation states (when, for example, TNCs' demands threaten the long-run viability of the system and hinder the legitimization function of the state) can and should be exploited. It is possible, for example, that a particular country could be deindustrialized partly owing to the nature of its (financial) transnational capital, as has been suggested in the case of the UK (see Coates and Hillard, 1986). Such possibilities provide common ground for an alliance between nationally oriented groups, labour, small-scale domestic capitals, and often the state, to try and devise policies constraining and/or challenging the power of the TNC.

NOTES

1 See Cantwell, in chapter 2 of this volume, for a discussion of the difference in the use of the terms.
2 This need not be the case if markets are perfectly contestable; see Baumol (1982) and Pitelis (1989a) for a critique pertaining to the actions of TNCs.
3 On top of extending Hymer's contribution (see Cantwell in this volume), however, Cowling and Sugden also discuss 'divide and rule' ideas, as in Sugden in this volume, as well as demand-side incentives, as in Pitelis (1987a) and this volume.
4 It is worth emphasizing here that the concept of internalization has been used by others, for example Papandreou (1973). The *differentia specifica* between the latter and the 'internalization school' is that the latter propose or assert that

the *raison d'être* of the internalization of markets is the reduction of transaction costs.

5   Such claims presuppose a clear-cut distinction between the firm and the market as well as the pre-existence of the market. Both these assumptions have been criticized, e.g. by Cowling and Sugden (1987), Fourie (1989) and Hodgson (1988).

6   Such claims by Rugman fail to account for the fact that the extension of internalization to potentially structural market inefficiencies tends to sacrifice the efficiency-only aspect to the internalization-transaction costs theory. As I have already noted, it is the transaction costs aspect which gives its distinguishing efficiency features to the internalization-transaction costs theory, not the concept of internalization *per se*.

7   It is possible, for example, that the social costs from internalization may exceed the private benefits.

8   It is interesting to note that in his most recent book Dunning (1989) traces the origin of internalization of Coase-type costs as well as the internalization of labour markets to Marx (1959), first published in 1867! A similar depressing claim is made by Bowles (1985).

9   As I have noted elsewhere (Pitelis, 1990) the similarity of ideas with the Austrian and contestability of markets traditions here is striking; see also Pitelis (1989a) for a discussion of these latter traditions.

10   It should be noted that monopolization and socialization of capital tendencies need not be the only reasons for demand-side deficiencies. In the Keynesian and neoclassical tradition, for example, such differences can arise for reasons related to changes in consumer tastes, investor attitudes and/or monetary policies such as increases in interest rates.

11   Another interesting insight of the oligopolistic rivalry scenario is the possibility of global collusion by TNCs; see Graham in chapter 7 of this volume and Pitelis (1989a). This possibility provides a link between this tradition, Hymer's focus on 'rivalry reduction' and the insights of the 'global reach' approach. In this sense it further questions the focus on unidimensional theories of the TNC.

12   I ignore here the important question concerning the extent to which TNCs are 'nationalistic' and/or whether their increased power poses a threat to the (or some) nation state(s). Such issues are discussed in Radice (1975). Suffice it to note here that the mobility of TNCs does tend to increase their bargaining power over 'their' nation state as well as over 'host' countries; see Pitelis (1990).

REFERENCES

Adams, S. (1985) *La-Roche* v. *Adams*, London: Fontana.

Agarwal, J.P. (1980) 'Determinants of foreign direct investment: a survey', *Weltwirtschaftliches Archiv* 116.

Baran, P.A., and Sweezy, P. (1966) *Monopoly Capital*, Harmondsworth: Penguin.

Baumol, W. (1982) 'Contestable markets', *American Economic Review* 72: 1–15.

Bleaney, M. (1976) *Underconsumption Theories*, London: Lawrence & Wishart.

Bowles, J. (1985) 'The production process in a competitive economy', *American Economic Review* 75.

Brewer, A. (1980) *Marxist Theories of Imperialism*, London: Routledge.

Buckley, P.J., and Casson, M. (1976) *The Future of the Multinational Enterprise*, London: Macmillan.

Calvet, A.L. (1981) 'A synthesis of foreign direct investment theories and theories of the multinational firm', *Journal of International Business Studies*.

Cantwell, J. (1988) Theories of International Production, University of Reading Discussion Papers in International Investment and Business Studies, No. 122.

Casson, M. (1987) 'Multinational firms', in R. Clarke and T. McGuiness (eds.), *The Economics of the Firm*, Oxford: Blackwell.

Caves, R.F. (1971) 'International corporations: the industrial economics of foreign investment', *Economica* 38: 1–27.

—— (1982) *Multinational Enterprise and Economic Analysis*, Cambridge: Cambridge University Press.

Coase, R.H. (1937) 'The nature of the firm', *Economica* 4: 386–405.

Coates, D., and Hillard, J. (1986), *The Economic Decline of Britain*, Brighton: Wheatsheaf.

Cowling, K. (1982) *Monopoly Capitalism*, London: Macmillan.

—— (1985) *The Internationalization of Production and Deindustrialization*, Warwick Economic Research Papers, No. 256.

Cowling, K., and Sugden, R. (1987) *Transnational Monopoly Capitalism*, Brighton: Wheatsheaf.

Dunning, J. (1958) *American Investment in British Manufacturing Industry*, London: Allen & Unwin.

—— (1981) *International Production and the Multinational Enterprise*, London: Allen & Unwin.

—— (1988) 'The eclectic paradigm of international production', *Journal of International Business Studies* 19: 1–31.

—— (1989) *Explaining International Production*, London: Unwin Hyman.

Dunning, J., and Rugman, A. (1985), 'The Influence of Hymer's dissertation on the theory of foreign direct investment', *American Economic Review* 75: 228–39.

Fieldhouse, D. (1986) 'The multinational: a critique of a concept', in A. Teichova, M. Levy-Leboyer and H. Nussbaum (eds.) *Multinational Enterprise in Historical Perspective*, Cambridge: Cambridge University Press.

Fourie, F.C.V.N. (1989) 'The nature of firms and markets: do transaction approaches help?, *South African Journal of Economics* 157, 2: 142–60.

Graham, E.M. (1978) Transnational investment by multinational firms: a rivalistic phenomenon?, *Journal of Post-Keynesian Economics* 1, 1: 82–99.

Gray, H.P. (1985) 'Macroeconomic theories of foreign direct investment: an assessment', in A. Rugman (ed.) *New Theories of Multinational Enterprise*, London: Croom Helm.

Hennart, J.F. (1982) *A Theory of Multinational Enterprise*, Ann Arbor, Mich.: University of Michigan Press.

Hilferding, R. (1981) *Finance Capital*, London: Routledge.

Hodgson, G. (1988) *Economics and Institutions*, Oxford: Polity Press.

Hood N., and Young J. (1979) *The Economics of Multinational Enterprise*, London: Longman.

Hymer, S.H. (1976) *The International Operations of National Firms: Study of Foreign Direct Investment*, Cambridge, Mass.: MIT Press.

Jenkins, R. (1987) *Transnational Corporations and Uneven Development: the Internationalisation of Capital and the Third World*, London and New York: Methuen.

Kalecki, M. (1971) *Dynamics of the Capitalist Economy*, Cambridge: Cambridge University Press.

Kindleberger, C.P. (1969) *International Business Abroad*, New Haven, Conn.: Yale University Press.

—— (1984) *Multinational Excursions*, Cambridge, Mass.: MIT Press.

Knickerbocker, F.T. (1973) *Oligopolistic Reaction and the Multinational Enterprise*, Cambridge, Mass.: Harvard University Press.

Koutsoyiannis, A. (1982) *Non-price Decisions*, London: Macmillan.

Lenin, V.I. (1917) *Imperialism: the Highest Stage of Capitalism*, Moscow.

Luxemburg, R. (1963) *The Accumulation of Capital*, London: Routledge.

Malcolmson, J. (1984) 'Efficient labour organisation: incentives, power and the transaction costs approach', in F. Stephen (ed.) *Firms, Organization and Labour, Approaches to the Economics of Labour Organization*, London: Macmillan.

Marglin, S. (1974) 'What do bosses do? The origins and functions of hierarchy in capitalist production', *Review of Radical Political Economics*, summer.

McManus, J.C. (1972) 'The theory of the Multinational firm', in G. Paquet (ed.) *The Multinational Firm and the Nation State*, Don Mills, Ont.: Collier-Macmillan.

Marx, K. (1959) *Capital* I, London: Lawrence & Wishart.

Newfarmer, R. ed. (1985) *Profits, Progress and Poverty: Case Studies of International Industries in Latin America*, Notre Dame, Ind.: Notre Dame University Press.

Papandreou, A. (1973) 'Multinational corporations and empire', *Social Praxis* 1, 2.

Pitelis, C. N. (1985) 'The Tendency towards the Socialisation of the Ownership of the Means of Production and the Realisation of Profits in the Post-war UK Economy', paper presented at the Conference of Socialist Economists, Manchester.

—— (1987a) *Corporate Capital: Control Ownership, Saving and Crisis*, Cambridge: Cambridge University Press.

—— (1987b), Internalization and the Transnational Corporation: a Critique, University of Nottingham Discussion Paper in Industrial Economics.

—— (1989a), Neoclassical models of industrial organization', in H. Schenk *et al. Perspectives in Industrial Organization*, Amsterdam: Kluwer.

—— (1989b), 'Competition theory and competition policy: a strategy for Europe, forthcoming in *Costs and Benefits of Europe*, Europe 12 group (ed.), Pinter.

—— (1990) 'The transnational corporation: a synthesis', *Review of Radical Political Economics*, forthcoming.

Radice, H., ed. (1975) *International Firms and Modern Imperialism*, Harmondsworth: Penguin.

Rowthorn, B. (1981) 'Demand, real wages and economic growth', *Thames Papers in Political Economy*, Autumn.

Rugman, A.M. (1986) 'New theories of the multinational enterprise: an assessment of internalisation theory', *Bulletin of Economic Research* 35: 101–18.

Servan-Schreiber, J. (1968) *The American Challenge*, London: Hamish Hamilton.

Steindl, J. (1952) *Maturity and Stagnation in American Capitalism*, London: Oxford University Press.

Stopford, J.M., and Dunning J. (1983) *Multinationals: Company Performance and Global Trends*, London: Macmillan.

Sugden, R. (1983) *Why Transnational Corporations?* Warwick Economic Research Papers, No. 222, Coventry: University of Warwick.

Teece, D.J. (1981) 'The multinational enterprise: market failure and market power considerations', *Sloan Management Review*, 99, 3.

—— (1982) A Transaction Cost Theory of the Multinational Enterprise, University of Reading Discussion Papers in International Investment and Business Studies, No. 66.

Tugenhat, T. (1971) *The Multinationals*, Harmondsworth: Penguin.

Vaitsos, K. (1974) *Inter-country Income Distribution and Transnational Enterprises*, Oxford: Clarendon.

Vernon, R. (1966) 'International investment and international trade in the product cycle', *Quarterly Journal of Economics* 80: 90–207.'

—— (1971) *Sovereignty at Bay*, Harlow: Longman.

—— (1981) ' "*Sovereignty at Bay*" ten years after', *International Organisation* 35, 3.

Williamson, O.E. (1975) *Markets and Hierarchies: Analysis and Antitrust Implications*, New York: Free Press.

—— (1981) 'The modern corporation: origins, evolution, attributes', *Journal of Economic Literature* 19, 4: 1537–68.

ACKNOWLEDGEMENTS

This chapter relies and builds upon Pitelis (1987b, 1990). I am grateful to Keith Cowling, Hugo Radice, Roger Sugden and Mohammad Yamin for comments on earlier drafts.

Name index

General index